SPIRITUAL TRILLIONAIRE:
Cherishing the Breath of Life while Simultaneously Preparing for the Blow of Death!

CHILDREN OF THE MOST HIGH:
PRISTINE YOUTH AND FAMILY SOLUTIONS, LLC.
SONS AND DAUGHTERS OF THE MOST HIGH PUBLISHERS ®

OH, GRACIOUS MOST HIGH HEAVENLY FATHER, HOLY IS YOUR NAME, YOUR WILL BE DONE NOW AND FOREVER!

By

Woodie Hughes Jr.
CEO & Founder of the Children of the Most High:
Pristine Youth and Family Solutions LLC.
Sons and Daughters of the Most High Publishers®
Mr. Hughes is a Servant of the Most High, and a Teacher
of the Most High's Doctrine.

I0155720

Table of Contents

I

Table of Contents

Table of Contents

Greetings:

We greet all members of humanity in peace! Nothing would exist if you Oh Gracious Most High Heavenly Father, The Creator didn't create it. You are alone in Your Greatness; you have no partners that share in your grace. To you all sovereignty is due and you are all powerful over everything. We seek refuge in you, the ever watchful Most High who hears and knows all things! Glory be to you as many times as the number of things you have created! All gratitude is due to you oh gracious Most High Heavenly Father, you are the Creator and Sustainer of all the boundless universes. You are the Yielder, and the most Merciful. The Ruler of the Day of Decision. It's you whom we worship and it is you alone whom we beseech for help, oh Guide, guide us to the narrow path **which reflects moral integrity and positive character traits in action** of the ones who stand straight, the narrow path of those who earned your grace not inclusive of those who brought an everlasting curse on themselves, those who conceal the facts of that which they know to be true in order to lead the **sincere-hearted seekers** of your truth astray. Amen

What does the phrase: "those who earned your grace" mean as oppose to saying "those who receive your grace?"

The word: "**grace**" in the King James Version (KJV) bible book of Genesis chapter 6 verse 8 is: חֵן **Khane** or **chen** pronounced as **khān (KJV bible Hebrew Strong's Concordance#2580).** The word: "חֵן **Khane** or **chen**" means "**favor, kindness.**" The word: "**grace**" in the KJV bible book of John chapter 1 verse 17 is: χάρις **Kharece** or **charis** pronounced as **khä'-rēs (KJV** bible Greek Strong's Concordance#5485). The word: "χάρις Kharece or **charis**" means "**joy, delight.**" So, the phrase: "**those who earned your grace**" is in reference **to those people who are no longer physically alive that have transitioned to a higher life** such as: **Yashu'a (Jesus), John the Baptist, Yowkhanan Bar Zebedee (John Son of Zebedee who was Yashu'a (Jesus) beloved disciple),** or **Ab-Ra-Kham (Abraham).** The phrase: "**those who receive your grace**" is in reference **to any person or people** who the Most High Heavenly Father bestows <u>**favor**</u> on by allowing them to still be physically alive, and to have an opportunity to experience <u>**joy**</u> while still be physically alive.

v

Dedication

The "Spiritual Trillionaire: Cherishing the Breath of Life while Simultaneously Preparing for the Blow of Death!" book is dedicated to all youth and all adults who are children of the Most High that want to learn the doctrine of the **Most High (ELYOWN עֶלְיוֹן EL אֵל)** in a way that reflects the original languages of the bible before being translated, and that reflects the original Most High Heavenly Father's doctrine that Yashu'a Ha Mashiakh (Jesus the Messiah) taught.

Acknowledgements

We thank the Most High Heavenly Father who is: The Most High Heavenly One, the Sustainer, the Nourisher, the Provider of Life, and the Creator of the boundless universes, thank you for sending the Messiah Yashu'a (Jesus) who was a willing sacrifice, and for your angelic-beings that protect us, inspire us and guide us to obey you, inclusive of the Sun of Righteousness (**Shemesh** צְדָקָה pronounced **sheh'·mesh Tsĕdaqah** שֶׁמֶשׁ pronounced **tsed·ä·kä'**) who arises with healing in his wings as stated in the King James Version (KJV) bible book of **Malachi chapter 4 verse 2**, and we thank the Most High Heavenly One for life, for health and for everything else!

A Special Thank You to: My Dad (The Honorable: Mr. Woodie Hughes Sr.), and Mom (the Noble: Mrs. Annette Hughes) for accepting the Messiah Yashu'a (Jesus) and raising me and my brothers in a Godly home filled with love as they like the Messiah Yashu'a (Jesus); willingly sacrificed their youth and many worldly possessions to ensure that my brothers and I had the greatest opportunity to achieve the maximum levels of success in all areas of our lives; **thank you Mom and Dad**! A Special Thank You to: My Beloved Wife and best friend (Mrs. Tonya L. Hughes) who sacrificed her health and well-being to give birth to our children. Our children inspire me every day to keep working hard for our family and to continuously work hard to help uplift members of humanity so that we can work together to help people and the planet earth to maintain, and sustain positive health and balance for that great day, when: "Thy kingdom will come to earth as it is in heaven." We also thank the many other family members, friends, colleagues, mentors, and global spiritual family who are the children of the Most High and who are in the body of Christ. They are some of the peacemakers who are referred to in the KJV bible books of Psalms chapter 82 verses 6 and 7, John chapter 10 verse 34, and Matthew chapter 5 verse 9), who are always being persecuted by the children of Devil, who are mentioned in the KJV bible book of John Chapter 8 verse 44.

In the KJV bible book of Psalms chapter 82 verses 6 and 7; it states: "I have said, Ye are gods (אֱלֹהִים 'Elohiym); and all of you are children of the Most High. But ye shall die like men, and fall like one of the princes." In the KJV bible book of John chapter 10 verse 34; Yashu'a (Jesus) said: "Is it not written in your law, I said, Ye are gods (θεός Theos)?" In the KJV bible book of Matthew chapter 5 verse 9; Yashu'a (Jesus) said: "Blessed μακάριος Makarios are the peacemakers εἰρηνοποιός eirēnopoios for ὅτι hoti they αὐτός autos shall be called καλέω kaleō καλέω the children υἱός huios υἱός of God θεός Theos." In the KJV bible book of John chapter 8 verse 44; Yashu'a (Jesus) said: "Ye are of your father the devil, and the lusts of your father ye will do. He was a murderer from the beginning, and abode not in the truth, because there is no truth in him. When he speaketh a lie, he speaketh of his own: for he is a liar, and the father of it."

So, the children of the devil exhibit the characteristics of: heinous murder, lying, lust, slothful, wrath, pride, greed, hopeless-fear-disobedience, and wickedness. The children of the Most High exhibit the characteristics of: love, joy, peace, longsuffering (μακροθυμία makrothymía, patience, endurance, constancy, steadfastness, perseverance), gentleness, goodness, faith, meekness (πραότης praotēs, humility), and temperance (ἐγκράτεια enkráteia, self-control).

Who are the Children of the Most High Pristine Youth and Family Solutions, LLC.?

We are teachers of the doctrine of the Most High; the doctrine that the real Messiah Yashu'a (Jesus) taught. In the KJV bible book of John chapter 7 verse 16; the Messiah Yashu'a (Jesus) stated: "My doctrine isn't mine, but his that sent me." The Children of the Most High, Pristine Youth and Family Solutions, LLC. purpose is to do the Most High Heavenly Father's will only! We exist and work under the authority of the Most High Heavenly Father, who is the Creator and the Ruler of all of the boundless universes! We acknowledge the Messiah Jesus as our Savior who **we refer to** in his original Judean/Galilean Aramic (Hebrew) language birth name **Yasu'a** or **Yashu'a** (ישׁוע) meaning "**Savior**" and **Jesus,** who is **the Son of God** in English. **We have accepted the Lord Jesus Christ (Yashu'a Ha Mashiakh – Jesus the Messiah or Yehoshu'a, which means Yahayyu is Salvation or Yahayyu Saves) as our Savior and we are in the Body of Christ!**

CHILDREN OF THE MOST HIGH:
PRISTINE YOUTH AND FAMILY SOLUTIONS, LLC.
SONS AND DAUGHTERS OF THE MOST HIGH PUBLISHERS ®

What is the Mission, Vision, and Motto of the Children of the Most High; Pristine Youth and Family Solutions, LLC?

The Mission: To inspire and empower all children of the Most High to pristinely make the world a safe and healthy place for all members of humanity.

The Vision: To create a world that is ruled by Love and the "Will" of the Most High, void of negative emotions, greed, lusts and love of money.

According to the KJV bible book of Matthew chapter 19 verse 26, the Messiah Yashu'a (Jesus) said unto them, "With men this is impossible; but with God all things are possible." According to the KJV bible book of Philippians chapter 4 verse 13; it states: "I can do all things through Christ which strengthened me." Therefore; with God and through Christ, the children of the Most High Pristine Youth and Family Solutions, LLC. Mission and Vision can become a reality for the children of the Most High!

Motto: There is no right way to do the wrong thing!

Who is the Most High to the Children of the Most High Pristine Youth and Family Solutions, LLC.?

The Most High Heavenly Father is Love, the Sustainer, the Nourisher, the Provider of all Life, and the Omnipotent and the Omnipresent Creator of the boundless universes.

The Most High Heavenly Father encompasses and interpenetrates all existence inclusive of every part of nature both visible as well as invisible. Oh, Most High Heavenly Father, you are all, and there is nothing nearer to us than you; for you encompass all things! Glory be to you alone!

In the KJV bible book of John chapter 4 verse 23; the Messiah Yashu'a (Jesus) said: "God is a Spirit: and they that worship him must worship him in spirit and in truth." In the KJV bible book of Genesis, chapter 14 verse 18; it states: "And Melchizedek (**Malkiy-Tsedeq**, מַלְכִּי־צֶדֶק) king of Salem brought forth bread and wine: and he was the priest of the **Most High** (ELYOWN עֶלְיוֹן EL אֵל) God."

Who is the Real Messiah Jesus to the Children of the Most High Pristine Youth and Family Solutions, LLC.?

The Children of the Most High, Pristine Youth and Family Solutions, LLC., acknowledges the Real Messiah Jesus as our Savior who **we refer to** in his original Galilean/Judean Aramic (Hebrew) language, original birth name **Yasu'a (يسوع)** or **Yashu'a (ישוע)** meaning "**Savior**" also spelled Yeshua or Yehoshu'a, **Iesous** (Ἰησοῦς) in the Greek translation and as **Kurios** (Greek word for Lord), and **Issa** or **Isa** in Ashuric Syriac (Arabic). Now when **Yehoshu'a** is translated in the Hebrew language it translates as **Yahayyu Saves** or simply **Joshua**, and in the Galilean language as Yashu'a or **Yasu'a** Inar Rab (which translates as **Jesus Son of the Sustainer**), **Yashu'a Bar Yahayyu** (يا حيى, **Existing One**) in Modern Hebrew translates as **Savior Son of the Everliving** or **Savior Son of the**

xi

Existing One or **Living One**, **Yasu'** and **Haru** as **Karast** "Christ" to the **Ancient** original indigenous Egyptian people of what is called: "Egypt" today, not to be confused with the Egyptians who are the nonindigenous people who migrated to what is now known as Egypt. Yashu'a called **Jesus, is the Son of God** in English. Yashu'a (Jesus), **the Son of the Most High God** is the way back to the Most High. In the KJV bible book of John chapter 14 verse 6; the Messiah Yashu'a (Jesus) said: "I am the way, the truth, and the life: no man (the words: "no man" is not in the original language that this verse was revealed in. The original word for "no man" in the Greek KJV bible translation is: "**Oudeis**" (οὐδείς, Oudeis (is the KJV bible Greek Strong's Concordance#**3762**) means: *__not one; no one, nothing__*. So, this phrase is inclusive of males and females, not just males) cometh unto the Father, but by me." However, according to the Messiah Yashu'a (Jesus), no one can come to him unless the Most High Heavenly Father sends them to him. Yashu'a (Jesus) said in the KJV bible book of John chapter 6 verse 44: "No man (οὐδείς *oudeis*) can (δύναμαι *dynamai*) come (ἔρχομαι *erchomai*) to (πρός *pros*) me (μέ mé, meh), except (ἐὰν μή *ean mē*; KJV bible Greek Strong's Concordance#**3362** meaning: **if not, unless, whoever... not**) the Father which hath sent me draw (ἕλκω *helkō*; KJV bible Greek Strong's Concordance#**1670** meaning: **to draw by inward power, lead, impel; to drag (literally or figuratively)** him: and I will raise him up at the last day." Again, in the aforementioned verse, the words: "no man" is not in the original language that this verse was revealed in. The original word for "no man" is: "**Oudeis**" (οὐδείς, Oudeis (KJV bible

Greek Strong's Concordance#**3762**) means: _**not one**_; _**no one,**_ _**nothing**_.

What does the Children of the Most High Pristine Youth and Family Solutions, LLC. do?

The Children of the Most High; Pristine Youth and Family Solutions LLC. does the will of the Most High Heavenly Father. **Our targeted audiences are youth and adults who are children of the Most High**. They are celestial beings by nature and by the spirit of the Most High that is in them. The children of the Most High willingly allows love to dwell in them which automatically makes them to love others. In the KJV bible book of 1st John chapter 4 verses 7-10; it states: "Beloved, let us love one another: for love is of God; and every one that loveth is born of God, and knoweth God. He that loveth not, knoweth not God; for God is love. In this was manifested the love of God toward us, because that God sent his only begotten Son into the world, that we might live through him. Herein is love, not that we loved God, but that he loved us, and sent his Son to be the propitiation for our sins."

According to the Children of the Most High; Pristine Youth and Family Solutions LLC., what is the difference between celestial beings and terrestrial beings? According to the Online American Heritage Dictionary (2019), the word "**Celestial**" comes from the Old Latin word "Caelum" meaning "Heaven" or that which relates to the heavens, and heaven is an

Anglo-Saxon word, meaning "the region or expanse which surrounds the Planet Earth" and is ethereal, immortal, angelic, divine, or divination. The word "**Terrestrial**" is that which is within Earth's atmosphere, that which is earthly or worldly."

Celestial beings who are children of the Most High, define success as: "**the Most High's "Will" being done!**" Celestial beings are not drawn to what society defines as fun, Celestial beings' idea of fun, is doing the "**Will**" of the Most High. **Terrestrial** beings are driven to think, do and feel from that which society defines as: power, money, lusts, intoxication, and fun as recreation (**re-creation** of that which **wrecks-creation**; and over time causes damage to your body, mind, and spirit and can lead to the destruction of your body that God (אֱלֹהִים 'Elohiym) created. The Children of the Most High; Pristine Youth and Family Solutions LLC. teaches youth and adults True Vine Yashu'a (Jesus) positive life skills nonformal education known as: "**9X9 True Vine "Yashu'a" (Jesus) B.A.-K.A.-R.E. Sequential Order of Learning Habits of Success**" to help them succeed in life in the form of 21st century workshops, presentations and questions and answers study of the Most High's Scriptures from the original languages that the scriptures were revealed in. This method is utilized to explore how we can learn the Most High's doctrine and apply it in every aspect of our lives to ensure overall success in the eyesight of the Most High.

Why does the Children of the Most High Pristine Youth and Family Solutions, LLC. refer to themselves as Teachers / Administers of the Most High Heavenly Father's Doctrine instead of Preachers?

The Children of the Most High Pristine Youth and Family Solutions, LLC. refer to themselves as Teachers and **Administers of the Most High Heavenly Father's Doctrine** that Yashu'a (Jesus) taught instead of Preachers because the Most High inspired and endowed them with the knowledge and with the ability to teach with the True-Vine (Yashu'a, Jesus) Spirit of the Word of Knowledge in the KJV bible book of 1st Corinthians chapter 12 verse 8 to teach the Most High's Doctrine as mentioned in the KJV bible book of John chapter 7 verse 16. In the KJV bible book of Matthews chapter 28 verses 19-20, the Messiah Yashu'a (Jesus) said: "Go ye therefore, and teach all nations, baptizing them in the name of the Father, and of the Son, and of the Holy Ghost. Teaching them to observe all things whatsoever I have commanded you: and, lo, I am with you always, even unto the end of the world. Amen."

The word in the aforementioned KJV bible book of Matthews chapter 28 verse 19 for *teach* is: the **KJV bible Greek Strong's Concordance#3100 mathēteuō (μαθητεύω) which means: teach, instruct, be disciple.** The word in the book of Matthews chapter 28 verse 20 for *Teaching* is: the **KJV bible Greek Strong's Concordance#1321 didaskō (διδάσκω) which means: to teach, to hold discourse with others in order to instruct them, deliver didactic discourses, to be a teacher, to** discharge the office of a teacher, <u>conduct one's self as a teacher,</u> to teach one, to impart instruction, <u>instill doctrine into one,</u> the thing taught or enjoined, to explain or expound a thing, to teach one something. The word for **"Preach"** in **the KJV bible book of Matthew chapter 11 verse 1** is: the **KJV bible Greek Strong's Concordance#2784 kēryssō (κηρύσσω) which means to: preach, publish, and proclaim**.

In the KJV bible book of Matthew chapter 11 verse 1; it states: "And it came to pass, when Jesus had made an end of commanding his twelve disciples, he departed thence to **teach** and to **preach** in their cities. The plural noun of "teach" is "Teachers": the **KJV bible Greek Strong's Concordance#1320 didaskalos (διδάσκαλος,** meaning one who teaches or teachers) and has the same root foundation as the word for "Teach" (the **KJV bible Greek Strong's Concordance#1321 didaskō (διδάσκω)** in the book of Acts chapter 13 verse 1; and states:

"Now there were in the church that was at Antioch certain prophets and **teachers**; as Barnabas, and Simeon that was called **Niger**, and Lucius of Cyrene, and Manaen, which had been brought up with Herod the tetrarch, and Saul." In the aforementioned verse, the word: "Niger" is the **KJV Bible Greek Strong's Concordance#3526 Νίγερ (Niger)** which means: **Νίγερ Níger, neeg'-er; of Latin origin; black; Niger, a Christian**: **Niger**. According to the African American Registry (2019): "The history of the word **nigger is often traced to the Latin word Niger, meaning Black**. This word became the noun, Negro (Black person) in English." The KJV bible book of Hosea, chapter 4 verse 6; states: "My people are destroyed for lack of knowledge: because thou hast rejected knowledge, I will also reject thee, that thou shalt be no priest to me: seeing thou hast forgotten the law of thy God, I will also forget thy children." The KJV bible book of Isaiah, chapter 5 verse 13; states: "Therefore my people are gone into captivity, because they have no knowledge: and their honorable men are famished, and their multitude dried up with thirst."

So, the Children of the Most High Pristine Youth and Family Solutions, LLC. refer to themselves as **Teachers** instead of **Preachers** because after over 25 years of teaching and studying the scriptures in the languages that they were originally revealed in, the children of the Most High don't find themselves **preaching**, they found themselves **teaching**.

According to the Online American Heritage Dictionary, teaching means; instructing, explaining, and elaborating. So, we teach in an effort to ensure that the children of the Most High do their best to make the doctrine of the Most High clear in the minds of people who want to learn the original message or messages of the scriptures before they were translated into other languages. Why do the children of the Most High: Pristine Youth and Family Solutions, LLC. also refer to themselves as **Administers** of the Most High's Doctrine that the Messiah Yashu'a (Jesus) taught?

According to the Online American Heritage Dictionary (2019), Administer is defined as:

ad·min·is·ter (ăd-mĭnⁱĭ-stər)
v. **ad·min·is·tered, ad·min·is·ter·ing, ad·min·is·ters**
v.tr.
1. To have charge of; manage.
2.a. To apply as a remedy: *administer a sedative.*
1. To manage as an administrator.
2. To minister: *administering to their every whim.*

––––––––––––

[Middle English *administren*, from Old French *administrer*, from Latin *administrāre*: *ad*, ad- + *ministrāre*, to manage (from *minister, ministr-*, servant; see <u>MINISTER</u>).]

So, we are "**Administers of the Most High's Doctrine**" by way of the Most High Heavenly Father giving the Children of the Most High: Pristine Youth and Family Solutions, LLC. **charge of managing the administering** of his Doctrine to inspire and empower all children of the Most High to pristinely make the world a safe and healthy place for all members of humanity. Which occurs by **applying** the Doctrine of the Most High **as a remedy** to create a world that is ruled by Love and the "Will" of the Most High, void of negative emotions, greed, lusts and love of money.

Why does the work that the Children of the Most High Pristine Youth and Family Solutions, LLC. do Matter?

In order for the Children of the Most High; Pristine Youth and Family Solutions LLC. to be obedient to the Most High Heavenly Father, we seek to be positive difference makers who helps and teach youth and adults: to apply the doctrine of the Most High in all that they aspire to do and to teach them how to create positive predetermined goals, how to achieve positive success according to what positive success means to them, how to achieve positive happiness according to what positive happiness means to them, and how to learn to work together with members of humanity to create a world where all youth and all adults are happy, healthy, and balanced mentally, spiritually, physically, emotionally, financially, personally, professionally, and socially.

"Happiness is associated with and precedes numerous successful outcomes, as well as behaviors paralleling success, Lyubomirsky, King, & Diener, (2005). Furthermore, the evidence suggests that positive affect is the hallmark of well-being and may be the cause of many of the desirable characteristics, resources, and successes correlated with happiness, (Lyubomirsky, King, & Diener, (2005)." It also matters for our youth to receive the protection from the Most High Heavenly Father from all harm during the pre-adult years and beyond, in order to have an opportunity to become adults that can continue to create a world where all youth and all adults are happy, healthy, and balanced mentally, spiritually, physically, emotionally, financially, personally, professionally, and socially.

According the bible, this can only occur if our youth learn God's knowledge and God's laws. According to the KJV bible book of Hosea chapter 4 verse 6, the LORD states: "**My people are destroyed for lack of knowledge**: because thou hast rejected knowledge, I will also reject thee, that thou shalt be no priest to me: <u>**seeing thou hast forgotten the law of thy God, I will also forget thy children**</u>." So, according to the aforementioned verse, in order to best prepare today's youth to survive and thrive until adulthood and beyond, they need to learn **God's (אלהים Elôhîym)** knowledge (**Elôhîym, אלהים is the original word for "God" before being translated as the word: "God" in the KJV bible book of Genesis chapter 1 verse 1**), and **God's (אלהים Elôhîym)** laws to be eligible to receive **God's (אלהים Elôhîym)** protection from all harm. Therefore, today's youth must be informed with **God's (אלהים Elôhîym) A̲ll, W̲ise, A̲bundant, R̲ight, E̲xact (A.W.A.R.E.) Knowledge**. How do you know? Because God's **A.W.A.R.E.** knowledge is **best, accurate, correct (right, healthy)** and **exact** and best to guide and protect all of the global children of the Most High from all harm. For this reason, **God's (אלהים Elôhîym) A.W.A.R.E. Knowledge** gives the children of the Most High the ability to develop the habit of **positive thinking** or correct **(right, healthy) thinking** as oppose to **negative thinking** or **wrong thinking**. A person with **wrong knowledge** thinks negatively by having **wrong I. D. E. A. S. (I̲**mpure **D̲**esires **E̲**motionally **A̲**ctivated **S̲**equentially) or negative thoughts continuously, which leads to negative thinking, negative speaking, negative actions, and negative character. **Learning, applying and obeying the laws of Elohiym (God), activates the will of the Most High Heavenly Father in the mind which initiates all thoughts, and a person acts and speaks, as he or she thinks!** This is why in the KJV bible book of Hebrews chapter 8 verse 10; it states: "For this is the covenant that I will make with the house of Israel after those days, saith the Lord; **I will put my laws into their mind, and write them in their hearts**: and I will be to them a God, and they shall be to me a people."

In the KJV bible book of Revelation chapter 22 verses 12-16; Yashu'a (Jesus) stated: "And, behold, I come quickly; and my reward is with me, to give every man according as his work shall be. I am Alpha and Omega, the beginning and the end, the first and the last. Blessed are they that do his [the Most High, Heavenly Father's, **ELYOWN** עֶלְיוֹן **EL** אֵל] commandments, that they may have right to the tree of life,

xxi

and may enter in through the gates into the city. For without are dogs, and sorcerers, and whoremongers, and murderers, and idolaters, and whosoever loveth and maketh a lie. I Jesus [Yashu'a] have sent mine angel to testify unto you these things in the churches. I am the root and the offspring of David, and the bright and morning star."

Hence, **God's (אלהים Elôhîym) A.W.A.R.E. Knowledge** is the **best knowledge** for our youth to be taught in order for them to have the best opportunity to be recipients of **Elohiym** (God's) protection, and to help ensure that our youth will become the future positive leaders of tomorrow, today!

SPIRITUAL TRILLIONAIRE:
Cherishing the Breath of Life while Simultaneously
Preparing for the Blow of Death!

CHILDREN OF THE MOST HIGH:
PRISTINE YOUTH AND FAMILY SOLUTIONS, LLC.
SONS AND DAUGHTERS OF THE MOST HIGH PUBLISHERS ®

OH, GRACIOUS MOST HIGH HEAVENLY FATHER, HOLY IS YOUR
NAME, YOUR WILL BE DONE NOW AND FOREVER!

Introduction:

The Children of the Most High: Pristine Youth and Family Solutions, LLC. is putting forth this book entitled: "Spiritual Trillionaire: Cherishing the Breath of Life While Simultaneously Preparing for the Blow of Death" by the will of the Most High Heavenly Father to **inspire** ALL youth and ALL adults who are children of the Most High to attain, maintain and sustain positive spiritual health and positive spiritual wealth on the path to becoming a **Spiritual Trillionaire!** In order for this to occur, today's youth and adults must have the necessary knowledge needed to achieve success in all of their endeavors. What is success? Success is doing the "Will" of the Most High, success is being obedient to the Most High, and success is the progressive realization of a worthy idea which works in conjunction with the virtues of seriousness and sincerity. To possess these virtues, is to have tranquility, which is the mental, emotional and spiritual foundation for clarity, patience, and perseverance.

1

SPIRITUAL TRILLIONAIRE:
Cherishing the Breath of Life while Simultaneously
Preparing for the Blow of Death!

CHILDREN OF THE MOST HIGH:
PRISTINE YOUTH AND FAMILY SOLUTIONS, LLC.
SONS AND DAUGHTERS OF THE MOST HIGH PUBLISHERS ®

OH, GRACIOUS MOST HIGH HEAVENLY FATHER, HOLY IS YOUR NAME, YOUR WILL BE DONE NOW AND FOREVER!

The attributes of clarity, patience, and perseverance; helps' a person to create and work towards achieving their positive predetermined goals that are required for them to succeed in life. Goals inform people of the directions to where they want to go in life. Goals also help people to create the necessary plans or strategic steps in their minds that they must take, and know in order to make all of their dreams come true. Thought initiates all actions. The key to success and failure is that people become a reflection of their most dominant and most frequent thoughts. The choices that people make will determine what their actions will be. Consequences are the result of positive or negative actions. Consequences follow as a natural effect or a result of a previous action. Successful completion of goals, especially long-termed goals, requires patience. Patience is a virtue; of what? Patience is a virtue of success! So, it is important that we as true followers of the Real Messiah Yashu'a (Jesus Son of God) utilize this book as a 9X9 True Vine "Yashu'a" (Jesus) B.A.-K.A.-R.E. Sequential Order of Learning that **helps all youth and all adults who are children of the Most High to learn how to work together to create a world that is ruled by love and not ruled by negative emotions, greed, lusts and love of money**; a world where all youth and all adults are happy,

2

SPIRITUAL TRILLIONAIRE:
**Cherishing the Breath of Life while Simultaneously
Preparing for the Blow of Death!**

CHILDREN OF THE MOST HIGH:
PRISTINE YOUTH AND FAMILY SOLUTIONS, LLC.
SONS AND DAUGHTERS OF THE MOST HIGH PUBLISHERS ®

OH, GRACIOUS MOST HIGH HEAVENLY FATHER, HOLY IS YOUR
NAME, YOUR WILL BE DONE NOW AND FOREVER!

healthy, and balanced mentally, spiritually, physically, emotionally, financially, socially, personally, and professionally.

What is the English etymology of the word **inspire and spirit**? According to the Online Etymology Dictionary (2019), **inspire (v.)** mid-14c., enspiren, "*to fill (the mind, heart, etc., with grace*, etc.);*" also "*to prompt or induce (someone to do something*)," from Old French enspirer (13c.), from Latin inspirare "blow into, breathe upon," figuratively "inspire, excite, inflame," from in- "in" (from PIE root *en "in") + spirare "to breathe" (see spirit (n.). The Latin word was used as a loan-translation of Greek pnein in the Bible. General sense of **"influence or animate with an idea or purpose"** is from late 14c. Also, sometimes used in literal sense in Middle English. Related: Inspires; inspiring."

spirit (n.)
mid-13c., "animating or vital principle in man and animals," from Anglo-French spirit, Old French espirit "spirit, soul" (12c., Modern French esprit) and directly from Latin spiritus

SPIRITUAL TRILLIONAIRE:
Cherishing the Breath of Life while Simultaneously
Preparing for the Blow of Death!

CHILDREN OF THE MOST HIGH:
PRISTINE YOUTH AND FAMILY SOLUTIONS, LLC.
SONS AND DAUGHTERS OF THE MOST HIGH PUBLISHERS ®

OH, GRACIOUS MOST HIGH HEAVENLY FATHER, HOLY IS YOUR
NAME, YOUR WILL BE DONE NOW AND FOREVER!

"*a breathing* (<u>respiration, and of the wind</u>), breath; breath of a god," hence "*inspiration*; *breath of life*," hence "*life*;" also "*disposition, character; high spirit, vigor, courage; related to spirare* "*to breathe*," perhaps from PIE *(s) peis- "*to blow*."

The aforementioned correlation between the words *inspire* and *spirit* relate to *breathing* and *breath of life*. Therefore, we hope that the words in this book fill each reader's spirit with courage, soul with zest, mind with successful resolutions to life issues, and to **animate** (to give life) to thoughts that remind all members of humanity that: "**All the wealth in the world can't bring one person back from the dead! <u>From a moral integrity point of view; a person's life is worth more than all of the money and all of the wealth in the world! A person's life is more precious than all the pleasures in the world, and each person's life is truly invaluable</u>**!

What does **invaluable** mean? According to the Online American Heritage Dictionary (2019), **invaluable** is defined as: *Of inestimable value*; *priceless*."

4

SPIRITUAL TRILLIONAIRE:
Cherishing the Breath of Life while Simultaneously
Preparing for the Blow of Death!

CHILDREN OF THE MOST HIGH:
PRISTINE YOUTH AND FAMILY SOLUTIONS, LLC.
SONS AND DAUGHTERS OF THE MOST HIGH PUBLISHERS ®

OH, GRACIOUS MOST HIGH HEAVENLY FATHER, HOLY IS YOUR NAME, YOUR WILL BE DONE NOW AND FOREVER!

Therefore, the Children of the Most High: Pristine Youth and Family Solutions LLC. are working to inspire all members of humanity to discover their inner potential, and to develop their potential in a positive creative way that will help them to achieve all of their predetermined goals, while simultaneously helping other people to do the same.

The Children of the Most High: Pristine Youth and Family Solutions LLC. are also working diligently to **W**arn, **I**nform and **T**each youth and adults how to solve or successfully work through difficult problems or issues or situations by utilizing the **Children of the Most High Pristine Youth and Family Solutions, LLC. 9X9 True Vine "Yashu'a" (Jesus) B.A.-K.A.-R.E. ("RE" is pronounced as "RAY") Sequential Order of Learning**.

5

SPIRITUAL TRILLIONAIRE:
Cherishing the Breath of Life while Simultaneously Preparing for the Blow of Death!

CHILDREN OF THE MOST HIGH:
PRISTINE YOUTH AND FAMILY SOLUTIONS, LLC.
SONS AND DAUGHTERS OF THE MOST HIGH PUBLISHERS ®

OH, GRACIOUS MOST HIGH HEAVENLY FATHER, HOLY IS YOUR NAME, YOUR WILL BE DONE NOW AND FOREVER!

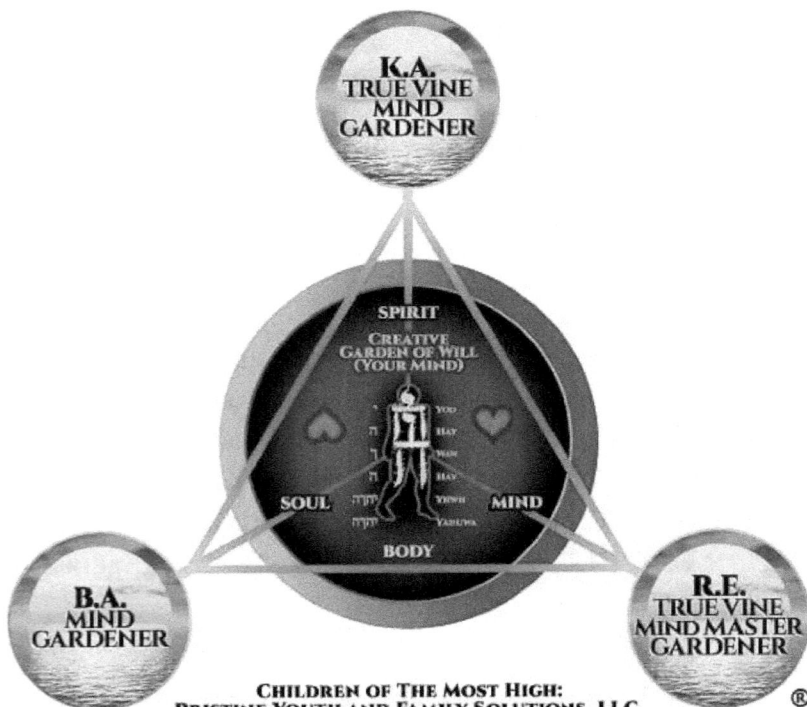

CHILDREN OF THE MOST HIGH:
PRISTINE YOUTH AND FAMILY SOLUTIONS, LLC.
9X9 TRUE VINE "YASHU'A" (JESUS) B.A.-K.A.-R.E.
SEQUENTIAL ORDER OF LEARNING®

6

SPIRITUAL TRILLIONAIRE:
Cherishing the Breath of Life while Simultaneously
Preparing for the Blow of Death!

CHILDREN OF THE MOST HIGH:
PRISTINE YOUTH AND FAMILY SOLUTIONS, LLC.
SONS AND DAUGHTERS OF THE MOST HIGH PUBLISHERS ®

OH, GRACIOUS MOST HIGH HEAVENLY FATHER, HOLY IS YOUR NAME, YOUR WILL BE DONE NOW AND FOREVER!

It is one of our greatest hopes that this publication will reach **50%** of the world's population over the next **9** years and that **50%** of the world's population will practice the **Children of the Most High Pristine Youth and Family Solutions, LLC. 9X9 True Vine "Yashu'a" (Jesus) B.A.-K.A.-R.E. Sequential Order of Learning Habits of Success** for **99** consecutive days! It is our hope that this publication inspires youth and adults to read or to continue the habit of reading. Also, it is our greatest hope that the information in this book helps to lead the children of the Most High back to the Most High Heavenly Father through the acceptance of the Messiah Yashu'a (Jesus), and sincere-hearted repentance to the Most High for all of their unforgiven sins in order to help them to achieve, maintain and sustain eternal success. The Children of the Most High: Pristine Youth and Family Solutions, LLC. **thanks' you so much for purchasing this book! May the Most High bless you with a peace of mind and pristine health!**

Is it possible to become a Spiritual Trillionaire?

SPIRITUAL TRILLIONAIRE:
Cherishing the Breath of Life while Simultaneously
Preparing for the Blow of Death!

CHILDREN OF THE MOST HIGH:
PRISTINE YOUTH AND FAMILY SOLUTIONS, LLC.
SONS AND DAUGHTERS OF THE MOST HIGH PUBLISHERS ®

OH, GRACIOUS MOST HIGH HEAVENLY FATHER, HOLY IS YOUR
NAME, YOUR WILL BE DONE NOW AND FOREVER!

Some may say: "it is **impossible** to become a Spiritual Trillionaire," right? The Children of the Most High: Pristine Youth and Family Solutions, LLC. merely ask; does the word: **Im-possible** spell **I'm-possible**? In the KJV bible book of Matthew chapter 19 verse 26; the Messiah Yashu'a (Jesus) said: "With men this is impossible, with God, all things are possible." According to the bible, is money evil? Or is the love of money evil? In the KJV bible book of 1st Timothy chapter 6 verse 10; it states: "For *the love of money* is the root of all evil: which while some coveted after, they have erred from the faith, and pierced themselves through with many sorrows."

~OH, MOST HIGH HEAVENLY FATHER,
HELP US TO NOT WASTE TIME AND TO NOT GIVE IN TO
DISAGREEABLE THOUGHTS. AMEN~

SPIRITUAL TRILLIONAIRE:
Cherishing the Breath of Life while Simultaneously
Preparing for the Blow of Death!

CHILDREN OF THE MOST HIGH:
PRISTINE YOUTH AND FAMILY SOLUTIONS, LLC.
SONS AND DAUGHTERS OF THE MOST HIGH PUBLISHERS ®

OH, GRACIOUS MOST HIGH HEAVENLY FATHER, HOLY IS YOUR
NAME, YOUR WILL BE DONE NOW AND FOREVER!

Chapter 1: Do You Value Money? Why? Or Why not?

Yashu'a (Jesus) said: "After this manner therefore pray ye:
Our Father which art in heaven, hallowed (Holy) be thy
name. Thy kingdom come, thy will be done in earth, as it is
in heaven. Give us this day our daily bread. And forgive us
our debts, as we forgive our debtors. And lead us not into
temptation, but deliver us from evil: For thine is the
kingdom, and the power, and the glory, forever. Amen."

What is money? According the Online American Heritage
Dictionary (2019), money is defined as: "A medium that can be
exchanged for goods and services and is used as a measure of
their values on the market, including among its forms a
commodity such as gold, an officially issued coin or note, or a
deposit in a checking account or other readily liquefiable

SPIRITUAL TRILLIONAIRE:
Cherishing the Breath of Life while Simultaneously Preparing for the Blow of Death!

CHILDREN OF THE MOST HIGH:
PRISTINE YOUTH AND FAMILY SOLUTIONS, LLC.
SONS AND DAUGHTERS OF THE MOST HIGH PUBLISHERS ®

OH, GRACIOUS MOST HIGH HEAVENLY FATHER, HOLY IS YOUR NAME, YOUR WILL BE DONE NOW AND FOREVER!

account. **What is the purpose of money**? On the top front left side of an American $1 bill, it says: *"this note is legal tender for all debts, public and private"*?

So, according to the statement on the top front left side of an American $1dollar bill, the **purpose** of having money is **to pay for all debts, public and private**. Is having a lot of money important to you? If so, why is it important to you? If not, why is it not important to you to have a lot of money? Are you financially wealthy or rich? If not, do you aspire to be wealthy or rich? As it relates to financial wealth, are you a millionaire? billionaire? Or trillionaire? If not, do you intentionally work hard to become a millionaire or billionaire or trillionaire?

SPIRITUAL TRILLIONAIRE:
**Cherishing the Breath of Life while Simultaneously
Preparing for the Blow of Death!**

CHILDREN OF THE MOST HIGH:
PRISTINE YOUTH AND FAMILY SOLUTIONS, LLC.
SONS AND DAUGHTERS OF THE MOST HIGH PUBLISHERS ®

OH, GRACIOUS MOST HIGH HEAVENLY FATHER, HOLY IS YOUR
NAME, YOUR WILL BE DONE NOW AND FOREVER!

If you are not a millionaire, billionaire or trillionaire, what would you do with your money if you became a millionaire, or billionaire, or trillionaire? Have you ever thought about becoming a trillionaire? If not, why not? What is the definition of: **wealthy**, **rich**, **millionaire**, **billionaire**, and **trillionaire**?

According to the Online American Heritage Dictionary (2019), wealthy is defined as:

wealth·y (wĕl′thē)

adj. **wealth·i·er**, **wealth·i·est**

SPIRITUAL TRILLIONAIRE:
**Cherishing the Breath of Life while Simultaneously
Preparing for the Blow of Death!**

CHILDREN OF THE MOST HIGH:
PRISTINE YOUTH AND FAMILY SOLUTIONS, LLC.
SONS AND DAUGHTERS OF THE MOST HIGH PUBLISHERS ®

OH, GRACIOUS MOST HIGH HEAVENLY FATHER, HOLY IS YOUR
NAME, YOUR WILL BE DONE NOW AND FOREVER!

1. Having wealth; rich. See Synonyms at <u>rich</u>.

2. Marked by abundance: *a wealthy land.*

3. Well supplied: *wealthy in compassion.*

n.

(used with a pl. verb) Rich people considered as a group. Often used with *the* **wealth'i·ly** *adv. And* **wealth'i·ness** *n.*

According to the Online American Heritage Dictionary (2019), rich is defined as:

rich (rĭch)

adj. **rich·er, rich·est**

1. Having great material wealth: *He was so rich he didn't have to work.*

2. a. Having great worth or value: *a rich harvest.*

b. Made of or containing valuable materials: *rich cabinetry.*

c. Magnificent; sumptuous: *a rich banquet.*

SPIRITUAL TRILLIONAIRE:
Cherishing the Breath of Life while Simultaneously
Preparing for the Blow of Death!

CHILDREN OF THE MOST HIGH:
PRISTINE YOUTH AND FAMILY SOLUTIONS, LLC.
SONS AND DAUGHTERS OF THE MOST HIGH PUBLISHERS ®

OH, GRACIOUS MOST HIGH HEAVENLY FATHER, HOLY IS YOUR
NAME, YOUR WILL BE DONE NOW AND FOREVER!

3. Abundant or productive, as:

a. Having an abundant supply: *Meat is rich in protein.*

b. Abounding in natural resources: *a rich region.*

c. Having many nutrients for plant growth; fertile: *rich land.*

d. Very productive and therefore financially profitable: *rich seams of coal.*

4. a. Containing a large amount of choice ingredients, such as butter, sugar, or eggs, and therefore unusually heavy or sweet: *a rich dessert.*

b. Strong in aroma or flavor: *a rich coffee.*

c. Containing a large proportion of fuel to air: *a rich gas mixture.*

5. a. Pleasantly full and mellow: *a rich tenor voice.*

b. Warm and strong in color: *a rich brown velvet.*

6. a. Highly varied: *a museum showcasing a rich assortment of artworks.*

13

SPIRITUAL TRILLIONAIRE:
**Cherishing the Breath of Life while Simultaneously
Preparing for the Blow of Death!**

CHILDREN OF THE MOST HIGH:
PRISTINE YOUTH AND FAMILY SOLUTIONS, LLC.
SONS AND DAUGHTERS OF THE MOST HIGH PUBLISHERS ®

OH, GRACIOUS MOST HIGH HEAVENLY FATHER, HOLY IS YOUR
NAME, YOUR WILL BE DONE NOW AND FOREVER!

b. Highly developed or complex: *rich musical harmonies.*

7. *Informal* Highly amusing, often for being absurd or preposterous.
n. (used with a pl. verb) Wealthy people considered as a group. Often used with *the*: *taxes paid by the very rich.*

[Middle English *riche*, from Old French (of Germanic origin) and from Old English *rīce*, strong, powerful; see **reg-** in the Appendix of Indo-European roots.]

rich'ly *adv.*
rich'ness *n.*

According to the Online American Heritage Dictionary (2019), millionaire is defined as:

mil·lion·aire - (mĭl'yə-nâr')

n. A person whose wealth amounts to at least a million dollars, pounds, or the equivalent in other currency.

SPIRITUAL TRILLIONAIRE:
**Cherishing the Breath of Life while Simultaneously
Preparing for the Blow of Death!**

CHILDREN OF THE MOST HIGH:
PRISTINE YOUTH AND FAMILY SOLUTIONS, LLC.
SONS AND DAUGHTERS OF THE MOST HIGH PUBLISHERS ®

OH, GRACIOUS MOST HIGH HEAVENLY FATHER, HOLY IS YOUR
NAME, YOUR WILL BE DONE NOW AND FOREVER!

[French *millionnaire*, from *million*, million, from Old French *milion*; see MILLION.]

According to the Online American Heritage Dictionary (2019), billionaire is defined as:

bil·lion·aire - (bĭl′yə-nâr', bĭl′yə-nâr')

n. A person whose wealth amounts to at least a billion dollars, pounds, or the equivalent in other currency.

trill·lion·aire - (trĭll′yə-nâr', trĭll′yə-nâr')

n. A person whose wealth amounts to at least a trillion dollars, pounds, or the equivalent in other currency.

After reviewing the aforementioned definitions, if you became a millionaire, billionaire or trillionaire of financial assets, **would you utilize your wealth to create 21st century safe, sustainable agriculture farms nationally and/or internationally to help end world hunger?**

15

SPIRITUAL TRILLIONAIRE:
Cherishing the Breath of Life while Simultaneously
Preparing for the Blow of Death!

CHILDREN OF THE MOST HIGH:
PRISTINE YOUTH AND FAMILY SOLUTIONS, LLC.
SONS AND DAUGHTERS OF THE MOST HIGH PUBLISHERS ®

OH, GRACIOUS MOST HIGH HEAVENLY FATHER, HOLY IS YOUR
NAME, YOUR WILL BE DONE NOW AND FOREVER!

Why does sustainable agriculture matter to every person in the world? Sustainable agriculture matters because if there is no agriculture, there is no food. According to the United States of America Congress, how is **sustainable agriculture** defined? Congress defines **sustainable agriculture** as: "an integrated system of plant and animal production practices having a site-specific application that will, over the long term:

16

SPIRITUAL TRILLIONAIRE:
**Cherishing the Breath of Life while Simultaneously
Preparing for the Blow of Death!**

CHILDREN OF THE MOST HIGH:
PRISTINE YOUTH AND FAMILY SOLUTIONS, LLC.
SONS AND DAUGHTERS OF THE MOST HIGH PUBLISHERS ®

OH, GRACIOUS MOST HIGH HEAVENLY FATHER, HOLY IS YOUR
NAME, YOUR WILL BE DONE NOW AND FOREVER!

1. Satisfy human food and fiber needs.

2. Enhance environmental quality and the natural resource base upon which the agricultural economy depends.

3. Make the most efficient use of nonrenewable resources and on-farm resources and integrate, where appropriate, natural biological cycles and controls.

4. Sustain the economic viability of farm operations.

5. Enhance the quality of life for farmers and society as a whole."

If you are a millionaire, billionaire or trillionaire of financial assets, **do you utilize your wealth to provide free health care for vulnerable populations of youth and adults nationally and/or internationally to help them improve their overall physical and mental well-being?**

According to the National Institute of Food and Agriculture (NIFA), United States Department of Agriculture (USDA, 2018), "**Vulnerable populations** are groups and communities

17

SPIRITUAL TRILLIONAIRE:
Cherishing the Breath of Life while Simultaneously
Preparing for the Blow of Death!

CHILDREN OF THE MOST HIGH:
PRISTINE YOUTH AND FAMILY SOLUTIONS, LLC.
SONS AND DAUGHTERS OF THE MOST HIGH PUBLISHERS ®

OH, GRACIOUS MOST HIGH HEAVENLY FATHER, HOLY IS YOUR
NAME, YOUR WILL BE DONE NOW AND FOREVER!

a higher risk for poor health as a result of the barriers they experience to social, economic, political and environmental resources, as well as limitations due to illness or disability. The well-being of the United States depends upon the well-being of our children and youth. At present, populations of young people may be identified as vulnerable based on situational characteristics such as early parenthood, disconnection from school and work, homelessness, and involvement in the juvenile justice and foster care systems.

"Support for healthy development is an integral part of a solid foundation for young people. But data sources suggest that specific populations, including but not limited to those growing up in low-income households, children and youth of color, legal immigrants and their children, and children and youth with (dis)abilities, are significantly under-served. These vulnerable populations — which comprise of a large and growing percentage of our country's young people — disproportionately contend with conditions that often compromise healthy development and access to support for it, even as they carry rich cultural resources and cultivate strength and insight through adversity."

SPIRITUAL TRILLIONAIRE:
Cherishing the Breath of Life while Simultaneously
Preparing for the Blow of Death!

CHILDREN OF THE MOST HIGH:
PRISTINE YOUTH AND FAMILY SOLUTIONS, LLC.
SONS AND DAUGHTERS OF THE MOST HIGH PUBLISHERS ®

OH, GRACIOUS MOST HIGH HEAVENLY FATHER, HOLY IS YOUR
NAME, YOUR WILL BE DONE NOW AND FOREVER!

If you are **not** a millionaire, billionaire or trillionaire of financial assets, **do you advocate that humanity practice being just to the afflicted and needy? Do you advocate that humanity practice defending the poor, motherless and fatherless from all injustices? Do you volunteer or work professionally to empower, inspire, teach or feed the most vulnerable members of humanity?**

Dr. George Washington Carver said: "We have become ninety-nine percent money mad. The method of living at home modestly and within our income, laying a little by systematically for the proverbial rainy day which is due to come, can almost be listed among the lost arts. How far you go in life depends on your being tender with the young, compassionate with the aged, sympathetic with the striving and tolerant of the weak and strong. Because someday in your life you will have been all of these. There is no short cut to achievement. It is not the style of clothes one wears, neither the kind of automobile one drives, nor the amount of money one has in the bank, that counts. These mean nothing. It is simply service that measures success."

SPIRITUAL TRILLIONAIRE:
Cherishing the Breath of Life while Simultaneously
Preparing for the Blow of Death!

CHILDREN OF THE MOST HIGH:
PRISTINE YOUTH AND FAMILY SOLUTIONS, LLC.
SONS AND DAUGHTERS OF THE MOST HIGH PUBLISHERS ®

OH, GRACIOUS MOST HIGH HEAVENLY FATHER, HOLY IS YOUR
NAME, YOUR WILL BE DONE NOW AND FOREVER!

If you are **not** a millionaire, billionaire or trillionaire of financial assets, are you a person or do you know a person that has worked hard for many years and has no source of income? Or has a fixed monthly income that is not enough money to buy the daily food they need and not enough to pay for their mandatory monthly expenses?

Or are you a person or do you know a person who works more than one job and still lives paycheck to paycheck, or do you know a person who does not make enough money to save any of it, and has no disposable cash or very limited disposable cash to do something with instead of paying bills?

If so, are we working to pay bills and buy food to eat or are we working to create financial wealth or both? If the majority of people who have jobs or careers spend the best hours of the day for 30 to 80 years of their lives working to accumulate financial wealth, to take care of themselves, and/or family and/or friends, paying bills, and buying food to feed their physical bodies; **how much quality time do you spend each day to feed yourselves spiritually to obtain and sustain a positive spiritual health status? And what does that mean to you?**

20

SPIRITUAL TRILLIONAIRE:
Cherishing the Breath of Life while Simultaneously
Preparing for the Blow of Death!

CHILDREN OF THE MOST HIGH:
PRISTINE YOUTH AND FAMILY SOLUTIONS, LLC.
SONS AND DAUGHTERS OF THE MOST HIGH PUBLISHERS ®

OH, GRACIOUS MOST HIGH HEAVENLY FATHER, HOLY IS YOUR
NAME, YOUR WILL BE DONE NOW AND FOREVER!

If a person who lives in a capitalistic society, says: "I need money to pay for my monthly bills that provides me with the ability to financially take care of my family and myself; according to the bible, **what is wrong with me loving the money that I need to pay my monthly bills that provides me with the ability to financially take care of my family and myself?**"

According the KJV bible book of Ecclesiastics chapter 5 verse 10; it states: "He that loveth *silver* כסף (**Keseph**) **money**) shall not be satisfied with silver כסף (**Keseph**) **money**); nor he that loveth abundance with increase: this is also vanity." **What does this verse mean in the original Aramic (Hebrew) it was originally revealed in?**

- "He that **loveth** "אהב אהב" 'âhab 'âhêb). The original Aramic (Hebrew) word for the translated English word: "loveth or love" is: "אהב אהב" 'âhab 'âhêb, aw-*hab', aw-habe';* אהב אהב is the KJV bible Hebrew Strong's Concordance **#157.** It has a primitive root meaning; to *have affection* for (sexually or otherwise), Usage: to love, (be-) love (-d, -ly, -r), like, friend."

21

SPIRITUAL TRILLIONAIRE:
**Cherishing the Breath of Life while Simultaneously
Preparing for the Blow of Death!**

CHILDREN OF THE MOST HIGH:
PRISTINE YOUTH AND FAMILY SOLUTIONS, LLC.
SONS AND DAUGHTERS OF THE MOST HIGH PUBLISHERS ®

OH, GRACIOUS MOST HIGH HEAVENLY FATHER, HOLY IS YOUR
NAME, YOUR WILL BE DONE NOW AND FOREVER!

He that loveth **silver** (כסף (**keseph**), keh'-sef (**money**); כסף – the word for **silver** is the KJV bible Hebrew Strong's Concordance#**3701**) and means keh'-sef (**money**). In the KJV bible book of **Ecclesiastics chapter 5 verse 10** in other bible translations, it states:

Christian Standard Bible
"The one who loves silver is never satisfied with silver, and whoever loves wealth is never satisfied with income. This too is futile."

Contemporary English Bible Version
"If you love money and wealth, you will never be satisfied with what you have. This doesn't make a bit of sense."

Good News Translation
"If you love money, you will never be satisfied; if you long to be rich, you will never get all you want. It is useless." In the KJV bible book of **1st Timothy chapter 6 verse 10**; it states: "For *the love of money* is the root of all evil: which while some coveted after, they have erred from the faith, and pierced themselves through with many sorrows."

22

SPIRITUAL TRILLIONAIRE:
Cherishing the Breath of Life while Simultaneously
Preparing for the Blow of Death!

CHILDREN OF THE MOST HIGH:
PRISTINE YOUTH AND FAMILY SOLUTIONS, LLC.
SONS AND DAUGHTERS OF THE MOST HIGH PUBLISHERS ®

OH, GRACIOUS MOST HIGH HEAVENLY FATHER, HOLY IS YOUR
NAME, YOUR WILL BE DONE NOW AND FOREVER!

However, it is also important to be made aware that the lack of money or the lack of things money can buy, inclusive of health care, can lead to much preventable suffering. In the KJV bible book of 1ˢᵗ John chapter 2 verses 15-17; it states: **"Love not the world, neither the things that are in the world. If any man loves the world, the love of the <u>Father</u> (ELYOWN עֶלְיוֹן EL אֵל, the Most High) is not in him.** For all that is in the world, the lust of the flesh, and the lust of the eyes, and the pride of life, **is not of the Father (ELYOWN עֶלְיוֹן EL אֵל, the Most High**), but is of the world. And the world passeth away, and the lust thereof: **<u>but he that doeth the will of God abideth forever</u>."**

So, in response to the statement: "A person who lives in a capitalistic society, who says: "I need money to pay for my monthly bills that provides me with the ability to financially take care of my family and myself; according to the aforementioned bible verses, if a person loves money, **the love of the Most High Heavenly Father is not in him or her,** and he or she will not ever be satisfied because the love of money is rooted in **the Deadly Venom <u>desire</u> of greed** and greed is unsatisfiable!

SPIRITUAL TRILLIONAIRE:
Cherishing the Breath of Life while Simultaneously
Preparing for the Blow of Death!

CHILDREN OF THE MOST HIGH:
PRISTINE YOUTH AND FAMILY SOLUTIONS, LLC.
SONS AND DAUGHTERS OF THE MOST HIGH PUBLISHERS ®

OH, GRACIOUS MOST HIGH HEAVENLY FATHER, HOLY IS YOUR
NAME, YOUR WILL BE DONE NOW AND FOREVER!

This is why the **Good News Translation** of the bible says: "If you love money, you will never be satisfied; if you long to be rich, you will never get all you want. It is **useless** (meaning: **futile, pointless, purposeless, impractical, vain, in vain, to no purpose, to no avail, unavailing, hopeless, unusable, ineffectual, fruitless, unprofitable, profitless, unproductive, unachievable**)."

A man once stated to **Siddhartha Gautama "Buddha"**, "**I want happiness.**" Buddha said, "**First remove "I," that's Ego, then remove "want," that's Desire. See now, you are left with only "Happiness."** Siddhartha Gautama "Buddha" also said: "**Desire is the lead to all suffering.**"

SPIRITUAL TRILLIONAIRE:
Cherishing the Breath of Life while Simultaneously
Preparing for the Blow of Death!

CHILDREN OF THE MOST HIGH:
PRISTINE YOUTH AND FAMILY SOLUTIONS, LLC.
SONS AND DAUGHTERS OF THE MOST HIGH PUBLISHERS ®

OH, GRACIOUS MOST HIGH HEAVENLY FATHER, HOLY IS YOUR
NAME, YOUR WILL BE DONE NOW AND FOREVER!

The Children of the Most High, Pristine Youth and Family
Solutions LLC. refer to **greed** as **1 of the 9 Deadly Venoms of
Desires of the great dragon, that old serpent called the devil
and satan which deceiveth the whole world.**

25

SPIRITUAL TRILLIONAIRE:
**Cherishing the Breath of Life while Simultaneously
Preparing for the Blow of Death!**

CHILDREN OF THE MOST HIGH:
PRISTINE YOUTH AND FAMILY SOLUTIONS, LLC.
SONS AND DAUGHTERS OF THE MOST HIGH PUBLISHERS ®

OH, GRACIOUS MOST HIGH HEAVENLY FATHER, HOLY IS YOUR
NAME, YOUR WILL BE DONE NOW AND FOREVER!

Therefore, it is not possible for a person to attain positive spiritual health and positive spiritual wealth if a person is caught in the devil's web or if a person is poisoned emotionally (heart), mentally (mind) or possessed spiritually (spirit) by **greed** or any of **the 9 Deadly Venoms of the Desires of the great dragon, that old serpent called the devil and satan which deceiveth the whole world.**

SPIRITUAL TRILLIONAIRE:
**Cherishing the Breath of Life while Simultaneously
Preparing for the Blow of Death!**

CHILDREN OF THE MOST HIGH:
PRISTINE YOUTH AND FAMILY SOLUTIONS, LLC.
SONS AND DAUGHTERS OF THE MOST HIGH PUBLISHERS

OH, GRACIOUS MOST HIGH HEAVENLY FATHER, HOLY IS YOUR
NAME, YOUR WILL BE DONE NOW AND FOREVER!

THE DEVIL'S WEB

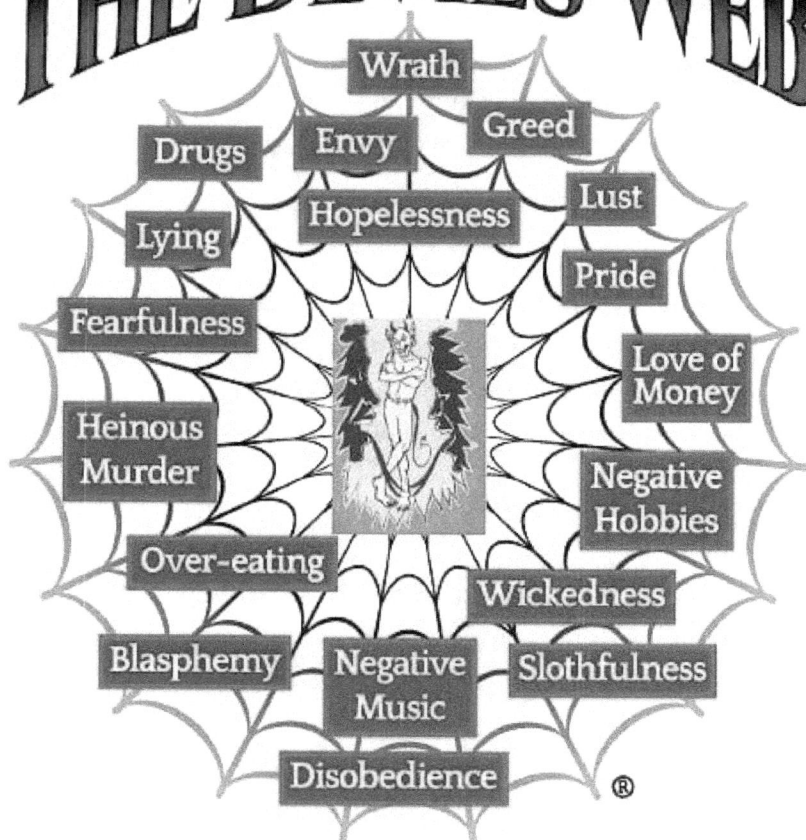

Wrath

Envy

Greed

Drugs

Hopelessness

Lust

Lying

Pride

Fearfulness

Love of Money

Heinous Murder

Negative Hobbies

Over-eating

Wickedness

Blasphemy

Negative Music

Slothfulness

Disobedience

®

27

SPIRITUAL TRILLIONAIRE:
Cherishing the Breath of Life while Simultaneously
Preparing for the Blow of Death!

CHILDREN OF THE MOST HIGH:
PRISTINE YOUTH AND FAMILY SOLUTIONS, LLC.
SONS AND DAUGHTERS OF THE MOST HIGH PUBLISHERS ®

OH, GRACIOUS MOST HIGH HEAVENLY FATHER, HOLY IS YOUR
NAME, YOUR WILL BE DONE NOW AND FOREVER!

How does Desires and Discipline Influence how we utilize our "Will" to make moment to moment Decisions?

Siddhartha Gautama "Buddha" also said: "**Desire is the lead to all suffering**." According the American Heritage Online Dictionary (2019), desire is defined as:

de·sire (dĭ-zīr)

tr.v. **de·sired, de·sir·ing, de·sires**
1. To wish or long for; want: *a reporter who desires an interview; a teen who desires to travel.*
2. To want to have sex with (another person).

3. To express a wish for; request.
n.
1. a. The feeling of wanting to have something or wishing that something will happen.
b. An instance of this feeling: *She had a lifelong desire to visit China.*

2. Sexual appetite; passion.

28

SPIRITUAL TRILLIONAIRE:
**Cherishing the Breath of Life while Simultaneously
Preparing for the Blow of Death!**

CHILDREN OF THE MOST HIGH:
PRISTINE YOUTH AND FAMILY SOLUTIONS, LLC.
SONS AND DAUGHTERS OF THE MOST HIGH PUBLISHERS ®

OH, GRACIOUS MOST HIGH HEAVENLY FATHER, HOLY IS YOUR
NAME, YOUR WILL BE DONE NOW AND FOREVER!

3. An object of such feeling or passion: *A quiet evening with you is my only desire.*

4. *Archaic* A request or petition.

[Middle English *desiren*, from Old French *desirer*, from Latin *dēsīderāre*, to observe or feel the absence of, miss, desire: *dē-*, de- +, *-sīderāre* (as in *cōnsīderāre*, to observe attentively, contemplate; see CONSIDER).]

de·sir·er *n.*

Synonyms: **desire, covet, crave, want, wish**
These verbs mean to have a strong longing for: *desire peace; coveted the new car; craving fame and fortune; wanted a drink of water; wished that she had gone to the beach.*

As we see from the aforementioned meanings of the word **"desire"**, it is critical to our acquisition of maintaining and sustaining of positive spiritual health and positive spiritual wealth that we eliminate of all desires that will lead our lives into preventable sufferings and misery!

29

SPIRITUAL TRILLIONAIRE:
**Cherishing the Breath of Life while Simultaneously
Preparing for the Blow of Death!**

CHILDREN OF THE MOST HIGH:
PRISTINE YOUTH AND FAMILY SOLUTIONS, LLC.
SONS AND DAUGHTERS OF THE MOST HIGH PUBLISHERS ®

OH, GRACIOUS MOST HIGH HEAVENLY FATHER, HOLY IS YOUR
NAME, YOUR WILL BE DONE NOW AND FOREVER!

In the Aramic (Hebrew) language of the KJV bible book of Deuteronomy chapter 5 verse 21; the word for "**desire**" is **Khaw'mad** חָמַד, **KJV Bible Hebrew Strong's Concordance#2530. Khaw'mad** חָמַד means to "**desire, to take pleasure, to delight**. In the KJV bible book of Deuteronomy chapter 5 verse 21; it states: "Neither shalt thou **desire** thy neighbor's wife, neither shalt thou covet thy neighbor's house, his field, or his manservant, or his maidservant, his ox, or his ass, or any*thing* that *is* thy neighbor's."

In the Greek language of the KJV bible book of Ephesians chapter 2 verse 3, the word for "**desire**" is "**Thelema**" (θέλημα). "**Thelema**" (θέλημα) means "**Will, Desire, Pleasure, Denoting the Inward Affection of the Mind, Rather than the External Object.**" In the KJV bible in the book of Ephesians chapter 2 verse 3; it states: "Among whom also we all had our conversation in times past in the lusts of our flesh, fulfilling the **desires** of the flesh and of the mind; and were by nature the children of wrath, even as others."

30

SPIRITUAL TRILLIONAIRE:
**Cherishing the Breath of Life while Simultaneously
Preparing for the Blow of Death!**

CHILDREN OF THE MOST HIGH:
PRISTINE YOUTH AND FAMILY SOLUTIONS, LLC.
SONS AND DAUGHTERS OF THE MOST HIGH PUBLISHERS ®

OH, GRACIOUS MOST HIGH HEAVENLY FATHER, HOLY IS YOUR
NAME, YOUR WILL BE DONE NOW AND FOREVER!

According to the Online American Heritage Dictionary (2019),
desire is the counterpart of **discipline**. **Discipline** is defined as:

dis·ci·pline (dĭs-ə-plĭn)
n.

1. Training expected to produce a specific character or pattern
of behavior, especially training that produces moral or mental
improvement: *was raised in the strictest discipline.*

2. a. Control obtained by enforcing compliance or order:
military discipline.
b. Controlled behavior resulting from disciplinary training;
self-control: *Dieting takes a lot of discipline.*
c. A state of order based on submission to rules and authority:
a teacher who demanded discipline in the classroom.

3. Punishment intended to correct or train: *subjected to harsh
discipline.*

SPIRITUAL TRILLIONAIRE:
**Cherishing the Breath of Life while Simultaneously
Preparing for the Blow of Death!**

CHILDREN OF THE MOST HIGH:
PRISTINE YOUTH AND FAMILY SOLUTIONS, LLC.
SONS AND DAUGHTERS OF THE MOST HIGH PUBLISHERS

OH, GRACIOUS MOST HIGH HEAVENLY FATHER, HOLY IS YOUR
NAME, YOUR WILL BE DONE NOW AND FOREVER!

4. A set of rules or methods, as those regulating the practice of a church or monastic order.

5. A branch of knowledge or teaching: *the discipline of mathematics.*
tr.v. **dis·ci·plined, dis·ci·plin·ing, dis·ci·plines**

1. To train by instruction and practice, as in following rules or developing self-control: *The sergeant disciplined the recruits to become soldiers.* See Synonyms at <u>teach</u>.

2. To punish in order to gain control or enforce obedience. See Synonyms at <u>punish</u>.

3. To impose order on: *needed to discipline their study habits.*

[Middle English, from Old French *descepline*, from Latin *disciplīna*, from *discipulus*, pupil; see <u>DISCIPLE</u>.]

Dis·ci·pli·nal (-plə-nəl) *adj.*
Dis·ci·plin'er *n.*

SPIRITUAL TRILLIONAIRE:
Cherishing the Breath of Life while Simultaneously
Preparing for the Blow of Death!

CHILDREN OF THE MOST HIGH:
PRISTINE YOUTH AND FAMILY SOLUTIONS, LLC.
SONS AND DAUGHTERS OF THE MOST HIGH PUBLISHERS ®

OH, GRACIOUS MOST HIGH HEAVENLY FATHER, HOLY IS YOUR
NAME, YOUR WILL BE DONE NOW AND FOREVER!

Being disciplined, can help a person to overcome life traumas, life changing events, or doing your best to overcome a difficult situation, or working through burdensome responsibilities or to overcome the temptations of **the 9 Deadly Venoms of the Desires of the great dragon, that old serpent called the devil and satan which deceiveth the whole world. How?**

**ON THE MOST HIGH HEAVENLY
FATHER!**

By keeping our minds and hearts focused on loving the Most High Heavenly Father, obeying the Most High Heavenly Father's commandments, only doing the Most High Heavenly Father's "**Will**", being a willing obedient instrument of the Most High Heavenly Father's "**Will**" above all else, and through loving the Messiah Yashu'a (Jesus), and adhering to the Most High's Heavenly Father's Doctrine that he taught.

SPIRITUAL TRILLIONAIRE:
Cherishing the Breath of Life while Simultaneously
Preparing for the Blow of Death!

CHILDREN OF THE MOST HIGH:
PRISTINE YOUTH AND FAMILY SOLUTIONS, LLC.
SONS AND DAUGHTERS OF THE MOST HIGH PUBLISHERS ®

OH, GRACIOUS MOST HIGH HEAVENLY FATHER, HOLY IS YOUR
NAME, YOUR WILL BE DONE NOW AND FOREVER!

In the KJV bible book of John chapter 7 verse 16; the Messiah Yashu'a (Jesus) stated: "My doctrine isn't mine, but his that sent me." In the KJV bible book of Matthew chapter 22 verses 37-38; the Messiah Yashu'a (Jesus) stated: "Thou shalt love the Lord thy God with all thy heart, and with all thy soul, and with all thy mind. This is the first and great commandment."

In the KJV bible book of Matthew chapter 10 verses 34-40; the Messiah Yashu'a (Jesus) stated: "Think not that I am come to send peace on earth: I came not to send peace, but a sword. For I am come to set a man at variance against his father, and the daughter against her mother, and the daughter in law against her mother-in-law. And a man's foes shall be they of his own household. He that loveth father or mother more than me is not worthy of me: and he that loveth son or daughter more than me is not worthy of me. And he that taketh not his cross, and followeth after me, is not worthy of me. He that findeth his life shall lose it: and he that loseth his life for my sake shall find it. He that receiveth you receiveth me, and he that receiveth me receiveth him that sent me."

SPIRITUAL TRILLIONAIRE:
Cherishing the Breath of Life while Simultaneously
Preparing for the Blow of Death!

CHILDREN OF THE MOST HIGH:
PRISTINE YOUTH AND FAMILY SOLUTIONS, LLC.
SONS AND DAUGHTERS OF THE MOST HIGH PUBLISHERS ®

OH, GRACIOUS MOST HIGH HEAVENLY FATHER, HOLY IS YOUR
NAME, YOUR WILL BE DONE NOW AND FOREVER!

R.E.
TRUE VINE
MIND MASTER
GARDENER

What is Active Discipline?

Active discipline is doing what you may or may not want to do when you need to do it. Have you ever heard the phrase: **"burning with desire"**? It is the craving or wanting that fuels our desires like an internal fire. Active discipline helps us to intentionally work each moment to not give in to the desires of all people, all places, all things, all issues, and all circumstances that goes against the commandments and the **"Will"** of the Most High Heavenly Father. Therefore, we are on the path of acquiring positive spiritual health and positive spiritual wealth when we are learning how to practice active discipline and patience through our obedience to the commandments and to the **"Will"** of the Most High Heavenly Father.

SPIRITUAL TRILLIONAIRE:
Cherishing the Breath of Life while Simultaneously
Preparing for the Blow of Death!

CHILDREN OF THE MOST HIGH:
PRISTINE YOUTH AND FAMILY SOLUTIONS, LLC.
SONS AND DAUGHTERS OF THE MOST HIGH PUBLISHERS ®

OH, GRACIOUS MOST HIGH HEAVENLY FATHER, HOLY IS YOUR
NAME, YOUR WILL BE DONE NOW AND FOREVER!

How? As **P.A.S.S.I.O.N.A.T.E. P.A.T.H.F.I.N.D.E.R.S.** of
the Most High who are on an inner journey on the narrow path
**which reflects moral integrity and positive character traits
in action** of the ones who stand straight.

The KJV bible book of Matthew chapter 7 verses 13-14; states:
"Enter ye in at the strait gate: for wide is the gate, and broad is
the way, that leadeth to destruction, and many there be which
go in there at: Because strait is the gate, and **narrow is the way**,
which leadeth unto life, and few there be that find it." In the
KJV bible book of John chapter 14 verse 6; The Messiah
Yashu'a (Jesus) saith unto him, "I am the way, the truth, and
the life: no man [**no person**] cometh unto the Father, but by
me."

~OH, MOST HIGH HEAVENLY FATHER, IF WE, MEMBERS OF
HUMANITY MUST DESIRE, GUIDE US TO ONLY DESIRE TO
OBEY YOUR COMMANDMENTS, TO DO YOUR WILL ONLY, TO
REPENT TO YOU FOR ALL OF OUR UNFORGIVEN SINS, AND TO
SEEK PROTECTION IN YOU FROM ALL HARM, ALL DISEASES,
AND FROM ALL THAT IS DISAGREEABLE AND FROM ALL
THAT IS WICKED IN YOUR EYESIGHT NOW AND FOREVER,
AMEN. ~

SPIRITUAL TRILLIONAIRE:
**Cherishing the Breath of Life while Simultaneously
Preparing for the Blow of Death!**

CHILDREN OF THE MOST HIGH:
PRISTINE YOUTH AND FAMILY SOLUTIONS, LLC.
SONS AND DAUGHTERS OF THE MOST HIGH PUBLISHERS ®

OH, GRACIOUS MOST HIGH HEAVENLY FATHER, HOLY IS YOUR
NAME, YOUR WILL BE DONE NOW AND FOREVER!

Chapter 2: Who are the P.A.S.S.I.O.N.A.T.E. P.A.T.H.F.I.N.D.E.R.S. of the Most High?

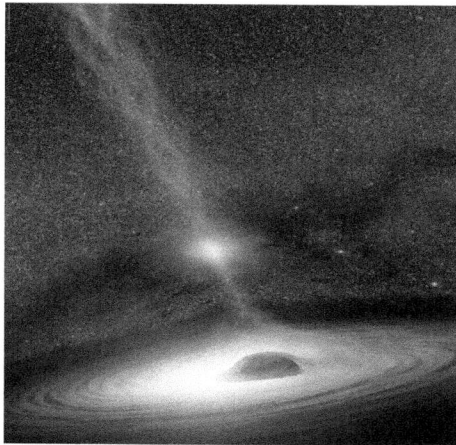

~OH, MOST HIGH HEAVENLY FATHER, ALLOW US TO
EXPERIENCE A PEACE OF MIND AND TRUE INNER
HEART PARADISE ONLY WHEN DOING YOUR WILL,
NOW AND FOREVER, AMEN.~

SPIRITUAL TRILLIONAIRE:
Cherishing the Breath of Life while Simultaneously
Preparing for the Blow of Death!

CHILDREN OF THE MOST HIGH:
PRISTINE YOUTH AND FAMILY SOLUTIONS, LLC.
SONS AND DAUGHTERS OF THE MOST HIGH PUBLISHERS ®

OH, GRACIOUS MOST HIGH HEAVENLY FATHER, HOLY IS YOUR
NAME, YOUR WILL BE DONE NOW AND FOREVER!

In the process of obtaining positive spiritual health and positive spiritual wealth, a person must be willing to work diligently, intentionally, and patiently each moment to become a **"P.A.S.S.I.O.N.A.T. E. - P.A.T.H.F.I.N.D.E.R. of the Most High."** Passionate Pathfinders of the Most High are people who are devout to the Most High Heavenly Father and obey the Most High's will and commandments on their inner journey on the narrow path back to the Most High through the Messiah Yashu'a (Jesus). Passionate Pathfinders of the Most High are those who stand up straight in character, exhibit moral integrity and seek to help uplift humanity. Also, Passionate Pathfinders of the Most High are conscientious of the choices they make which determine their intentional actions and are aware of the inevitable consequences they will reap from their sown thoughts and deeds. **P.A.S.S.I.O.N.A.T.E. - P.A.T.H.F.I.N.D.E.R. are also the acronyms for: Positive, Attitude, Smiling, Seeker, Improving, Optimistically, Now, Actively, Thriving, Efficiently, - Persevering, Agreeably, Thankful, Happy, Faithful, Inspired, Noble, Devoted, Empowered, Resiliency.**

SPIRITUAL TRILLIONAIRE:
Cherishing the Breath of Life while Simultaneously
Preparing for the Blow of Death!

CHILDREN OF THE MOST HIGH:
PRISTINE YOUTH AND FAMILY SOLUTIONS, LLC.
SONS AND DAUGHTERS OF THE MOST HIGH PUBLISHERS ®

OH, GRACIOUS MOST HIGH HEAVENLY FATHER, HOLY IS YOUR
NAME, YOUR WILL BE DONE NOW AND FOREVER!

Therefore, a "**Passionate Pathfinder of the Most High** utilizes God's (אלהים Elôhîym) <u>A</u>ll <u>W</u>ise <u>A</u>bundant <u>R</u>ight <u>E</u>xact (**A.W.A.R.E) Knowledge**, and practices the habit of positive thinking or correct (right, healthy) thinking as oppose to negative thinking or wrong thinking. The habit of positive thinking is essential to obtaining and sustaining positive spiritual health and positive spiritual wealth. A person with wrong knowledge thinks negatively by having wrong **I. D. E. A. S. (<u>I</u>mpure <u>D</u>esires <u>E</u>motionally <u>A</u>ctivated <u>S</u>equentially)** or negative thoughts continuously, which leads to negative speaking, and negative actions. **What is the main difference between positive spiritual health and positive spiritual wealth, and negative spiritual health and negative spiritual wealth?** The main difference between positive (benevolent) spiritual health and **positive (benevolent)** spiritual wealth, and **negative (malevolent (evil)** spiritual health and **negative (malevolent (evil)** spiritual wealth <u>is the root of where it comes from</u>. **Positive (benevolent)** spiritual health and **positive (benevolent)** spiritual wealth comes from the Most High (**ELYOWN** עֶלְיוֹן **EL** אֵל) God." According to the KJV bible book of 1st Timothy chapter 6 verse 10; it states: "<u>the love of money is the root of all evil.</u>"

39

SPIRITUAL TRILLIONAIRE:
Cherishing the Breath of Life while Simultaneously
Preparing for the Blow of Death!

CHILDREN OF THE MOST HIGH:
PRISTINE YOUTH AND FAMILY SOLUTIONS, LLC.
SONS AND DAUGHTERS OF THE MOST HIGH PUBLISHERS ®

OH, GRACIOUS MOST HIGH HEAVENLY FATHER, HOLY IS YOUR
NAME, YOUR WILL BE DONE NOW AND FOREVER!

So, the aforementioned are some of the inner qualities of **Passionate Pathfinders** of the Most High that are essential elements of obtaining and sustaining positive spiritual health and positive spiritual wealth throughout the process of becoming a **Mind Gardner, True Vine (Yashu'a, Jesus) Mind Gardener**, onto a **True Vine (Yashu'a, Jesus) Mind Master Gardener** which is taught through the **Children of the Most High Pristine Youth and Family Solutions, LLC. 9X9 True Vine "Yashu'a" (Jesus) B.A.-K.A.-R.E. Sequential Order of Learning Habits of Success**. This level of teaching is expounded on in meticulous detail during **True Vine "Yashu'a" (Jesus) Mind Master Gardener <u>Workshops that will only be made available to those who have had an opportunity to intensely study and apply the God (אלהים Elôhîym) A.W.A.R.E. knowledge in the Children of the Most High Pristine Youth and Family Solutions, LLC. Class A, B, C, D, and E publications.</u>** So, our desires and discipline influences how we utilize our "**will**" to make moment to moment decisions which occurs in what the Children of the Most High: Pristine Youth and Family Solutions, LLC. refer to as the: "**Creative Garden of Will (Your Mind).**"

SPIRITUAL TRILLIONAIRE:
**Cherishing the Breath of Life while Simultaneously
Preparing for the Blow of Death!**

CHILDREN OF THE MOST HIGH:
PRISTINE YOUTH AND FAMILY SOLUTIONS, LLC.
SONS AND DAUGHTERS OF THE MOST HIGH PUBLISHERS ®

OH, GRACIOUS MOST HIGH HEAVENLY FATHER, HOLY IS YOUR
NAME, YOUR WILL BE DONE NOW AND FOREVER!

Moment to moment discipline in the obedient service to the Most High Heavenly Father's **Will**; is an essential element in overcoming and in resisting the temptations of the **9 Deadly Venoms of the Desires of the great dragon, that old serpent called the devil and satan which deceiveth the whole world**; which can prevent a person from obtaining positive spiritual health and positive spiritual wealth. Therefore, if we discipline ourselves to learn and apply **God's (אלהים Elôhîym) <u>A</u>ll <u>W</u>ise <u>A</u>bundant <u>R</u>ight <u>E</u>xact (A.W.A.R.E)** Knowledge, we will reap the benefit of acquiring the ability to develop the habit of **positive thinking**, combined with **active discipline** in obeying the laws of **God (אלהים Elôhîym)**. Thereby, activating the "**Will**" of the Most High Heavenly Father in our mind which initiates all thoughts and all actions. The way that a person acts and speaks is a reflection of how he or she thinks!

A person who utilizes **incorrect** or **wicked** or **wrong knowledge**; thinks negatively by having **wrong I. D. E. A. S. (<u>I</u>mpure <u>D</u>esires <u>E</u>motionally <u>A</u>ctivated <u>S</u>equentially)** or negative thoughts continuously, which leads to negative speaking, and negative actions. It is not possible to maintain and sustain being obedient to the Most High Heavenly Father

SPIRITUAL TRILLIONAIRE:
Cherishing the Breath of Life while Simultaneously
Preparing for the Blow of Death!

CHILDREN OF THE MOST HIGH:
PRISTINE YOUTH AND FAMILY SOLUTIONS, LLC.
SONS AND DAUGHTERS OF THE MOST HIGH PUBLISHERS ®

OH, GRACIOUS MOST HIGH HEAVENLY FATHER, HOLY IS YOUR
NAME, YOUR WILL BE DONE NOW AND FOREVER!

without being intentionally disciplined to do so. It's like a person who is physically out shape and who has not ever worked out trying to do a three-day triathlon. Is that out of shape person prepared to do a three-day triathlon? Of course not, just like if an out of shape person who may be in the habit of eating unhealthy physically, may suffer from poor health, like a person who does not diligently work to improve themselves each day is not prepared to acquire positive spiritual health and positive spiritual wealth. So, whether it is in reference to physical health or spiritual health, proper preparation is essential.

Preparation to acquire, maintain and sustain positive spiritual health and positive spiritual wealth is rooted in the desire to only do the **Will** of the Most High Heavenly Father. This is initiated through discipline of voluntary utilization of one's "**will**", and activated "**Spiritual Majesty**" that is inspired, empowered, influenced and embraced through "**Divine Love**" for the **Most High Heavenly Father only**, and through our love for **Yasu'a** or **Yashu'a** (ישוע) meaning "**Savior**" also called **Jesus Christ (Yashu'a Ha Mashiakh – Jesus the Messiah or Yehoshu'a – Yahayyu is Salvation or Yahayyu Saves),** who is **the Son of God** in English.

42

SPIRITUAL TRILLIONAIRE:
Cherishing the Breath of Life while Simultaneously
Preparing for the Blow of Death!

CHILDREN OF THE MOST HIGH:
PRISTINE YOUTH AND FAMILY SOLUTIONS, LLC.
SONS AND DAUGHTERS OF THE MOST HIGH PUBLISHERS ®

OH, GRACIOUS MOST HIGH HEAVENLY FATHER, HOLY IS YOUR
NAME, YOUR WILL BE DONE NOW AND FOREVER!

There is a portion of the Most High Heavenly Father which is a: "**Spiritual Majesty**" that exists in each person that is dormant in many of us and it waits for us to utilize the "**will**" that the Most High Heavenly Father instilled in us to invoke the portion of the Most High Heavenly Father in us through "**Divine Love**" for the Most High. Positive thinking and the perpetual habit of only allowing positive thoughts to exists and flow through our minds, allows us the opportunity to acquire, maintain and sustain positive spiritual health and positive spiritual wealth.

What is "**Divine Love**", "**Spiritual Majesty**" and "**Will**"?

"**Divine Love (ISHQ)**" is a spiritual love, affection, passion for the Most High only that is from the Most High. There are various forms of love, however "**Divine Love (ISHQ)**" **is for the Most High only**!

How can a portion of the Most High be in a person and a person not know that it exists within him or her?

SPIRITUAL TRILLIONAIRE:
Cherishing the Breath of Life while Simultaneously
Preparing for the Blow of Death!

CHILDREN OF THE MOST HIGH:
PRISTINE YOUTH AND FAMILY SOLUTIONS, LLC.
SONS AND DAUGHTERS OF THE MOST HIGH PUBLISHERS ®

OH, GRACIOUS MOST HIGH HEAVENLY FATHER, HOLY IS YOUR
NAME, YOUR WILL BE DONE NOW AND FOREVER!

In the KJV bible book of John chapter 1verses 1-5; answers that question for us. The KJV bible book of John chapter 1verses 1-5; states: "In the beginning was the Word, and the Word was with God, and the Word was God. The same was in the beginning with God. All things were made by him; and without him was not anything made that was made. In him was life (**breath of life from the Lord God**); and the life (**from the Lord God made people into living souls**) was the light (**Neshamaw Khayyeem** נשמה חיים **- Divine Breath of Life**) of <u>men</u> (meaning human beings).

The **KJV bible Hebrew Strong's Concordance#444** word for "men" is: ἄνθρωπος anthrōpos which means a human being). And the light (**portion of the Most High that exists in every person**) shineth in darkness (**is inside the body of every person**); and the darkness (**the body and the mind in many people lack of the knowledge of how a portion of the Most High exists in every person**) comprehended it not.

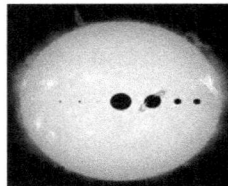

44

SPIRITUAL TRILLIONAIRE:
Cherishing the Breath of Life while Simultaneously
Preparing for the Blow of Death!

CHILDREN OF THE MOST HIGH:
PRISTINE YOUTH AND FAMILY SOLUTIONS, LLC.
SONS AND DAUGHTERS OF THE MOST HIGH PUBLISHERS ®

OH, GRACIOUS MOST HIGH HEAVENLY FATHER, HOLY IS YOUR
NAME, YOUR WILL BE DONE NOW AND FOREVER!

So, there is a portion of the Most High Heavenly Father which is a: "**Spiritual Majesty**" that exists in each person that is dormant in many of us. How did **the light shineth in darkness; and the darkness comprehended it not** get inside of us? The KJV bible book of **Genesis chapter 2 verse 7** answers that question; it states: "And the Lord God formed man of the dust of the ground, and breathed into his nostrils the breath of life; and man became a living soul."

So, according to the previous bible verses, the connection occurred when the **Yehovah (LORD) Elohiym (God)** breathed the **Khay** or **Hayy (Neshamaw Khayyeem** נשמה, חיים - Divine Breath of Life) into the nostrils of אָדָם **'Adam** (the **KJV bible Hebrew Strong's Concordance#120** word **"Adam"** means a human being) and Adam became a **Nephesh Khay** which in the Aramic (Hebrew) language, **Nephesh** is "Spirit" and **Rooahk** or **Ruwach** "Soul". **Why are the words spirit and soul so confusing to differentiate in the English language? The words spirit and soul are confusing to differentiate in the English language** because the words **Nephesh** is "Spirit" and **Rooahk** or **Ruwah** "Soul" and **mind** are sometimes interchangeably translated in English as the same words.

SPIRITUAL TRILLIONAIRE:
Cherishing the Breath of Life while Simultaneously
Preparing for the Blow of Death!

CHILDREN OF THE MOST HIGH:
PRISTINE YOUTH AND FAMILY SOLUTIONS, LLC.
SONS AND DAUGHTERS OF THE MOST HIGH PUBLISHERS ®

OH, GRACIOUS MOST HIGH HEAVENLY FATHER, HOLY IS YOUR
NAME, YOUR WILL BE DONE NOW AND FOREVER!

For example: in the KJV bible book of Genesis chapter 1:1, the Aramic (Hebrew) language word **Rooahk** or **Ruwah** "Soul" is translated in English as "spirit" and in Genesis (KJV) chapter 2:7, the Aramic (Hebrew) language word **Nephesh** which is "**Spirit**" is translated in English as "**Soul**".

Genesis (KJV) Chapter 1:1

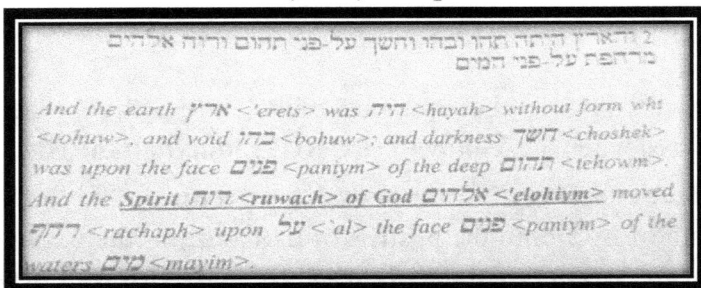

Genesis (KJV) 2:7

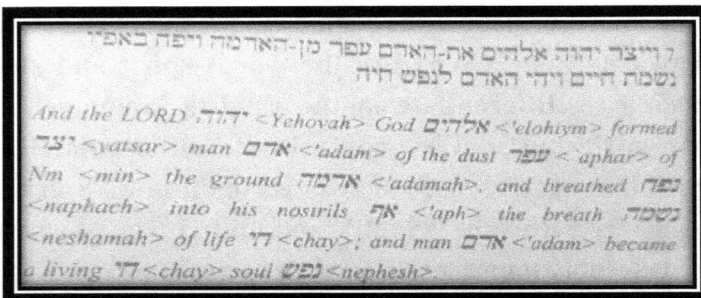

SPIRITUAL TRILLIONAIRE:
Cherishing the Breath of Life while Simultaneously
Preparing for the Blow of Death!

CHILDREN OF THE MOST HIGH:
PRISTINE YOUTH AND FAMILY SOLUTIONS, LLC.
SONS AND DAUGHTERS OF THE MOST HIGH PUBLISHERS ®

OH, GRACIOUS MOST HIGH HEAVENLY FATHER, HOLY IS YOUR
NAME, YOUR WILL BE DONE NOW AND FOREVER!

What is "**Spiritual Majesty**"?

Spiritual Majesty is a portion of the Most High that exists in each person as an inner quality that when it is intentionally organized and directed towards positive accomplishments, it activates our higher potential that helps us to conquer adverse situations. Unfortunately, **Spiritual Majesty** is usually not allowed to function in our lives due to many of us living most days according to people, places and worldly things, and other people plans for our lives that may not have our best interest; rather than becoming aware of the preordained Most High's plan for each of our lives and learning to only live in the world, but not of the world by the "**Will**" and commandments of the Most High. When our **Spiritual Majesty** is intentionally organized and directed towards positive accomplishments, it activates the ability to create positive life achievements that afford us the opportunity to get more out of life by sacrificing of ourselves in a positive healthy manner to give more to life.

What is "**Will**"? The word for "**Will**" in Galilean Ashuric/Syriac (Arabic) is: "**Mashiyya**" which to the eyes may

47

SPIRITUAL TRILLIONAIRE:
Cherishing the Breath of Life while Simultaneously
Preparing for the Blow of Death!

OH, GRACIOUS MOST HIGH HEAVENLY FATHER, HOLY IS YOUR NAME, YOUR WILL BE DONE NOW AND FOREVER!

appear to look like the Aramic (Hebrew) words: "**Mashiakh**" for "**Messiah**" and "Yashu'a" (Jesus) combined.

Mashiyya (مشية) Which Comes From The Root Word Shayaa-A (شاء) Or Yashaa-A (يشاء) And Means: *"By Which One*

deliberately chooses or decides upon a course of action; an instance of exercising this faculty; a deliberate decision or conclusion; choice.

"**Will**" is to do what one chooses, to have one's way and to see fit to one's own thinking. However, in order to acquire, maintain and sustain positive spiritual health and positive spiritual wealth, it is imperative to only focus on doing the "**Will**" of the Most High Heavenly Father and to focus on the works that are in alignment with the "**Will**" of the Most High Heavenly Father's "**Will**" only, now and forever!

In KJV bible book of Matthew chapter 19 verse 26; Yashu'a (Jesus) said: "With men this is impossible; but with God all things are possible." God gave many members of humanity the gift of the ability to think, which **behooves** us to not misuse it or under use the gift of the ability to think!

48

SPIRITUAL TRILLIONAIRE:
**Cherishing the Breath of Life while Simultaneously
Preparing for the Blow of Death!**

CHILDREN OF THE MOST HIGH:
PRISTINE YOUTH AND FAMILY SOLUTIONS, LLC.
SONS AND DAUGHTERS OF THE MOST HIGH PUBLISHERS ®

OH, GRACIOUS MOST HIGH HEAVENLY FATHER, HOLY IS YOUR
NAME, YOUR WILL BE DONE NOW AND FOREVER!

One of the most powerful forces in the universe is: "**Thought**" because thought initiates all actions which is maximized through divine love for the Most High Heavenly Father, true-prayer supplication and true-faith in the Most High. The highest level of knowledge throughout the boundless universes is: "**LOVE**" and **the Most High Heavenly Father is "LOVE"**. In the KJV bible book of Matthew chapter 22 verses 37-38; Yashu'a (Jesus) said: "Thou shalt love the Lord thy God with all thy heart, and with all thy soul, and with all thy mind. This is the first and great commandment".

In KJV bible book of Matthew chapter 10 verses 30-40; Yashu'a (Jesus) said: "But the very hairs of your head are all numbered. Fear ye not therefore, ye are of more value than many sparrows. Whosoever therefore shall confess me before men, him will I confess also before my Father

SPIRITUAL TRILLIONAIRE:
Cherishing the Breath of Life while Simultaneously
Preparing for the Blow of Death!

CHILDREN OF THE MOST HIGH:
PRISTINE YOUTH AND FAMILY SOLUTIONS, LLC.
SONS AND DAUGHTERS OF THE MOST HIGH PUBLISHERS ®

OH, GRACIOUS MOST HIGH HEAVENLY FATHER, HOLY IS YOUR
NAME, YOUR WILL BE DONE NOW AND FOREVER!

which is in heaven. But whosoever shall deny me before men, him will I also deny before my Father which is in heaven. <u>Think not that I am come to send peace on earth: I came not to send peace, but a sword</u>. For I am come to set a man at variance against his father, and the daughter against her mother, and the daughter in law against her mother-in-law. And a man's foes shall be they of his own household. He that loveth father or mother more than me is not worthy of me: and he that loveth son or daughter more than me is not worthy of me. And he that taketh not his cross, and followeth after me, is not worthy of me. He that findeth his life shall lose it: and he that loseth his life for my sake shall find it. He that receiveth you receiveth me, and he that receiveth me receiveth him that sent me.

Therefore, only in obeying this first and great commandment of loving the Lord thy God with all thy heart, and with all thy soul, and with all thy mind, loving the Messiah Yashu'a **(Jesus)** more than our mothers, fathers and children, taking our cross and following the Messiah Yashu'a **(Jesus)**; or living our lives in accordance with the example of how the Messiah Yashu'a (Jesus) lived his life, and by **receiving** or

SPIRITUAL TRILLIONAIRE:
Cherishing the Breath of Life while Simultaneously
Preparing for the Blow of Death!

CHILDREN OF THE MOST HIGH:
PRISTINE YOUTH AND FAMILY SOLUTIONS, LLC.
SONS AND DAUGHTERS OF THE MOST HIGH PUBLISHERS ®

OH, GRACIOUS MOST HIGH HEAVENLY FATHER, HOLY IS YOUR
NAME, YOUR WILL BE DONE NOW AND FOREVER!

accepting the Messiah Yashu'a (Jesus) as our Savior; can a person acquire, maintain and sustain positive spiritual health and positive spiritual wealth. The **KJV bible Strong's Concordance#1209** is the word "**receiveth**" is: δέχομαι **déchomai, dekh'-om-ahee**; middle voice of a primary verb; to receive (in various applications, literally or figuratively): — **accep**t, **receive**, take; Yashu'a (Jesus) said: "he that receiveth me receiveth him that sent me."

SPIRITUAL TRILLIONAIRE:
Cherishing the Breath of Life while Simultaneously
Preparing for the Blow of Death!

CHILDREN OF THE MOST HIGH:
PRISTINE YOUTH AND FAMILY SOLUTIONS, LLC.
SONS AND DAUGHTERS OF THE MOST HIGH PUBLISHERS ®

OH, GRACIOUS MOST HIGH HEAVENLY FATHER, HOLY IS YOUR
NAME, YOUR WILL BE DONE NOW AND FOREVER!

What is the Children of the Most High Pristine Youth and Family Solutions, LLC. 9X9 True Vine "Yashu'a" (Jesus) B.A.-K.A.-R.E. Sequential Order of Learning Habits of Success?

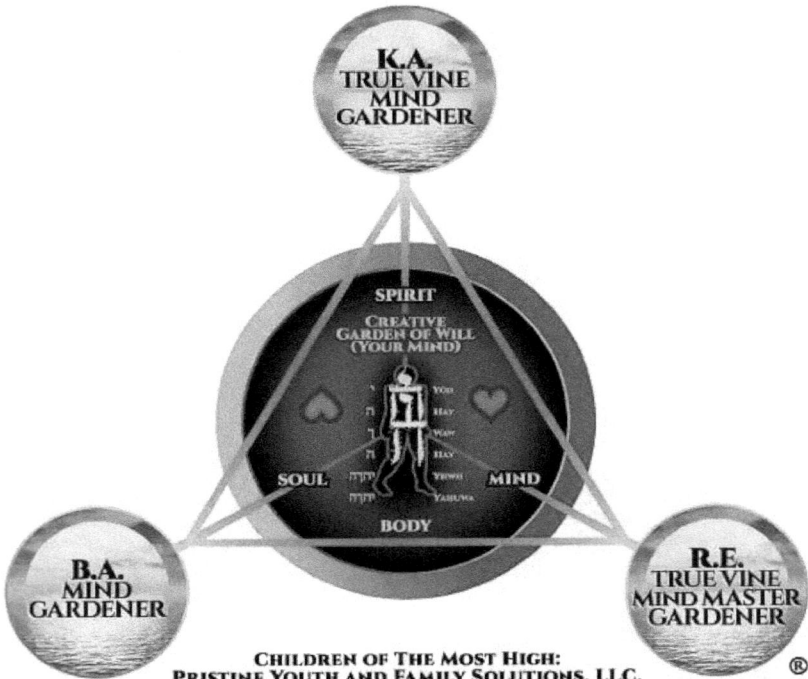

CHILDREN OF THE MOST HIGH:
PRISTINE YOUTH AND FAMILY SOLUTIONS, LLC.
9X9 TRUE VINE "YASHU'A" (JESUS) B.A.-K.A.-R.E.
SEQUENTIAL ORDER OF LEARNING®

SPIRITUAL TRILLIONAIRE:
Cherishing the Breath of Life while Simultaneously
Preparing for the Blow of Death!

CHILDREN OF THE MOST HIGH:
PRISTINE YOUTH AND FAMILY SOLUTIONS, LLC.
SONS AND DAUGHTERS OF THE MOST HIGH PUBLISHERS

OH, GRACIOUS MOST HIGH HEAVENLY FATHER, HOLY IS YOUR
NAME, YOUR WILL BE DONE NOW AND FOREVER!

The Children of the Most High Pristine Youth and Family Solutions, LLC. 9X9 True Vine "Yashu'a" (Jesus) B.A.-K.A.-R.E. Sequential Order of Learning Habits of Success are the intentional, non-formal education sequential steps to teaching **youth and adults'** the True Vine Yashu'a (Jesus) doctrine of the Most High. This is taught to them in an effort to create an opportunity for them to learn how to apply the doctrine of the Most High in all that they aspire to do and to teach them how to create positive predetermined goals that may help then to achieve positive success. When we say "positive success", we mean according to what positive success means to them. We also seek to teach youth and adults' the True Vine Yashu'a (Jesus) doctrine of the Most High in an effort to learn how to work together with members of humanity to create a world where all youth and all adults are happy, healthy, and balanced mentally, spiritually, physically, emotionally, financially, personally, professionally, and socially.

SPIRITUAL TRILLIONAIRE:
Cherishing the Breath of Life while Simultaneously
Preparing for the Blow of Death!

CHILDREN OF THE MOST HIGH:
PRISTINE YOUTH AND FAMILY SOLUTIONS, LLC.
SONS AND DAUGHTERS OF THE MOST HIGH PUBLISHERS ®

OH, GRACIOUS MOST HIGH HEAVENLY FATHER, HOLY IS YOUR NAME, YOUR WILL BE DONE NOW AND FOREVER!

The **True Vine "Yashu'a" (Jesus) B.A.-K.A.-R.E. Sequential Order of Learning Habits of Success** must be taught in proper sequential order in an effort to not confuse the mind of the learner. **BA** is the Ancient African word for **Soul**, **KA** is the Ancient African word for **Spirit**, **RE (pronounced as RAY)** is the Ancient African word for **Sun**.

Psalms (KJV) 84:11 with Hebrew inserts:

כִּי שֶׁמֶשׁ וּמָגֵן יְהוָה אֱלֹהִים חֵן וְכָבוֹד יִתֵּן יְהוָה לֹא

יִמְנַע־טוֹב לַהֹלְכִים בְּתָמִים:

In the KJV bible book of **Psalms chapter 84 verse 11**; it states: "For the **LORD** (Yĕhovah, יְהוָה, Yahuwa) God (Elohiym אֱלֹהִים) is a "**Sun**" **Shemesh** שֶׁמֶשׁ and "**Shield**" **Magen** מָגֵן: the **LORD** (Yĕhovah, Yahuwa) will give grace and glory: no good thing will he withhold from them that walk uprightly **Tamiym** תָּמִים." The "**Sun**" (**RE**) is the light of the star that sustains all life on the planet earth.

SPIRITUAL TRILLIONAIRE:
Cherishing the Breath of Life while Simultaneously
Preparing for the Blow of Death!

CHILDREN OF THE MOST HIGH:
PRISTINE YOUTH AND FAMILY SOLUTIONS, LLC.
SONS AND DAUGHTERS OF THE MOST HIGH PUBLISHERS ®

OH, GRACIOUS MOST HIGH HEAVENLY FATHER, HOLY IS YOUR
NAME, YOUR WILL BE DONE NOW AND FOREVER!

In the True Vine "Yashu'a" (Jesus) B.A.-K.A.-R.E.
Sequential Order of Learning Habits of Success, the RE
(Sun) connects to the body as the light (RE) that shines in the
darkness (Body) that the darkness (Body) does not comprehend
in the KJV bible book of John chapter 1 verse 5, and as Yashu'a
(Jesus) said in the KJV bible book of Matthew chapter 6 verse
22 "the light (RE) of the body is the eye: if therefore thine
eye be single, thy whole body shall be full of light." So, B.A.-
K.A.-R.E. translates in English as: The Soul and Spirit, Sun-
Light of Life of Yĕhovah, Yahuwa, Yahweh, Yahovah,
Jehovah (Lord God), and Yahayyu in Modern Hebrew
translates as Existing One or Living One that sustains all life
on the planet earth, and it also translates as: "Glorious is the
Spirit of the Lord God (RE)." The acronyms of "B.A.-K.A.-
R.E." in English stands for: Become, Aware, Knowledge,
Apply, Reflect, Experience.

Therefore, the True Vine "Yashu'a" (Jesus) B.A.-K.A.-R.E.
Sequential Order of Learning Habits of Success youth and
adult learners Become Aware of the meaning of the KJV bible
book of Hosea chapter 4 verse 6: "My people (children of the
Most High) are being destroyed for lack of not knowing God's
(אלהים Elôhîym) A.W.A.R.E. knowledge."

55

SPIRITUAL TRILLIONAIRE:
Cherishing the Breath of Life while Simultaneously
Preparing for the Blow of Death!

CHILDREN OF THE MOST HIGH:
PRISTINE YOUTH AND FAMILY SOLUTIONS, LLC.
SONS AND DAUGHTERS OF THE MOST HIGH PUBLISHERS ®

OH, GRACIOUS MOST HIGH HEAVENLY FATHER, HOLY IS YOUR
NAME, YOUR WILL BE DONE NOW AND FOREVER!

By learning **God's (אלהים Elôhîym) All Wise Abundant Right Exact (A.W.A.R.E)** Knowledge with a sincere-heart and focused mind, they acquire the **God's (אלהים Elôhîym) All Wise Abundant Right Exact (A.W.A.R.E) K**nowledge which affords youth and adult learners the opportunity to **A**pply **God's (אלהים Elôhîym) A.W.A.R.E.** knowledge in order to receive the mental, spiritual and physical (mind, body, spirit, and soul), benefits in the process of acquiring positive spiritual health and positive spiritual wealth.

SPIRITUAL TRILLIONAIRE:
**Cherishing the Breath of Life while Simultaneously
Preparing for the Blow of Death!**

CHILDREN OF THE MOST HIGH:
PRISTINE YOUTH AND FAMILY SOLUTIONS, LLC.
SONS AND DAUGHTERS OF THE MOST HIGH PUBLISHERS ®

OH, GRACIOUS MOST HIGH HEAVENLY FATHER, HOLY IS YOUR
NAME, YOUR WILL BE DONE NOW AND FOREVER!

As the **Children of the Most High Pristine Youth and Family Solutions, LLC. 9X9 True Vine "Yashu'a" (Jesus) B.A.-K.A.-R.E. Sequential Order** of **Learning Habits of Success** continues to be applied and practiced over time by youth and adult learners, opportunities will occur for them to **R**eflect on their **E**xperiences as they share and process what they learned with others; in an ongoing process that may help youth and adults to develop new skills that enables them to best respond to daily life situations that may lead to successful outcomes. This also affords youth and adults opportunities to create new ways of how to utilize their newly acquired knowledge to successfully achieve all of their positive life aspirations and predetermined positive life goals.

SPIRITUAL TRILLIONAIRE:
Cherishing the Breath of Life while Simultaneously
Preparing for the Blow of Death!

CHILDREN OF THE MOST HIGH:
PRISTINE YOUTH AND FAMILY SOLUTIONS, LLC.
SONS AND DAUGHTERS OF THE MOST HIGH PUBLISHERS ®

OH, GRACIOUS MOST HIGH HEAVENLY FATHER, HOLY IS YOUR
NAME, YOUR WILL BE DONE NOW AND FOREVER!

The **Children of the Most High Pristine Youth and Family Solutions, LLC. 9X9 True Vine "Yashu'a" (Jesus) B.A.-K.A.-R.E. Sequential Order of Learning Habits of Success** also teaches youth and adults how to be aware of the children of the devil who advocate, teach and preach **the great dragon, that old serpent, called the Devil, and Satan, which deceiveth the whole world and his angels** (ἄγγελος Angelos, meaning **Messengers**), **messages** of the **9 Deadly Venoms of the Desires** of **the great dragon, that old serpent, called the Devil, and Satan, which deceiveth the whole world**. The **9 Deadly Venoms of Desires** are: **Slothful, Wrath, Pride, Greed, Lust, Hopeless Fear Disobedience, Lying, Heinous Murde**r, and **Wickedness**.

~OH, MOST HIGH, THANK YOU FOR EVERYTHING! AMEN~

SPIRITUAL TRILLIONAIRE:
**Cherishing the Breath of Life while Simultaneously
Preparing for the Blow of Death!**

CHILDREN OF THE MOST HIGH:
PRISTINE YOUTH AND FAMILY SOLUTIONS, LLC.
SONS AND DAUGHTERS OF THE MOST HIGH PUBLISHERS ®

OH, GRACIOUS MOST HIGH HEAVENLY FATHER, HOLY IS YOUR
NAME, YOUR WILL BE DONE NOW AND FOREVER!

Chapter 3: According to the Bible, who are the children of the Most High? And who are the children of the devil?

~OH, MOST HIGH HEAVENLY FATHER, YOU ALONE ARE
THE RULER OF THE BOUNDLESS UNIVERSES. LET US
NOT STRAY AWAY FROM YOU AS MANY HAVE
ALREADY STRAYED AWAY FROM YOUR GUIDANCE.
YOU ALONE PROTECT US FROM ALL WHO ARE EVIL IN
YOUR EYESIGHT. AMEN~

59

SPIRITUAL TRILLIONAIRE:
**Cherishing the Breath of Life while Simultaneously
Preparing for the Blow of Death!**

OH, GRACIOUS MOST HIGH HEAVENLY FATHER, HOLY IS YOUR
NAME, YOUR WILL BE DONE NOW AND FOREVER!

In the bible book of Genesis chapter 3 verse 15; it states: "And I will put enmity between thee and the woman, and between thy **seed (Zera`, זֶרַע)** and her **seed (Zera`, זֶרַע)**; it shall bruise thy head, and thou shalt bruise his heel." It is important to know that according to the bible, <u>**there are two separate children on the planet earth**</u>; <u>**the children of the Most High**</u> who are referred to as **Eve's seed (physical children)** and <u>**the children of the devil**</u> **(physical children)** referred to as the **serpent's seed (Zera`, זֶרַע)**. The **KJV bible Hebrew Strong's Concordance#2233** word for "seed" is "**Zera**" זֶרַע, which means: **seed, semen virile, child, carnally, fruitful, physical offspring, descendants, posterity, children, sowing, or physical children**). In the KJV bible book of Isaiah chapter 14 verses 12-16; it refers to **Lucifer** as **a man**: "How art thou fallen from heaven, O **Lucifer**; is this **the man** that made the earth to tremble, that did shake kingdoms." In the KJV bible book of Revelation chapter 13 verse 18; it states: "Here is wisdom. Let him that hath understanding count the **number of the beast**: <u>**for it is the number of a man**</u>; and his number is Six hundred threescore and six [**666**]."

SPIRITUAL TRILLIONAIRE:
**Cherishing the Breath of Life while Simultaneously
Preparing for the Blow of Death!**

CHILDREN OF THE MOST HIGH:
PRISTINE YOUTH AND FAMILY SOLUTIONS, LLC.
SONS AND DAUGHTERS OF THE MOST HIGH PUBLISHERS ®

OH, GRACIOUS MOST HIGH HEAVENLY FATHER, HOLY IS YOUR
NAME, YOUR WILL BE DONE NOW AND FOREVER!

The Messiah Yashu'a (Jesus) said in the KJV bible book of
John chapter 10 verse 34; "Is it not written in your law that I
said ye (you) are gods?" Which is supported in the KJV bible
book of Psalms chapter 82 verses 6-7; it states: "I have said, *Ye
are gods; and all of you are **children of the Most High**. But ye
shall die like men, and fall like one of the princes." The Messiah
Yashu'a when speaking to those who are now called Jews in the
KJV bible book of John chapter 8 verse 44; where Yashu'a
(Jesus) said: "Ye are of your father the devil, and the lusts of
your father ye will do. He was a murderer from the
beginning, and abode not in the truth, because there is no
truth in him. When he speaketh a lie, he speaketh of his
own: for he is a liar, and the father of it." This verse is
supported in the KJV bible book of Revelation chapter 2 verse
9 where Yashu'a (Jesus) said: "I know thy works, and
tribulation, and poverty, (but thou art rich) and I know the
blasphemy of them which say they are Jews, and are not,
but are the synagogue of Satan." In the KJV bible book of
Revelation chapter 3 verse 9; Yashu'a (Jesus) said: "Behold, I
will make them of the synagogue of Satan, which say they
are Jews, and are not, but do lie; behold, I will make them
to come and worship before thy feet, and to know that I have

SPIRITUAL TRILLIONAIRE:
Cherishing the Breath of Life while Simultaneously
Preparing for the Blow of Death!

CHILDREN OF THE MOST HIGH:
PRISTINE YOUTH AND FAMILY SOLUTIONS, LLC.
SONS AND DAUGHTERS OF THE MOST HIGH PUBLISHERS ®

OH, GRACIOUS MOST HIGH HEAVENLY FATHER, HOLY IS YOUR
NAME, YOUR WILL BE DONE NOW AND FOREVER!

loved thee." In the KJV bible book of 1st John chapter 3 verses 9-10; it states: "Whosoever is born of God doth not commit sin; for his **seed** remained in him: and he cannot sin, because he is born of God. In this **the children of God** are manifest, and **the children of the devil:** whosoever doeth not righteousness is not of God, neither he that loveth not his brother."

According to the bible, are people born wicked?

In the KJV bible book of Psalms chapter 58 verses 3-5; it states: "**The wicked are estranged from the womb. The KJV bible Hebrew Strong's Concordance #7358 for the word "estranged" is: רֶחֶם rechem meaning from the womb of a woman**), they go astray as soon as they be born, speaking lies. Their poison is like the poison of a serpent: they are like the deaf adder that stoppeth her ear; which will not hearken to the voice of charmers, charming never so wisely."

SPIRITUAL TRILLIONAIRE:
Cherishing the Breath of Life while Simultaneously
Preparing for the Blow of Death!

CHILDREN OF THE MOST HIGH:
PRISTINE YOUTH AND FAMILY SOLUTIONS, LLC.
SONS AND DAUGHTERS OF THE MOST HIGH PUBLISHERS ®

OH, GRACIOUS MOST HIGH HEAVENLY FATHER, HOLY IS YOUR
NAME, YOUR WILL BE DONE NOW AND FOREVER!

So, according to the aforementioned KJV bible verses, it is now clear who the children of the Most High are, and who the children of the devil are. In the KJV bible book of Matthew chapter 12 verses 48-50; the Messiah Yashu'a (Jesus) said: "Who is my mother? and who are my brethren? And he stretched forth his hand toward his disciples, and said, behold my mother and my brethren! For whosoever shall do the will of my Father which is in heaven, the same is my brother, and sister, and mother."

SPIRITUAL TRILLIONAIRE:
Cherishing the Breath of Life while Simultaneously
Preparing for the Blow of Death!

CHILDREN OF THE MOST HIGH:
PRISTINE YOUTH AND FAMILY SOLUTIONS, LLC.
SONS AND DAUGHTERS OF THE MOST HIGH PUBLISHERS ®

OH, GRACIOUS MOST HIGH HEAVENLY FATHER, HOLY IS YOUR
NAME, YOUR WILL BE DONE NOW AND FOREVER!

According to the bible, should people seek faith-based teachers and ministers to assist them with acquiring positive spirit health and positive spiritual wealth?

Well, it depends on whether or not they are teachers and **ministers of satan** who are **children of devil** or teachers and **administers of the Most High Heavenly Father's Doctrine** that Yashu'a (Jesus) taught who are **children of the Most High**. In the KJV bible book of 2ⁿᵈ Corinthians chapter 11 verses 14-15; it states: "**And no marvel; for Satan himself is transformed into an angel of light. Therefore, it is no great thing if his ministers also be transformed as the ministers of righteousness**; whose end shall be according to their works."

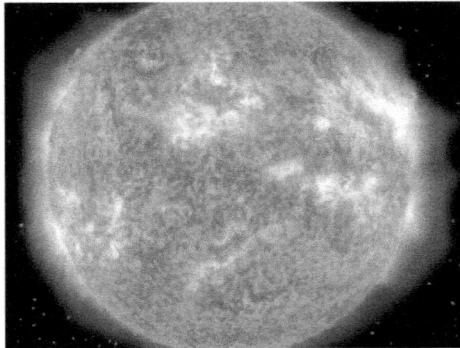

SPIRITUAL TRILLIONAIRE:
**Cherishing the Breath of Life while Simultaneously
Preparing for the Blow of Death!**

CHILDREN OF THE MOST HIGH:
PRISTINE YOUTH AND FAMILY SOLUTIONS, LLC.
SONS AND DAUGHTERS OF THE MOST HIGH PUBLISHERS ®

OH, GRACIOUS MOST HIGH HEAVENLY FATHER, HOLY IS YOUR
NAME, YOUR WILL BE DONE NOW AND FOREVER!

In the KJV bible book of 1st John chapter 3 verses 9-10; it states: **"Whosoever is born of God doth not commit sin; for his seed remained in him: and he cannot sin, because he is born of God. In this the children of God are manifest, and the children of the devil: whosoever doeth not righteousness is not of God, neither he that loveth not his brother."**

So, whether it is in reference to the children of the devil or the children of the Most High, our desires and discipline influence how we utilize our **"will"** to make moment to moment decisions! The greater a person's active mental power is, the greater are the things that he or she can and will do! Moment to moment discipline in the obedient service to the Most High Heavenly One's will is an essential element in overcoming and in resisting the temptations of the 9 Deadly Venoms of the Desires of the great dragon, that old serpent called the devil and satan which deceiveth the whole world which can prevent a person from attaining positive spiritual health and positive spiritual wealth.

SPIRITUAL TRILLIONAIRE:
Cherishing the Breath of Life while Simultaneously
Preparing for the Blow of Death!

CHILDREN OF THE MOST HIGH:
PRISTINE YOUTH AND FAMILY SOLUTIONS, LLC.
SONS AND DAUGHTERS OF THE MOST HIGH PUBLISHERS ®

OH, GRACIOUS MOST HIGH HEAVENLY FATHER, HOLY IS YOUR
NAME, YOUR WILL BE DONE NOW AND FOREVER!

In the KJV bible book of **Revelation** chapter **12** verses **7-9**; it states: "And there was war in heaven: **Michael and his angels** (ἄγγελος **Angelos, meaning Messengers** according to the KJV bible Greek Strong's Concordance#32) fought against the **dragon**; and **the dragon fought and his angels** (ἄγγελος **Angelos, meaning Messengers**, according to the KJV bible Greek Strong's#32), And prevailed not; neither was their place found any more in heaven. And the **great dragon** was cast out, that **old serpent, called the Devil, and Satan**, which deceiveth the whole world: he was cast out into the earth, and his **angels** (ἄγγελος **Angelos, meaning Messengers**, according to the KJV bible Greek Strong's# 32) were cast out with him.

Since angels are messengers, how does messages of the great dragon: that old serpent, called the Devil, and Satan, which deceiveth the whole world and his angels and the **messages of Michael and his angels** relate to all members of humanity?

A person actions can sometimes tell more about them than their words. The great dragon: that old serpent, called the Devil, and Satan, which deceiveth the whole world and his angels (ἄγγελος **Angelos, meaning Messengers**), spread **messages** of

SPIRITUAL TRILLIONAIRE:
Cherishing the Breath of Life while Simultaneously
Preparing for the Blow of Death!

CHILDREN OF THE MOST HIGH:
PRISTINE YOUTH AND FAMILY SOLUTIONS, LLC.
SONS AND DAUGHTERS OF THE MOST HIGH PUBLISHERS ®

OH, GRACIOUS MOST HIGH HEAVENLY FATHER, HOLY IS YOUR
NAME, YOUR WILL BE DONE NOW AND FOREVER!

the 9 Deadly Venoms of the Desires of the great dragon: that old serpent, called the Devil, and Satan, which are: **Slothful**, **Wrath**, **Pride**, **Greed**, **Lust**, **Hopeless Fear Disobedience**, **Lying**, **Heinous Murde**r, and **Wickedness**.

The messages of **Michael and his angels** (ἄγγελος **Angelos**) are in the KJV bible book of Hebrews chapter 8 verses 10-14; states: "**For this is the covenant that I will make with the house of Israel after those days, saith the Lord; I will put my laws into their mind, and write them in their hearts: and I will be to them a God, and they shall be to me a people. And they shall not teach every man his neighbour, and every man his brother, saying, Know the Lord: for all shall know me, from the least to the greatest. For I will be merciful to their unrighteousness, and their sins and their iniquities will I remember no more. In that he saith, a new covenant, he hath made the first old. Now that which decayeth and waxeth old is ready to vanish away.**" In the KJV bible book of Revelation chapter 22 verses 14-16; Yashu'a (Jesus) saith "Blessed are they that do his commandments, that they may have right to the tree of life, and may enter in through the gates into the city."

67

SPIRITUAL TRILLIONAIRE:
Cherishing the Breath of Life while Simultaneously
Preparing for the Blow of Death!

CHILDREN OF THE MOST HIGH:
PRISTINE YOUTH AND FAMILY SOLUTIONS, LLC.
SONS AND DAUGHTERS OF THE MOST HIGH PUBLISHERS &

OH, GRACIOUS MOST HIGH HEAVENLY FATHER, HOLY IS YOUR
NAME, YOUR WILL BE DONE NOW AND FOREVER!

In the KJV bible book of John chapter 14 verse 6; Yashu'a
(Jesus) saith unto him, "I am the way, the truth, and the life:
no man cometh unto the Father, but by me." In the KJV bible
book of Matthew chapter 22 verses 37-38; Yashu'a (Jesus) said
unto him: "Thou shalt love the Lord thy God with all thy
heart, and with all thy soul, and with all thy mind. This is
the first and great commandment." Therefore, each person
on the planet earth is either a knowing or unknowing advocate
of the **messages of the great dragon, that old serpent called
the devil and satan** which deceiveth the whole world **or an
advocate of the messages of the Arch Angelic-Being
Miykaa'iyl (Micha-El-means who dares to be like the Most
High (ELYOWN עֶלְיוֹן EL אֵל)** by the purpose of why and how
they live their lives, the way they think, the way they speak,
their actions and deeds.

> Watch your *thoughts;*
> they become words.
> Watch your *words;* they
> become actions.
> Watch your *actions;* they
> become habits.
> Watch your *habits;* they
> become character.
> Watch your *character;* it
> becomes your *destiny.*
> -Lao-Tze

SPIRITUAL TRILLIONAIRE:
**Cherishing the Breath of Life while Simultaneously
Preparing for the Blow of Death!**

CHILDREN OF THE MOST HIGH:
PRISTINE YOUTH AND FAMILY SOLUTIONS, LLC.
SONS AND DAUGHTERS OF THE MOST HIGH PUBLISHERS ®

OH, GRACIOUS MOST HIGH HEAVENLY FATHER, HOLY IS YOUR
NAME, YOUR WILL BE DONE NOW AND FOREVER!

Can unclean (malevolent) spirits make a person or people physically and spiritually unhealthy?

According to Yashu'a (Jesus), absolutely. In the KJV bible book of Mathew chapter 10 verse 1; the Messiah Yashu'a (Jesus): **"called unto him his twelve disciples, he <u>gave them power against unclean spirits</u>, <u>to cast them out</u>, <u>and to heal all manner of sickness and all manner of disease</u>."** Is there is a correlation between **<u>unhealthy</u>** and **<u>unclean</u>** which is the KJV bible Greek Strong's Concordance#169 **word: ἀκάθαρτος akathartos- meaning:** not cleansed, unclean; in a ceremonial sense: that which must be abstained from according to the Levitical law; **<u>in a moral sense: unclean in thought and life</u>**. Strong's Definitions (Strong's Definitions Legend) ἀκάθαρτος akáthartos, ak-ath'-ar-tos; from <u>G1</u> (as a negative particle) and a presumed derivative of <u>G2508</u> (meaning cleansed); **impure (ceremonially, morally (lewd-crude and offensive in a sexual way, vulgar, filthy, obscene, pornographic, wicked (evil or morally wrong), indecent)** or specially, **(demonic):—** foul, unclean).

SPIRITUAL TRILLIONAIRE:
**Cherishing the Breath of Life while Simultaneously
Preparing for the Blow of Death!**

CHILDREN OF THE MOST HIGH:
PRISTINE YOUTH AND FAMILY SOLUTIONS, LLC.
SONS AND DAUGHTERS OF THE MOST HIGH PUBLISHERS ®

OH, GRACIOUS MOST HIGH HEAVENLY FATHER, HOLY IS YOUR
NAME, YOUR WILL BE DONE NOW AND FOREVER!

In the First Testament or the [**Old**] Testament of the bible (**Old, what can be old to God?**), in the Aramic (Hebrew) language, the word for "**spirit**" is **Nephesh** which is sometimes translated in English as **Ruwach**, **soul** and **mind**. In the Second Testament or the [**New**] Testament of the bible, (**New, what can be new to God?**) the word for "**spirit**" is πνεῦμα **Pneuma**. So, is it possible that when a person's lungs become sick, it is from and **unhealthy "Pneuma πνεῦμα (Spirit)?"** The original Greek word for "**Spirit**" is "*Pneuma*" (**pronounced as: pnyoo' - mah**)" which is the root word for **Pneumonia**. According to the Online American Heritage Dictionary (2019), "**Pneumonia is "inflammation of the lungs," from pleumon "lung," and became pneumon "lung," from pnein "to breathe" literally "floater," probably cognate with Latin pulmo "lung(s)," from PIE root *pleu "to flow."**

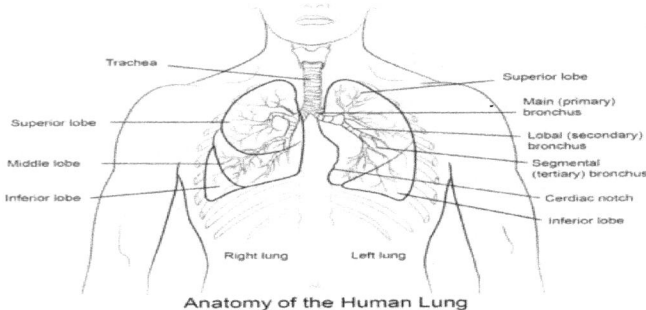

Trachea
Superior lobe
Main (primary) bronchus
Superior lobe
Lobal (secondary) bronchus
Middle lobe
Segmental (tertiary) bronchus
Inferior lobe
Cardiac notch
Inferior lobe
Right lung
Left lung

Anatomy of the Human Lung

70

SPIRITUAL TRILLIONAIRE:
Cherishing the Breath of Life while Simultaneously
Preparing for the Blow of Death!

CHILDREN OF THE MOST HIGH:
PRISTINE YOUTH AND FAMILY SOLUTIONS, LLC.
SONS AND DAUGHTERS OF THE MOST HIGH PUBLISHERS ®

OH, GRACIOUS MOST HIGH HEAVENLY FATHER, HOLY IS YOUR
NAME, YOUR WILL BE DONE NOW AND FOREVER!

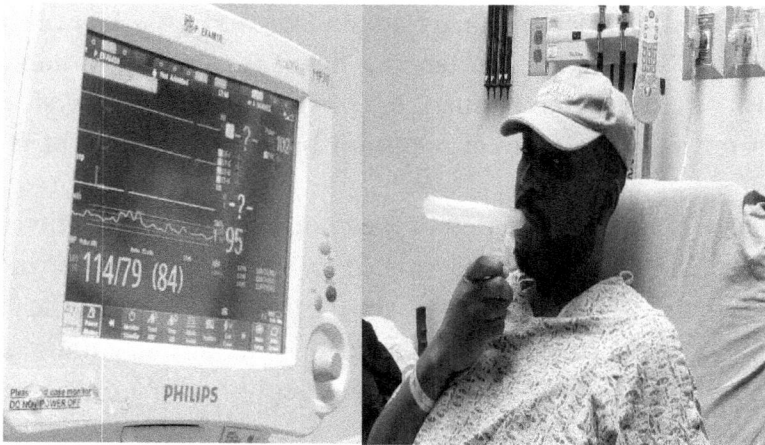

I was hospitalized twice for pneumonia in November and December 2018. I now have a much greater appreciation for my lungs and the ability to breathe without experiencing any discomfort. I thank the Most High Heavenly Father for healing me and bringing me through those experiences! So, according to the aforementioned verse, there is a direct correlation between **unclean spirits, and the elimination of unclean spirits** in order to heal **all** manner of sickness and **all** manner of diseases.

SPIRITUAL TRILLIONAIRE:
Cherishing the Breath of Life while Simultaneously
Preparing for the Blow of Death!

CHILDREN OF THE MOST HIGH:
PRISTINE YOUTH AND FAMILY SOLUTIONS, LLC.
SONS AND DAUGHTERS OF THE MOST HIGH PUBLISHERS ®

OH, GRACIOUS MOST HIGH HEAVENLY FATHER, HOLY IS YOUR
NAME, YOUR WILL BE DONE NOW AND FOREVER!

Why would a person focus on the Most High's Heavenly Father if they are experiencing heart issues or emotional pain or emotional trauma or physical pain or physical trauma or brain issues or mental trauma or a broken spirit?

A person who is experiencing emotional pain or emotional trauma would focus on the Most High's Heavenly Father who created the heart and has the ability to heal all of our heart issues, and can strengthen our hearts to overcome all emotional trauma if we ask the Most High Heavenly Father to do so in true-prayer supplication through true-faith. This is also inclusive of each person putting in the work that is essential to making a full recovery. A person who is experiencing physical pain or physical trauma would focus on the Most High's Heavenly Father who created the body and has the ability to heal all of our body issues if we ask the Most High Heavenly Father to do so in true-prayer supplication through true-faith. This is also inclusive of each person putting in the work that is essential to making a full recovery.

SPIRITUAL TRILLIONAIRE:
Cherishing the Breath of Life while Simultaneously
Preparing for the Blow of Death!

CHILDREN OF THE MOST HIGH:
PRISTINE YOUTH AND FAMILY SOLUTIONS, LLC.
SONS AND DAUGHTERS OF THE MOST HIGH PUBLISHERS ®

OH, GRACIOUS MOST HIGH HEAVENLY FATHER, HOLY IS YOUR
NAME, YOUR WILL BE DONE NOW AND FOREVER!

A person who is experiencing brain issues or mental trauma would focus on the Most High's Heavenly Father who created the brain and has the ability to heal all of our mental trauma and can gives us a peace of mind if we ask the Most High Heavenly Father to do so in true-prayer supplication through true-faith. A person who is experiencing a broken spirit would focus on the Most High's Heavenly Father who created all spirits and has the ability to **heal** and remove all of our broken spirit root causes if we ask the Most High Heavenly Father to do so in true-prayer supplication through true-faith. This is also inclusive of each person putting in the work that is essential to making a full recovery.

The first 4 letters in the word "Health,"
spell the word: "Heal." Therefore, the
ability to heal is essential to obtaining
and sustaining positive spiritual health
and positive spiritual wealth!

SPIRITUAL TRILLIONAIRE:
Cherishing the Breath of Life while Simultaneously
Preparing for the Blow of Death!

CHILDREN OF THE MOST HIGH:
PRISTINE YOUTH AND FAMILY SOLUTIONS, LLC.
SONS AND DAUGHTERS OF THE MOST HIGH PUBLISHERS &

OH, GRACIOUS MOST HIGH HEAVENLY FATHER, HOLY IS YOUR NAME, YOUR WILL BE DONE NOW AND FOREVER!

So, the Children of the Most High Pristine Youth and Family Solutions, LLC. ask that each person who is in the process of learning how to positively overcome or work through or live with life traumas, life changing events, or doing your best to overcome difficult situations or working through burdensome responsibilities consider the following: surrounding yourself with positive people who can become a positive support system that may be able to successfully help you get through difficult circumstances in your life or consider seeking profession help who can become a positive support system for yourself. The Children of the Most High: Pristine Youth and Family Solutions, LLC. are advocates of professional health for people who may need to receive professional medical care, professional therapy and/or professional counseling as recommended by the professionals in those fields of practice. Asking and excepting the help that we may need at different stages in our growth requires active discipline.

SPIRITUAL TRILLIONAIRE:
Cherishing the Breath of Life while Simultaneously
Preparing for the Blow of Death!

CHILDREN OF THE MOST HIGH:
PRISTINE YOUTH AND FAMILY SOLUTIONS, LLC.
SONS AND DAUGHTERS OF THE MOST HIGH PUBLISHERS ®

OH, GRACIOUS MOST HIGH HEAVENLY FATHER, HOLY IS YOUR
NAME, YOUR WILL BE DONE NOW AND FOREVER!

Is being unhealthy physically and/or spiritually always the result of spiritual circumstances?

Being unhealthy physically and/or spiritually is not always the result of spiritual circumstances. The Children of the Most High Pristine Youth and Family Solutions, LLC strongly **recommend that people consider** exploring all physical medical options with their physicians before ignoring illnesses that are believed to have a metaphysical origin. Sometimes or many times, our unhealthiness can result from poor eating, not eating, over eating, or due to living a busy lifestyle that neglects taking care of our bodies, or neglects getting enough hours of quality sleep each day, or not having enough money to buy food, and/or living in a geographic area where there is no food or limited healthy food like living in a food desert or a literal desert. **Why does what we put into our physical body affect us spiritually?** What we put into our physical body affects us spiritually because our bodies are the temples that house our souls and spirits.

SPIRITUAL TRILLIONAIRE:
Cherishing the Breath of Life while Simultaneously
Preparing for the Blow of Death!

CHILDREN OF THE MOST HIGH:
PRISTINE YOUTH AND FAMILY SOLUTIONS, LLC.
SONS AND DAUGHTERS OF THE MOST HIGH PUBLISHERS ®

OH, GRACIOUS MOST HIGH HEAVENLY FATHER, HOLY IS YOUR
NAME, YOUR WILL BE DONE NOW AND FOREVER!

In the KJV bible book of 1st Corinthians chapter 3 verses 16-17; it states:

"Know ye not that ye are the temple of God, and [that] the Spirit of God dwelleth in you? If any man defiles the temple of God, him shall God destroy; for the temple of God is holy, which [temple] ye are."

In the KJV bible book of 1st Corinthians chapter 6 verses 19-20; it states: "What? know ye not that your *body* is the *temple* of the Holy Ghost [which is] in you, which ye have of God, and ye are not your own?"

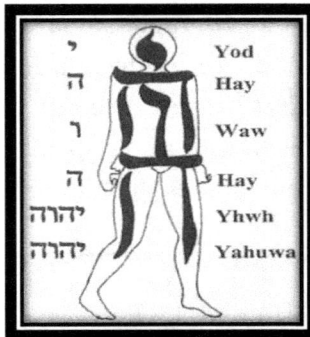

76

SPIRITUAL TRILLIONAIRE:
Cherishing the Breath of Life while Simultaneously
Preparing for the Blow of Death!

CHILDREN OF THE MOST HIGH:
PRISTINE YOUTH AND FAMILY SOLUTIONS, LLC.
SONS AND DAUGHTERS OF THE MOST HIGH PUBLISHERS ®

OH, GRACIOUS MOST HIGH HEAVENLY FATHER, HOLY IS YOUR
NAME, YOUR WILL BE DONE NOW AND FOREVER!

According to the Children of the Most High Pristine Youth and Family Solutions, LLC. what are the 9 Essential Elements in a Human Being and what are the 9 Essential Habits of Healing the physical body as it relates to acquiring positive spiritual health and positive spiritual wealth?

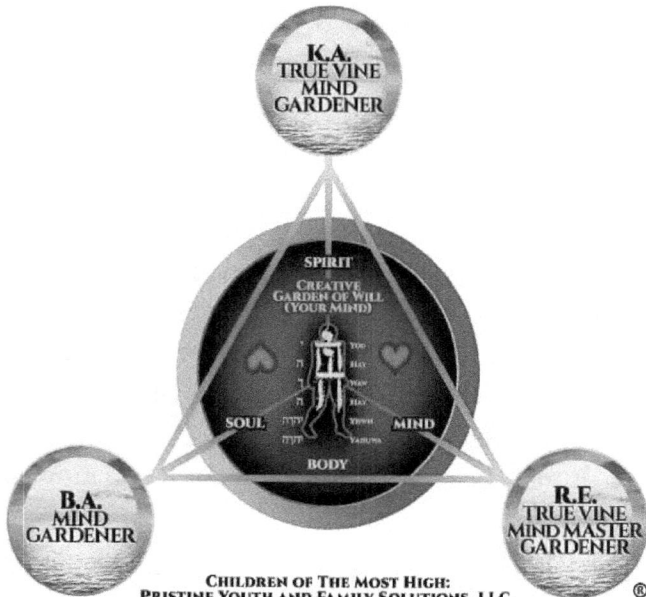

CHILDREN OF THE MOST HIGH:
PRISTINE YOUTH AND FAMILY SOLUTIONS, LLC.
9X9 TRUE VINE "YASHU'A" (JESUS) B.A.-K.A.-R.E.
SEQUENTIAL ORDER OF LEARNING®

SPIRITUAL TRILLIONAIRE:
Cherishing the Breath of Life while Simultaneously
Preparing for the Blow of Death!

CHILDREN OF THE MOST HIGH:
PRISTINE YOUTH AND FAMILY SOLUTIONS, LLC.
SONS AND DAUGHTERS OF THE MOST HIGH PUBLISHERS ®

OH, GRACIOUS MOST HIGH HEAVENLY FATHER, HOLY IS YOUR
NAME, YOUR WILL BE DONE NOW AND FOREVER!

According to the Children of the Most High Pristine Youth and Family Solutions, LLC., **the 9 Essential Elements in a Human Being** as it relates to positive spiritual health and positive spiritual wealth are:

1. Spirit (KJV bible book of Genesis chapter 2 verse 7).
2. Mind (KJV bible book of Mathew chapter 22 verses 37-38).
3. Body (KJV bible book of Genesis chapter 2 verse 7).
4. Soul (KJV bible book of Genesis chapter 2 verse 7).
5. Plasma in you or Plasmatic You (KJV bible book of Leviticus chapter 17 verses 13-14, Life is in the blood).
6. Etheric (ether) you, is a person's genetic spiritual link to their Ancestors, the Ancient Ones and the Old Ones. (KJV bible book of Psalms chapter 82 verses 6-7).
7. Physical Heart (KJV bible book of Proverbs chapter 3 verses 5-6).
8. Spiritual Heart (KJV bible book of Revelation chapter 3 verse 20).
9. Spark of Life – Lifeforce of all living things (KJV bible book of John chapter 1 verses 1-5).

SPIRITUAL TRILLIONAIRE:
**Cherishing the Breath of Life while Simultaneously
Preparing for the Blow of Death!**

CHILDREN OF THE MOST HIGH:
PRISTINE YOUTH AND FAMILY SOLUTIONS, LLC.
SONS AND DAUGHTERS OF THE MOST HIGH PUBLISHERS ®

**OH, GRACIOUS MOST HIGH HEAVENLY FATHER, HOLY IS YOUR
NAME, YOUR WILL BE DONE NOW AND FOREVER!**

According to the Children of the Most High Pristine Youth and Family Solutions, LLC., the **9 Essential Habits of Healing the physical body** as it relates to acquiring positive spiritual health and positive spiritual wealth are:

1. Daily intake of healthy food.
2. Daily intake of plenty healthy water.
3. Healthy – medical physician approved physical exercising 5 to 6 days a week.
4. Daily true-prayer supplication.
5. Daily meditation, healthy breathing and healthy relaxation.
6. Daily high-quality sufficient amounts of sleep.
7. Daily loving and obeying the Messiah Yashu'a (Jesus).
8. Daily having and practicing True-Faith in the Most High Heavenly Father.
9. Daily having and expressing divine love for the Most High Heavenly Father, loving and obeying the Most High Heavenly Father with all of your heart, with all your spirit, with all of your soul, and with all of your mind.

SPIRITUAL TRILLIONAIRE:
**Cherishing the Breath of Life while Simultaneously
Preparing for the Blow of Death!**

CHILDREN OF THE MOST HIGH:
PRISTINE YOUTH AND FAMILY SOLUTIONS, LLC.
SONS AND DAUGHTERS OF THE MOST HIGH PUBLISHERS ®

OH, GRACIOUS MOST HIGH HEAVENLY FATHER, HOLY IS YOUR
NAME, YOUR WILL BE DONE NOW AND FOREVER!

Also, our physical health and spiritual health can negatively be affected by stress from experiencing heart issues or emotional pain or emotional trauma or physical pain or physical trauma or brain issues or mental trauma or broken spirit or from stress we may experience from lack of money or from wanting more money or from the circumstances we experience in our careers or at our **J-O-B** or a multitude of life changing events such as losing a **J-O-B** or not having a **J-O-B**.

According to the Children of the Most High Pristine Youth and Family Solutions, LLC., how should a person best consider getting prepared for potential **J-O-B** stress or how should a person best consider continuing to stay prepared so they don't have to get ready as it relates to positively responding to **J-O-B** related stress? By reading the KJV book of the bible "**J-O-B**" and utilize **J-O-B's** example of **True-Faith in action**. If a person lacks **True-Faith in the Most High**, a person is afforded the opportunity to ask the Most High to increase their **True-Faith** in the Most High through the Messiah Yashu'a (Jesus) to counteract all of the **J-O-B** related stress and all other stressors in our lives.

SPIRITUAL TRILLIONAIRE:
Cherishing the Breath of Life while Simultaneously
Preparing for the Blow of Death!

CHILDREN OF THE MOST HIGH:
PRISTINE YOUTH AND FAMILY SOLUTIONS, LLC.
SONS AND DAUGHTERS OF THE MOST HIGH PUBLISHERS ®

OH, GRACIOUS MOST HIGH HEAVENLY FATHER, HOLY IS YOUR
NAME, YOUR WILL BE DONE NOW AND FOREVER!

The Children of the Most High Pristine Youth and Family
Solutions, LLC. refer to it as: the **True Vine** (Yashu'a, Jesus)
**Fruit of the Spirit Positive Character-Building Essentials,
known as the Fruit of the Spirit of "Faith"** in the KJV bible
book of Galatians chapter 5 verses 22-23; according to the KJV
bible Greek Strong Concordance# **G3982**; the word for "**Faith**"
is: πίστις pístis, Pis'-tis; and means: persuasion, i.e. credence;
moral conviction (of religious truth, or the truthfulness of God),
truth itself:—assurance, belief, believe, faith, fidelity."

Iyanla Vanzant stated: "**We each come into this life with a
spiritual curriculum. Our spiritual curriculum is chosen by
our souls to facilitate growth, learning and healing. If we
judge our spiritual curriculum as good or bad, right or
wrong, fair or unfair, we will miss the point of the lesson,
and we will repeat the class over and over. Once you get
clear about who you are, what you do, and what you are
being called to do, you become powerful.**"

I truly can relate to the fact that "serious illness experiences
often make people stand back and take account of where they
currently are and where they want to be in life.

81

SPIRITUAL TRILLIONAIRE:
Cherishing the Breath of Life while Simultaneously
Preparing for the Blow of Death!

CHILDREN OF THE MOST HIGH:
PRISTINE YOUTH AND FAMILY SOLUTIONS, LLC.
SONS AND DAUGHTERS OF THE MOST HIGH PUBLISHERS ®

OH, GRACIOUS MOST HIGH HEAVENLY FATHER, HOLY IS YOUR
NAME, YOUR WILL BE DONE NOW AND FOREVER!

On February 12, 2012, my wife rushed me to the Macon, Georgia Coliseum Hospital Emergency Ward. I was hospitalized for 9 days. Six months prior to my hospitalization, I was living on water and Ensure shakes. My stomach had experienced pain that became worse from 2007 to 2012. I had lost over 70 pounds 6 months prior to being rushed to the emergency ward by my wife. On February 14, 2012 while I was unconscious during an endoscopy procedure, my GI Doctor told my wife and mother that I was not going to survive the night. He stated that: "the inside of your husband's organs looks like stone, his pancreas according to the CT scan is 100% inflamed and can stop working at any moment, his liver is inflamed, the part of his stomach that connects to the upper intestine is blocked and the food that was in his stomach prior to this blockage had rotted and turned to poison; which is why he is malnourished. His upper intestine is completely ulcerated, inflamed and ready to burst at any moment."

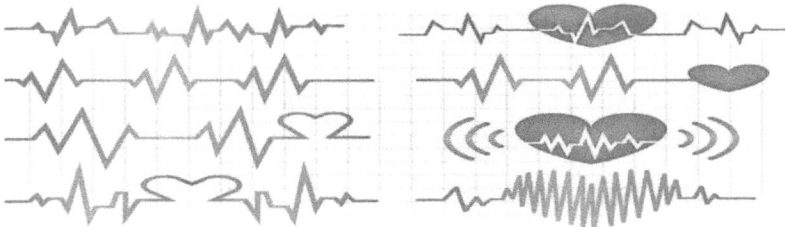

SPIRITUAL TRILLIONAIRE:
**Cherishing the Breath of Life while Simultaneously
Preparing for the Blow of Death!**

CHILDREN OF THE MOST HIGH:
PRISTINE YOUTH AND FAMILY SOLUTIONS, LLC.
SONS AND DAUGHTERS OF THE MOST HIGH PUBLISHERS ®

OH, GRACIOUS MOST HIGH HEAVENLY FATHER, HOLY IS YOUR
NAME, YOUR WILL BE DONE NOW AND FOREVER!

"I have tried for the past hour and a half to locate the area where the blockage is in an effort to open that area to release the poison from your husband's stomach. However; I have not been able to do so because it is dark and bloody in that area and there is no visibility even with a light. Do you have any last rites for your husband? My team and I are going to perform emergency surgery that will allow us to cut off the infected part of his upper intestine. However; due to his immune system being so weak, I do not anticipate your husband surviving this procedure."

On February 15, 2012, my GI Doctor came to my hospital bed and starred at me as if he had seen a ghost. He asked me: "how were you walking around for so long in all of that pain?" My GI Doctor said to me: "Last night, I told your wife and mother that you were not going to make it through the night. Right before I began surgery, something told me to try one more time to open the area of your stomach that was blocked."

SPIRITUAL TRILLIONAIRE:
**Cherishing the Breath of Life while Simultaneously
Preparing for the Blow of Death!**

CHILDREN OF THE MOST HIGH:
PRISTINE YOUTH AND FAMILY SOLUTIONS, LLC.
SONS AND DAUGHTERS OF THE MOST HIGH PUBLISHERS ®

OH, GRACIOUS MOST HIGH HEAVENLY FATHER, HOLY IS YOUR
NAME, YOUR WILL BE DONE NOW AND FOREVER!

"It was dark and bloody in that area and I could not see anything. I admit that by that time, I had become frustrated. I put the scope back in you and it just went there. I was able to open your stomach blockage area just enough so that the poison in your stomach would be released. That's why you are now experiencing a temperature of 103 degrees."

**Woodie Hughes Jr.
02/15/2012**

I was diagnosis with a rare onset of Chrohn's Disease. My GI Doctor said that "it is rare because typical Chrohn's Disease is in the lower intestine and falls under the Irritable Bowels Syndrome category." However, in 2012, I did not have any symptoms of Irritable Bowels Syndrome and my issue was in my upper intestine and I was physically eating healthy prior to not being able to physically eat solid food.

SPIRITUAL TRILLIONAIRE:
Cherishing the Breath of Life while Simultaneously
Preparing for the Blow of Death!

CHILDREN OF THE MOST HIGH:
PRISTINE YOUTH AND FAMILY SOLUTIONS, LLC.
SONS AND DAUGHTERS OF THE MOST HIGH PUBLISHERS ®

OH, GRACIOUS MOST HIGH HEAVENLY FATHER, HOLY IS YOUR
NAME, YOUR WILL BE DONE NOW AND FOREVER!

However; I allowed J-O-B stress, lack of financial resources to be able to pay monthly bills, and worrying about situations that I could not control to poison me mentally, spiritually, emotionally and physically which almost killed me!

I am truly blessed and thankful to the Most High Heavenly Father for bringing me through that experience!!! **Prior to that time of only being able to consume water and Ensure shakes, my diet was almost perfect**. I was only eating fruits, vegetables, lots of water, baked fish, baked chicken, healthy grains, no soda, no pork, no beef, no alcohol, no tobacco products, no illegal substances, and I was working out 4 to 6 days a week. However, at that time in my life, I was a worrier, full of anxiety, and wasted much time dwelling on past regrets, fearing future financial disasters, situations, and circumstances. I share this experience with you as an example of how positive thinking, true-faith in the Most High, and the Most High healing me at such a difficult time can also happen for you too! Why? In hopes that you may glorify the Most High. I had to get sick in order to get well which motivated me to work moment to moment each day to eliminate the habit of negative thinking, and decided that **"I cannot afford the luxury of a negative thought as my mom, Mrs. Annette Hughes, recites frequently."**

85

SPIRITUAL TRILLIONAIRE:
Cherishing the Breath of Life while Simultaneously
Preparing for the Blow of Death!

CHILDREN OF THE MOST HIGH:
PRISTINE YOUTH AND FAMILY SOLUTIONS, LLC.
SONS AND DAUGHTERS OF THE MOST HIGH PUBLISHERS ®

OH, GRACIOUS MOST HIGH HEAVENLY FATHER, HOLY IS YOUR
NAME, YOUR WILL BE DONE NOW AND FOREVER!

Which for me, later became "**I cannot afford the luxury of negative thinking**." This began the process of me reexamining all of my thoughts and perceptions that were negative and required me to immediately exchange them for their opposite positive reinforced thoughts. In November 2012, my GI Doctor stated: "all of your organs look brand new, keep doing whatever it is that you are doing." "Thought" is one of the most powerful forces in the universe because it initiates all actions. There is no sickness that there is not a physical or spiritual cure for or that can't be cured physically or spiritually. If we align ourselves back with the Most High spiritually by consistently doing the following: living a lifestyle that reflects the daily disciplines of true-prayer supplications, practicing true-faith, positive thinking, positive intentions, positive visualization, positive speaking, positive actions, obeying the Most High's laws and commandments, fasting of the mind from all disagreeableness, eating healthy, meditation, proper breathing, true scripture studying of the scriptures from the original languages they were revealed in, into the language or languages you speak most frequently, physical exercising and **physical fasting only according to your doctor's medical guidelines if possible**; we give ourselves the greatest opportunity to live a life that reflects positive overall wellness and wellbeing!

86

SPIRITUAL TRILLIONAIRE:
**Cherishing the Breath of Life while Simultaneously
Preparing for the Blow of Death!**

CHILDREN OF THE MOST HIGH:
PRISTINE YOUTH AND FAMILY SOLUTIONS, LLC.
SONS AND DAUGHTERS OF THE MOST HIGH PUBLISHERS ®

OH, GRACIOUS MOST HIGH HEAVENLY FATHER, HOLY IS YOUR
NAME, YOUR WILL BE DONE NOW AND FOREVER!

"When you spend time worrying about the things that you don't have or situations that you can't control, you rob yourself of experiencing, living in the NOW or living in the present! Which is the only TIME that change can occur. Therefore, NOW is the TIME that we have an opportunity to practice being thankful for what we do have, rather than creating a mental hell which is fueled by thoughts of what we don't have or can't control! (Hughes Mind Journal, 2001)."

SPIRITUAL TRILLIONAIRE:
**Cherishing the Breath of Life while Simultaneously
Preparing for the Blow of Death!**

CHILDREN OF THE MOST HIGH:
PRISTINE YOUTH AND FAMILY SOLUTIONS, LLC.
SONS AND DAUGHTERS OF THE MOST HIGH PUBLISHERS ®

OH, GRACIOUS MOST HIGH HEAVENLY FATHER, HOLY IS YOUR
NAME, YOUR WILL BE DONE NOW AND FOREVER!

Upholding your positive family obligations in an exquisite way, all of the time or as much as possible; utilizing time wisely, ensuring that your financial needs are met, obeying the Most High's doctrine, and living a life that reflects the characteristics and attributes of the life of the Messiah Yashu'a (Jesus) is paramount to a person who is on the path to becoming a Spiritual Trillionaire!

Many people want the blessings of righteousness while simultaneously living in sin. However, because of the law of nature that a person must reap what he or she sows, members of humanity cannot receive the blessings of righteousness while simultaneously living in sin. So, as it relates to acquiring, maintain and sustaining spiritual health and spiritual wealth, it is not possible for a person to accomplish these goals if he or she neglects self-care, over commits oneself to worldly affairs, and not utilize the blessed gift of time wisely. Remember: all of the money and wealth in the world cannot bring one person back from physical death, and cannot buy back one moment of time that has passed!

SPIRITUAL TRILLIONAIRE:
Cherishing the Breath of Life while Simultaneously
Preparing for the Blow of Death!

CHILDREN OF THE MOST HIGH:
PRISTINE YOUTH AND FAMILY SOLUTIONS, LLC.
SONS AND DAUGHTERS OF THE MOST HIGH PUBLISHERS ®

OH, GRACIOUS MOST HIGH HEAVENLY FATHER, HOLY IS YOUR
NAME, YOUR WILL BE DONE NOW AND FOREVER!

Practicing the aforementioned on a daily basis, may eliminate or decrease the amount of times a person becomes ill, it may strengthen a person mentally, physically, spiritually and emotionally in their pursuit to acquire, maintain and sustain positive spiritual health and positive spiritual wealth on the path to becoming a Spiritual Trillionaire.

What is self-care? According to the Online American Heritage Dictionary (2019), **self-care** is defined as: "The act of engaging in activities or behaviors that help one achieve or maintain good physical or mental health, especially to mitigate the effects of stress or trauma: "Self-care is not only an act of kindness toward yourself, it's also a necessary component of life now."

~Oh, Most High,
All Praises are Eternally due to You, Amen~

SPIRITUAL TRILLIONAIRE:
Cherishing the Breath of Life while Simultaneously
Preparing for the Blow of Death!

CHILDREN OF THE MOST HIGH:
PRISTINE YOUTH AND FAMILY SOLUTIONS, LLC.
SONS AND DAUGHTERS OF THE MOST HIGH PUBLISHERS ®

OH, GRACIOUS MOST HIGH HEAVENLY FATHER, HOLY IS YOUR
NAME, YOUR WILL BE DONE NOW AND FOREVER!

Chapter 4: What is the correlation between the 9 Deadly Venoms of the Desires of the great dragon, that old serpent called the devil and satan which deceiveth the whole world and Leviathan mentioned in the Bible?

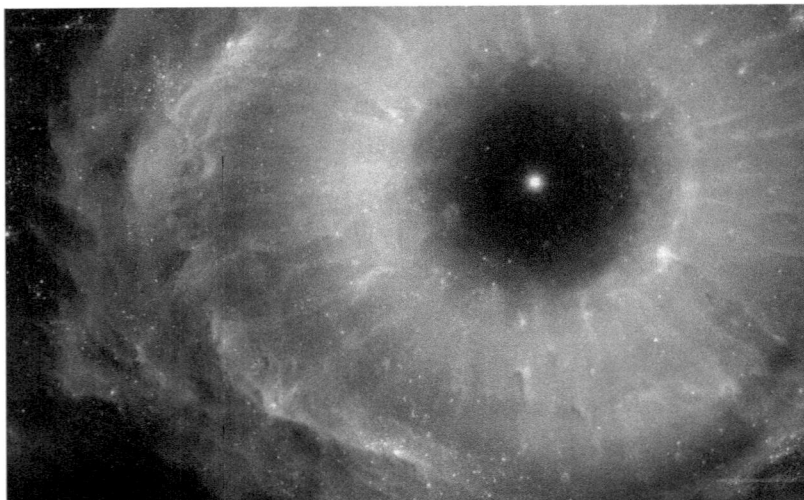

~Oh, Most High Heavenly Father, we eternally seek
protection in you from the great dragon, that old serpent
called the devil and satan which deceiveth the whole world.
Amen~

SPIRITUAL TRILLIONAIRE:
Cherishing the Breath of Life while Simultaneously
Preparing for the Blow of Death!

CHILDREN OF THE MOST HIGH:
PRISTINE YOUTH AND FAMILY SOLUTIONS, LLC.
SONS AND DAUGHTERS OF THE MOST HIGH PUBLISHERS ®

OH, GRACIOUS MOST HIGH HEAVENLY FATHER, HOLY IS YOUR
NAME, YOUR WILL BE DONE NOW AND FOREVER!

The **9 Deadly Venoms of the Desires of the great dragon, that old serpent called the devil and satan which deceiveth the whole world** are: **Slothful**, **Wrath**, **Pride**, **Greed**, **Lust**, **Hopeless-Fear-Disobedience**, **Lying**, **Heinous Murde**r, and **Wickedness**. These **9 Deadly Venoms of the Desires of** are the root causes that prevent the acquisition of positive spiritual health and positive spiritual wealth.

What is venom? According to the Online American Heritage Dictionary (2019), venom is defined as: **1.** A poisonous secretion of an animal, such as a snake, spider, or scorpion, usually transmitted to prey or to attackers by a bite or sting. **Is there a correlation between venom, Leviathan, the old Serpent and the Dragon mentioned in the Bible that can adversely impact a person's spiritual health and spiritual wealth status?**

In the KJV bible book of **Job** chapter **41** verse **1**: "Canst thou draw out **leviathan** with a hook? or his tongue with a cord which thou lettest down?"

SPIRITUAL TRILLIONAIRE:
Cherishing the Breath of Life while Simultaneously
Preparing for the Blow of Death!

CHILDREN OF THE MOST HIGH:
PRISTINE YOUTH AND FAMILY SOLUTIONS, LLC.
SONS AND DAUGHTERS OF THE MOST HIGH PUBLISHERS

OH, GRACIOUS MOST HIGH HEAVENLY FATHER, HOLY IS YOUR
NAME, YOUR WILL BE DONE NOW AND FOREVER!

In the KJV bible book of **Psalms** chapter **74** verse **14**: "Thou brakest the heads of **leviathan** in pieces, and gavest him to be meat to the people inhabiting the wilderness."

In the KJV bible book of **Psalms** chapter **104** verse **26**: "There go the ships: there is that **leviathan**, whom thou hast made to play therein."

In the KJV bible book of **Isaiah** chapter **27** verse **1**: "In that day the LORD with his sore and great and strong sword shall punish **leviathan** the piercing serpent, even leviathan that crooked serpent; and he shall slay the dragon that is in the sea."

SPIRITUAL TRILLIONAIRE:
Cherishing the Breath of Life while Simultaneously
Preparing for the Blow of Death!

CHILDREN OF THE MOST HIGH:
PRISTINE YOUTH AND FAMILY SOLUTIONS, LLC.
SONS AND DAUGHTERS OF THE MOST HIGH PUBLISHERS ®

OH, GRACIOUS MOST HIGH HEAVENLY FATHER, HOLY IS YOUR
NAME, YOUR WILL BE DONE NOW AND FOREVER!

Leviathan: From *The Klein's Comprehensive Etymological Dictionary Of The English Language.*

Late Latin From Hebrew **Liwayathan,** *"Serpent, Dragon, ˋLeviathan",* Prop, Tortuous, Which Is Related To ˋ**Liwya.** *"Wreath" From* Base L-W-H, *"To Wind, Turn, Twist",* Whence Also Arab, **Lawa,** *"The Wound, Turned, Twisted",* To Surround, Encircle.

Leviathan: From the *Webster's New Twentieth Century Dictionary Unabridged, Second Edition*

(Noun) Middle English - **Leuyethan,** *Late Latin (Ecclesiastic) Hebrew* **Liwayathan,** *base akin to Akkadian -* **Lawu,** *to surround, Arabic:* **Liyatu,** *Snake. 1. A large and powerful aquatic animal described in* **Job Chapter 4,** *and mentioned in other passages or*

scriptures: variously thought of as a whale or a reptile. 2. Anything huge of its kind.

Leviathan: From The *Webster's Second College Edition, New World Dictionary.*

(Noun) Middle English - **Leuyethan,** *Late Latin (Ecclesiastic) Hebrew* **Liwayathan,** *base akin to Akkadian -* **Lawu,** *to surround, Arabic:* **Liyatu,** *Snake. 1. Bible, a sea monster, variously thought of as a reptile or a whale. 2. Anything huge or very powerful. 3. a political treatise by Thomas Hobbes (1651 A.D.) dealing with the organization of the state.*

93

SPIRITUAL TRILLIONAIRE:
**Cherishing the Breath of Life while Simultaneously
Preparing for the Blow of Death!**

CHILDREN OF THE MOST HIGH:
PRISTINE YOUTH AND FAMILY SOLUTIONS, LLC.
SONS AND DAUGHTERS OF THE MOST HIGH PUBLISHERS

OH, GRACIOUS MOST HIGH HEAVENLY FATHER, HOLY IS YOUR
NAME, YOUR WILL BE DONE NOW AND FOREVER!

לִוְיָתָן (with the adj. termination ָן‎, like נְחֻשְׁתָּן brazen, from נְחֹשֶׁת, עֲקַלָּתוֹן from עֲקַלָּה), prop. an (animal), *wreathed, twisted in folds.*

(1) *a serpent* of a larger kind, Job 3:8 (as to this place see the root עוּר Pilel); Isa. 27:1 (where it is the symbol of the hostile kingdom of Babylon).

(2) specially, *a crocodile*, Job 40:25, seq.

(3) any *very large aquatic creature*, Ps. 104: 26; used for a fierce enemy, Psa. 74:14; comp. תַּנִּין Isa. 51:9; Ezek. 29:3; 32:2, 3. Bochart, Hieroz. P. ii. lib. v. cap. 16—18.

94

SPIRITUAL TRILLIONAIRE:
Cherishing the Breath of Life while Simultaneously
Preparing for the Blow of Death!

CHILDREN OF THE MOST HIGH:
PRISTINE YOUTH AND FAMILY SOLUTIONS, LLC.
SONS AND DAUGHTERS OF THE MOST HIGH PUBLISHERS ®

OH, GRACIOUS MOST HIGH HEAVENLY FATHER, HOLY IS YOUR
NAME, YOUR WILL BE DONE NOW AND FOREVER!

In the KJV bible book of **Revelation** chapter **12** verses **7-9**; it states: "And there was war in heaven: **Michael and his angels** (ἄγγελος **Angelos,** meaning **Messengers**, the KJV bible Greek Strong's#32) fought against the **dragon**; and **the dragon fought and his angels** (ἄγγελος **Angelos,** meaning **Messengers**, the KJV bible Greek Strong's# 32), And prevailed not; neither was their place found any more in heaven. And the **great dragon** was cast out, that **old serpent**, **called the Devil, and Satan**, which deceiveth the whole world: he was cast out into the earth, and his **angels** (ἄγγελος **Angelos,** meaning **Messengers**, the KJV bible Greek Strong's#32) were cast out with him.

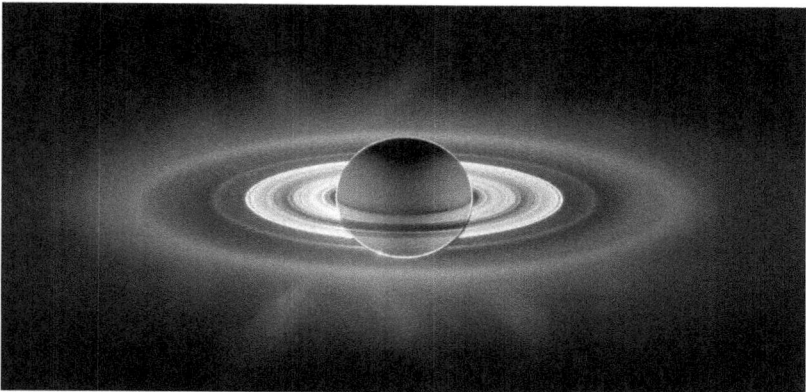

SPIRITUAL TRILLIONAIRE:
Cherishing the Breath of Life while Simultaneously
Preparing for the Blow of Death!

CHILDREN OF THE MOST HIGH:
PRISTINE YOUTH AND FAMILY SOLUTIONS, LLC.
SONS AND DAUGHTERS OF THE MOST HIGH PUBLISHERS ®

OH, GRACIOUS MOST HIGH HEAVENLY FATHER, HOLY IS YOUR
NAME, YOUR WILL BE DONE NOW AND FOREVER!

So, the answer to the question: Is there a correlation between venom, **Leviathan**, the **old Serpent** and the **Dragon** mentioned in the bible that can adversely impact a person's spiritual health and spiritual wealth status? **YES!!!** By biblical definitions, the **old** cunning **Serpent** and the **Dragon** called **Satan** and the **Devil** deceived the whole world.

Are some of the people of this world under some type of Serpent's spell or spell of Leviathan? Why do we ask this? It would seem unlikely that the **whole world** or everybody on the planet with the many intellectuals in the world would simultaneously be deceived unless the whole world was under some type of hypnotic spell (**which deceiveth the whole world**). **The spell of leviathan is another name for that great dragon, that old serpent called the devil and satan that deceiveth the whole world.**

According to the bible, Leviathan is in the atmosphere of the planet earth. "**Levi**" means "**Law**" and "**athan**" means "**sin**". Could Leviathan be the law that governed the **serpent** in the Garden of Eden in the KJV bible book of Genesis chapter 3 verse 1?

SPIRITUAL TRILLIONAIRE:
**Cherishing the Breath of Life while Simultaneously
Preparing for the Blow of Death!**

CHILDREN OF THE MOST HIGH:
PRISTINE YOUTH AND FAMILY SOLUTIONS, LLC.
SONS AND DAUGHTERS OF THE MOST HIGH PUBLISHERS ®

OH, GRACIOUS MOST HIGH HEAVENLY FATHER, HOLY IS YOUR
NAME, YOUR WILL BE DONE NOW AND FOREVER!

"Now the **serpent** was more subtil than any beast of the field
which the LORD God had made. And he said unto the woman,
Yea, hath God said, Ye shall not eat of every tree of the garden,
Genesis 3:1."

Many theologians and practitioners of Judaism, Christianity
and Islam refer to the **Serpent** in the KJV bible book of Genesis
as another title for **Lucifer** as mentioned in the KJV bible book
of Isaiah chapter 14 verses 12-16. So, Lucifer is sometimes
referred to as a serpent. The pluralization of **Lucifer** is
Luciferians or is sometimes referred to as **Legions**.

In the KJV bible book of Isaiah chapter 14 verses 12-16; it
states: "How art thou fallen from heaven, O **Lucifer**, son of the
morning! [how] art thou cut down to the ground, which didst
weaken the nations! For thou hast said in thine heart, I will
ascend into heaven, I will exalt my throne above the stars of
God: I will sit also upon the mount of the congregation, in the
sides of the north: I will ascend above the heights of the clouds;
I will be like the Most High. Yet thou shalt be brought down to
hell, to the sides of the pit. They that see thee shall narrowly

SPIRITUAL TRILLIONAIRE:
Cherishing the Breath of Life while Simultaneously
Preparing for the Blow of Death!

CHILDREN OF THE MOST HIGH:
PRISTINE YOUTH AND FAMILY SOLUTIONS, LLC.
SONS AND DAUGHTERS OF THE MOST HIGH PUBLISHERS ®

OH, GRACIOUS MOST HIGH HEAVENLY FATHER, HOLY IS YOUR
NAME, YOUR WILL BE DONE NOW AND FOREVER!

look upon thee, [and] consider thee, [saying, is] this the man that made the earth to tremble, that did shake kingdoms."

In the KJV bible book of Mark chapter 5 verse 9; Yashu'a (Jesus) asked him (**the unclean spirits inside the man that was possessed**): "What [is] thy name? And he answered, saying, my name [is] **Legion: for we are many**." The **KJV bible Greek Strong's Concordance#3003**, defines: "λεγιών **Legion**" as a body of soldiers whose number differed at different times. The **KJV bible Hebrew Strong's Concordance#03882**, defines: "**Leviathan**" לִוְיָתָן **livyâthân, liv-yaw-thawn'; as a sea monster, dragon from Lawwaw meaning: to unite, to remain.** In the KJV bible book of Isaiah chapter 27 verse 1; **Leviathan** is literally called the: "**piercing serpent**". The **KJV bible Strong's Hebrew Concordance# 5175**, defines: "**Serpent**" as נָחָשׁ **nachash or Nakhash** which is the same word used the KJV bible book of **Genesis chapter 3 verse 1** for "**the devil**".

נָחָשׁ m. — (1) *a serpent,* so called from its hissing (see the root) Gen. 3:1, seq.; Ex. 4:3; 7:15; 2 Ki. 18:4. Used of the constellation of the serpent or dragon in the northern part of the sky, Arab. حِيَّة Job 26:13.

SPIRITUAL TRILLIONAIRE:
Cherishing the Breath of Life while Simultaneously
Preparing for the Blow of Death!

CHILDREN OF THE MOST HIGH:
PRISTINE YOUTH AND FAMILY SOLUTIONS, LLC.
SONS AND DAUGHTERS OF THE MOST HIGH PUBLISHERS ®

OH, GRACIOUS MOST HIGH HEAVENLY FATHER, HOLY IS YOUR
NAME, YOUR WILL BE DONE NOW AND FOREVER!

In the KJV bible book of Mathew chapter 10 verse 1; the Messiah Yashu'a (Jesus): **"called unto him his twelve disciples, he gave them power against unclean spirits, to cast them out, and to heal all manner of sickness and all manner of disease."** The word **"unclean"** in this verse is KJV bible Greek Strong's Concordance#169 word: **"ἀκάθαρτος akathartos- meaning:** not cleansed, unclean; in a ceremonial sense: that which must be abstained from according to the Levitical law; **in a moral sense: unclean in thought and life**; impure **(ceremonially, morally (lewd-crude and offensive in a sexual way, vulgar, filthy, obscene, pornographic, wicked (evil or morally wrong), indecent)** or specially, **(demonic):** foul, unclean)." According to the aforementioned KJV bible verses, **Leviathan, the great dragon** is a **Legion** of **unclean** spirits also known as the **Sex Spirit Force** called **pórnē, por'- nay πόρνη** and pronounced as: **"Pornay"** that the Messiah Yashu'a (Jesus) spoke about in the KJV bible book of John chapter 8 verse 41 below with Greek inserts.

ὑμεῖς ποιεῖτε τὰ ἔργα τοῦ πατρὸς ὑμῶν εἶπον οὖν αὐτῷ Ἡμεῖς ἐκ πορνείας οὐ γεγεννήμεθα ἕνα πατέρα ἔχομεν τὸν θεόν **(KJV bible book of John chapter 8 verse 41).**

99

SPIRITUAL TRILLIONAIRE:
Cherishing the Breath of Life while Simultaneously
Preparing for the Blow of Death!

OH, GRACIOUS MOST HIGH HEAVENLY FATHER, HOLY IS YOUR
NAME, YOUR WILL BE DONE NOW AND FOREVER!

In the KJV bible book of John chapter 8 verses 41; Yashu'a
(Jesus) stated: "Ye do the deeds of your father. Then said they
to him, we be not born of **fornication**; we have one Father, even
God." In the above-mentioned verse, the word "**fornication**" is
the **KJV bible Greek Strong's Concordance#4202 πορνεία**
porneia **which means defined as illicit sexual intercourse,
adultery, fornication, homosexuality, lesbianism,
intercourse with animals etc.** "The word "fornication"
πορνεία *porneia*, is from the root word 'pornay", **KJV bible
Greek Strong's Concordance#4202 πόρνη pórnē, por'-nay**;
which means an idolater: —harlot, whore." In the KJV bible
book of John chapter 8 verses 44; Yashu'a (Jesus) stated: "Ye
are of *your* father the devil, and the lusts of your father ye
will do. He was a murderer from the beginning, and abode
not in the truth, because there is no truth in him. When he
speaketh a lie, he speaketh of his own: for he is a liar, and
the father of it."

SPIRITUAL TRILLIONAIRE:
Cherishing the Breath of Life while Simultaneously
Preparing for the Blow of Death!

CHILDREN OF THE MOST HIGH:
PRISTINE YOUTH AND FAMILY SOLUTIONS, LLC.
SONS AND DAUGHTERS OF THE MOST HIGH PUBLISHERS

OH, GRACIOUS MOST HIGH HEAVENLY FATHER, HOLY IS YOUR
NAME, YOUR WILL BE DONE NOW AND FOREVER!

The KJV bible book of John chapter 8 verses 44 with Greek inserts: ὑμεῖς ἐκ πατρὸς τοῦ διαβόλου ἐστὲ καὶ τὰς ἐπιθυμίας τοῦ πατρὸς ὑμῶν θέλετε ποιεῖν ἐκεῖνος ἀνθρωποκτόνος ἦν ἀπ᾽ ἀρχῆς καὶ ἐν τῇ ἀληθείᾳ οὐχ ἔστηκεν ὅτι οὐκ ἔστιν ἀλήθεια ἐν αὐτῷ ὅταν λαλῇ τὸ ψεῦδος ἐκ τῶν ἰδίων λαλεῖ ὅτι ψεύστης ἐστὶν καὶ ὁ πατὴρ αὐτοῦ.

In the above-mentioned verse, the word "**lusts**" is the **KJV bible Greek Strong's Concordance#1939 word: ἐπιθυμία** *epithymia*, which means: **desire, craving, longing, desire for what is forbidden, lust**.

So far, the KJV bible has established that **Leviathan, <u>the great dragon</u>** is a **Legion** (a body of soldiers or many unclean spiritual soldiers that can invade a body) also known as the **Sex Spirit Force** called **pórnē, por'-nay πόρνη** and pronounced as: "**Pornay**" that the Messiah Yashu'a (Jesus) spoke about in the KJV bible book of John chapter 8 verses 41-44. The bible also teaches us that this **Lucifer** who leads this **Legion** of **Luciferians, that old serpent (Leviathan)** who also **lived** during the time in the KJV bible book of **Genesis chapter 3 verse 1 called the Devil** (and **devil** spelled backwards is the

SPIRITUAL TRILLIONAIRE:
Cherishing the Breath of Life while Simultaneously
Preparing for the Blow of Death!

CHILDREN OF THE MOST HIGH:
PRISTINE YOUTH AND FAMILY SOLUTIONS, LLC.
SONS AND DAUGHTERS OF THE MOST HIGH PUBLISHERS ®

OH, GRACIOUS MOST HIGH HEAVENLY FATHER, HOLY IS YOUR
NAME, YOUR WILL BE DONE NOW AND FOREVER!

word: "**lived**"). So, this devil and his angels convey messages to humanity to influence humanity through the **Deadly Venom of the Desire** of "**Lust**" as the **Sex Spirit Force called Pornay**. This old dragon, was called the **devil** and **satan**. So, **Lucifer controls a Legion** of **Leviathans** or **Luciferians** and is also the leader as **Satan** over a **Legion** called **Satanists**. Therefore, it is essential for all members of humanity who seek to acquire, maintain and sustain positive spiritual health and positive spiritual wealth to do your best to not get trapped in the devil's web.

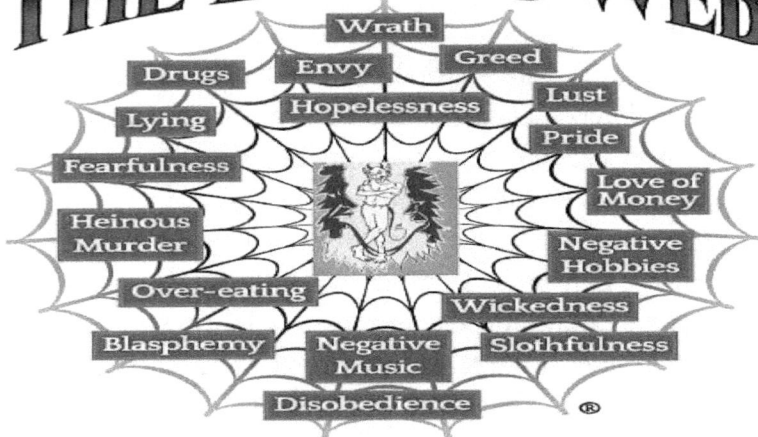

THE DEVIL'S WEB

Wrath
Envy · Greed
Drugs
Lust
Hopelessness
Lying
Pride
Fearfulness
Love of Money
Heinous Murder
Negative Hobbies
Over-eating
Wickedness
Blasphemy · Negative Music · Slothfulness
Disobedience ®

102

SPIRITUAL TRILLIONAIRE:
Cherishing the Breath of Life while Simultaneously
Preparing for the Blow of Death!

CHILDREN OF THE MOST HIGH:
PRISTINE YOUTH AND FAMILY SOLUTIONS, LLC.
SONS AND DAUGHTERS OF THE MOST HIGH PUBLISHERS ®

OH, GRACIOUS MOST HIGH HEAVENLY FATHER, HOLY IS YOUR
NAME, YOUR WILL BE DONE NOW AND FOREVER!

How does a person guard themselves against the **Luciferians** and **Satanists**? A person guards themselves against the **Luciferians** and **Satanists** by being obedient the Most High Heavenly Father! By doing so, a person learns to study the KJV bible Hebrew and Greek Strong's Concordance hidden meanings of the etymology of the English translated words or the translated words of any other language that their scriptures were translated into. By researching the original root meanings of the original languages that the scriptures were revealed in, **it affords a person an opportunity to acquire the original messages that Michael and his angels** according the KJV bible book of Revelation chapter 12, conveys to members of humanity. Thus, affording one to learn that the **Satanists** seek mind control and dominance and the **Luciferians** seek to control the energy of others. They are best described as "**Spiritual Vampires**" who draw energy from others which also can occur to a person who is striving to be positive while listening to negative speaking people or a negative speaking person.

SPIRITUAL TRILLIONAIRE:
Cherishing the Breath of Life while Simultaneously
Preparing for the Blow of Death!

CHILDREN OF THE MOST HIGH:
PRISTINE YOUTH AND FAMILY SOLUTIONS, LLC.
SONS AND DAUGHTERS OF THE MOST HIGH PUBLISHERS ®

OH, GRACIOUS MOST HIGH HEAVENLY FATHER, HOLY IS YOUR
NAME, YOUR WILL BE DONE NOW AND FOREVER!

Consequently, the messages of the great dragon, called the devil and satan are a part of a **Lucifer Conspiracy**. This **Lucifer** or **Luciferian Conspiracy** has succeeded under the **biblical disguise** of "Leviathan" by inflicting the **spell of Leviathan** which is **another name for the great dragon, that old serpent called the devil and satan** who controls what we see and hear in the media, on television, on the internet, on the radio and on the satellite radio. How? By utilizing what we see and hear in the media, on television, on the internet, on the radio and on the satellite radio to effect members of humanity in four ways:

1. **Meretricious Effect**: Making people unable to see the truth by masking it in lies and deception as apparently attractive, but in reality, having no value or moral integrity.

2. **Death-Dealing Effect**: Capable of causing death as the master orchestrator of chaos, conflict and illusions which causes 100% preventable global confusion amongst members of humanity.

SPIRITUAL TRILLIONAIRE:
Cherishing the Breath of Life while Simultaneously
Preparing for the Blow of Death!

CHILDREN OF THE MOST HIGH:
PRISTINE YOUTH AND FAMILY SOLUTIONS, LLC.
SONS AND DAUGHTERS OF THE MOST HIGH PUBLISHERS ®

OH, GRACIOUS MOST HIGH HEAVENLY FATHER, HOLY IS YOUR
NAME, YOUR WILL BE DONE NOW AND FOREVER!

3. **F**aint-hearted **E**xamples **A**mplifying **R**eality **(F.E.A.R.) Effect**: Killing unarmed, lawful abiding Black or Brown people or other marginalized members of humanity who are victims of the **deadly venom of desire of heinous murder**. This is done through terror or by a terrorizing force that instills fear in the hearts of Black, Brown people and other marginalized members of humanity who are family and friends of victims of heinous murder crimes. The reason for this is because they fear what might be done to them or to their loved ones or friends with no or little judicial consequences to those who commit heinous murder. Many marginalized members of humanity across the entire planet earth, denounce people who commit hate crimes, especially hate crimes against Black and Brown people. So, always remember that true-faith and trust in the Most High through the True Vine (Yashu'a, Jesus), increases your courage over time. Beware to not **enter fear** in your mind and heart, so that it will not **interfere** with acquiring and sustaining a peace of mind that won't depart; because you are uniquely and wonderfully made, allow the Most High to recreate anew you and don't be afraid!

SPIRITUAL TRILLIONAIRE:
**Cherishing the Breath of Life while Simultaneously
Preparing for the Blow of Death!**

CHILDREN OF THE MOST HIGH:
PRISTINE YOUTH AND FAMILY SOLUTIONS, LLC.
SONS AND DAUGHTERS OF THE MOST HIGH PUBLISHERS ®

OH, GRACIOUS MOST HIGH HEAVENLY FATHER, HOLY IS YOUR
NAME, YOUR WILL BE DONE NOW AND FOREVER!

We live in a day and time in which it has become more frequent to hear on the news that another **hate crime mass shooting** has occurred. Unbeknown, to some Black, Brown and other marginalized members of humanity, they may be praying to the same leviathan spiritual forces that incites hate and incites thoughts of feelings to commit hate crimes in the minds and hearts of the people that are the human vessels of the physical manifestation of evil heinous murders. These are the people who want to commit hate crimes and who commit hate crimes against Black, Brown and other marginalized members of humanity. So, aspiring Spiritual Trillionaires must ensure that when they **pray**, that they don't become the **prey** of leviathan spiritual forces. Aspiring Spiritual Trillionaires must guard their minds and hearts against the leviathan spiritual forces that incites hate and thoughts and feelings to commit hates crimes in the minds of those who worship the image of the beast and against Black, Brown, and other marginalized members of humanity, and others who worship the image of the beast.

106

SPIRITUAL TRILLIONAIRE:
**Cherishing the Breath of Life while Simultaneously
Preparing for the Blow of Death!**

CHILDREN OF THE MOST HIGH:
PRISTINE YOUTH AND FAMILY SOLUTIONS, LLC.
SONS AND DAUGHTERS OF THE MOST HIGH PUBLISHERS ®

OH, GRACIOUS MOST HIGH HEAVENLY FATHER, HOLY IS YOUR
NAME, YOUR WILL BE DONE NOW AND FOREVER!

In the KJV bible book of Revelation chapter 13 verses 15 and 18; it states: "And he had power to give life unto the image of the beast, that the image of the beast should both speak, and cause that as many as would not worship the image of the beast should be killed. Here is wisdom. Let him that hath understanding count the number of **the beast**: for it **is the number of a man**; and his number is **Six hundred threescore and six (666).**" The **F**aint-hearted **E**xamples **A**mplifying **R**eality (**F.E.A.R**) is strengthened through the **H.O.B.A. effect which is the Habit of Being Afraid (H.O.B.A.).**

**The KJV bible book of 2nd
Timothy chapter 1 verse 7 states:
"For God hath not given us the
spirit of fear; but of power, and of
love, and of a sound mind."**

107

SPIRITUAL TRILLIONAIRE:
**Cherishing the Breath of Life while Simultaneously
Preparing for the Blow of Death!**

CHILDREN OF THE MOST HIGH:
PRISTINE YOUTH AND FAMILY SOLUTIONS, LLC.
SONS AND DAUGHTERS OF THE MOST HIGH PUBLISHERS ®

OH, GRACIOUS MOST HIGH HEAVENLY FATHER, HOLY IS YOUR
NAME, YOUR WILL BE DONE NOW AND FOREVER!

4. <u>**C**</u>ulture <u>**O**</u>f <u>**A**</u>ccepting <u>**L**</u>ies (**C.O.A.L**) **Effect**: As the Messiah Yashu'a (Jesus) said: "Ye are of your father the devil, and the lusts of your father ye will do. He was a murderer from the beginning, and abode not in the truth, because there is no truth in him. When he speaketh a lie, he speaketh of his own: for he is a liar, and the father of it." So, the great dragon, the old serpent called the devil and satan is a liar and a deceiver **who can't ever be trusted!!!**

> The KJV bible book of John chapter 8 verse 44 states: "Ye are of your father the devil, and the lusts of your father ye will do. He was a murderer from the beginning, and abode not in the truth, because there is no truth in him. When he speaketh a lie, he speaketh of his own: for he is a liar, and the father of it."

SPIRITUAL TRILLIONAIRE:
Cherishing the Breath of Life while Simultaneously
Preparing for the Blow of Death!

CHILDREN OF THE MOST HIGH:
PRISTINE YOUTH AND FAMILY SOLUTIONS, LLC.
SONS AND DAUGHTERS OF THE MOST HIGH PUBLISHERS ®

OH, GRACIOUS MOST HIGH HEAVENLY FATHER, HOLY IS YOUR
NAME, YOUR WILL BE DONE NOW AND FOREVER!

Phonetically, what is the reverse of "Levi-athan"?

Phonetically, the reverse of **"Levi-athan"** is **"Anton LaVey"** which spelled backwards as: **LaVey Anton** is phonetically pronounced as: **"Leviathan"**. Who is Anton LaVey?

According to the **1972 TIME Magazine Article,**

"Anton LaVey is founder of the <u>Church of Satan in San Francisco in 1966</u>. But the existence of Satanists as an organized, public group in the United States is a much newer phenomenon, much of which can be largely traced to one man: **Anton Szandor La Vey**, author of 1969's **The Satanic Bible.**"

SPIRITUAL TRILLIONAIRE:
**Cherishing the Breath of Life while Simultaneously
Preparing for the Blow of Death!**

CHILDREN OF THE MOST HIGH:
PRISTINE YOUTH AND FAMILY SOLUTIONS, LLC.
SONS AND DAUGHTERS OF THE MOST HIGH PUBLISHERS ®

OH, GRACIOUS MOST HIGH HEAVENLY FATHER, HOLY IS YOUR
NAME, YOUR WILL BE DONE NOW AND FOREVER!

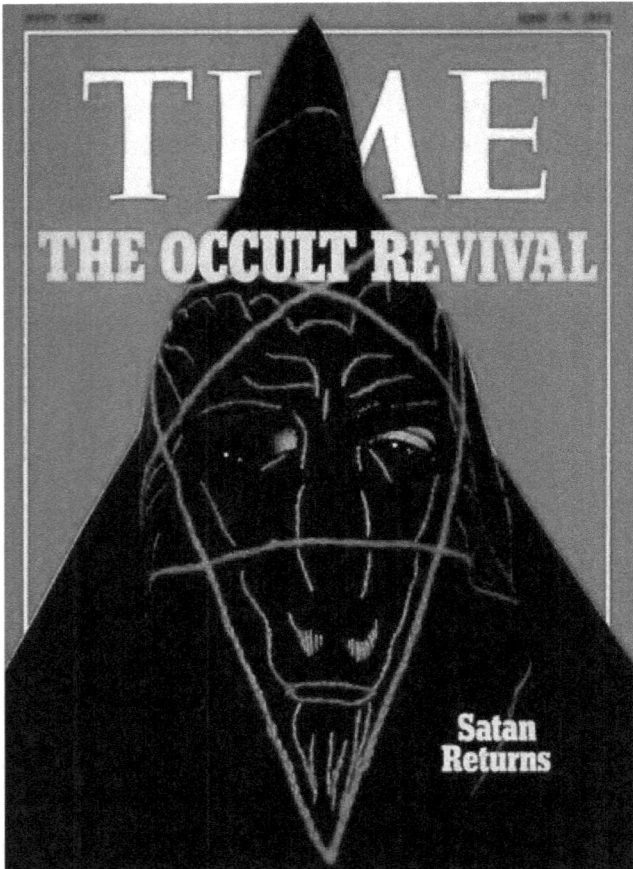

The June 19, 1972, cover of TIME

110

SPIRITUAL TRILLIONAIRE:
Cherishing the Breath of Life while Simultaneously
Preparing for the Blow of Death!

CHILDREN OF THE MOST HIGH:
PRISTINE YOUTH AND FAMILY SOLUTIONS, LLC.
SONS AND DAUGHTERS OF THE MOST HIGH PUBLISHERS ®

OH, GRACIOUS MOST HIGH HEAVENLY FATHER, HOLY IS YOUR
NAME, YOUR WILL BE DONE NOW AND FOREVER!

How does the poisonous venom Serpent's spell or the spell of Leviathan manifest in members of humanity? The poisonous venom **Serpent's spell** or the **spell of Leviathan** manifest in members of humanity through the dragon and his angels' messages. <u>**The great dragon that was cast out of heaven who is also known as: that old serpent, called the Devil, and Satan, which deceiveth the whole world and his angels**</u> (ἄγγελος **Angelos**, meaning: "Messengers" <u>**can only be messengers if they have a message or messages for the people on earth**</u>. In an ongoing effort to acquire, maintain and sustain positive spiritual health and positive spiritual wealth, it is critical to become aware of the root cause or root causes of why you or someone you care about may be or become **spiritually unhealthy**.

Are you or someone you care about affected, effected or infested by one, some, or all of **the 9 Deadly Venoms of Desires of great dragon that old serpent, called the Devil, and Satan, which deceiveth the whole world: Slothful, Wrath, Pride, Greed, Lust, Hopeless Fear Disobedience, Lying, Heinous Murde**r, and/or **Wickedness**?

SPIRITUAL TRILLIONAIRE:
Cherishing the Breath of Life while Simultaneously
Preparing for the Blow of Death!

CHILDREN OF THE MOST HIGH:
PRISTINE YOUTH AND FAMILY SOLUTIONS, LLC.
SONS AND DAUGHTERS OF THE MOST HIGH PUBLISHERS ®

OH, GRACIOUS MOST HIGH HEAVENLY FATHER, HOLY IS YOUR
NAME, YOUR WILL BE DONE NOW AND FOREVER!

What are the 9 Deadly Venoms of the Desires of the great
dragon, that old serpent called the devil and satan
which deceiveth the whole world?

1: The **1st** of the **9** Deadly Venoms of the Desires of the great
dragon, that old serpent called the devil and satan which
deceiveth the whole world is: **Slothful**, which is "the KJV bible
Hebrew Strong's Concordance#**6102** word: עָצֵל (atsel) -
sluggish, lazy Strong's Exhaustive Concordance. **slothful**,
sluggard. From atsal; indolent - **slothful**, sluggard. While
slothful is sometimes defined as physical laziness, mental and
spiritual laziness is emphasized. Failing to positively grow
mentally and spiritually is key to becoming guilty of
slothfulness." In the KJV bible book of Proverbs chapter 21
verses 25-26; it states: "**The desire of the slothful killeth him;
for his hands refuse to labour. "He coveteth greedily all the
day long: but the righteous giveth and spareth not.**"

SPIRITUAL TRILLIONAIRE:
Cherishing the Breath of Life while Simultaneously
Preparing for the Blow of Death!

CHILDREN OF THE MOST HIGH:
PRISTINE YOUTH AND FAMILY SOLUTIONS, LLC.
SONS AND DAUGHTERS OF THE MOST HIGH PUBLISHERS ®

OH, GRACIOUS MOST HIGH HEAVENLY FATHER, HOLY IS YOUR
NAME, YOUR WILL BE DONE NOW AND FOREVER!

In order to acquire, maintain and sustain positive spiritual health and positive spiritual wealth, a person has to be or become intentionally devout through the daily discipline of practicing positive thinking, positive visualization, positive speaking, positive actions, meditation, prayer, studying of the Most High's scriptures, recitation of the Most High's scriptures, fasting of the mind, fasting from food or liquid or both for short periods of time **if you are healthy enough to do so and have your medical physicians' consent to fast prior to doing any physical fasting**. These daily devout disciplines of practice assist in the process of making a person responsible for their own mental and spiritual well-being and places them in control of their own positive spiritual health and positive spiritual wealth destiny. If we lack the intentional, daily devout discipline of practices, physical, mental and spiritual laziness becomes one of our habits of the 9 **Deadly Venoms of Desires of the great dragon, that old serpent called the devil and satan which deceiveth the whole world called: "Slothful".**

113

SPIRITUAL TRILLIONAIRE:
Cherishing the Breath of Life while Simultaneously
Preparing for the Blow of Death!

CHILDREN OF THE MOST HIGH:
PRISTINE YOUTH AND FAMILY SOLUTIONS. LLC.
SONS AND DAUGHTERS OF THE MOST HIGH PUBLISHERS ®

OH, GRACIOUS MOST HIGH HEAVENLY FATHER, HOLY IS YOUR
NAME, YOUR WILL BE DONE NOW AND FOREVER!

The **Children of the Most High Pristine Youth and Family Solutions, LLC. 9X9 True Vine (Yashu'a, Jesus) B.A.-K.A.-R.E. Sequential Order of Learning Habits of Success** utilizes the **True Vine** (Yashu'a, Jesus**) Fruit of the Spirit of Positive Character-Building Essential** of "**Gentleness** – *Chrēstotēs (χρηστότης)* in action to overcome and resist "**Slothful**".

"**Gentleness** – *Chrēstotēs (χρηστότης)* is the KJV Bible Strong's Greek Concordance#**5544** which means khray-stot'-ace; from G5543; **usefulness**, i.e. morally, excellence (in character or demeanor):—gentleness, good(-ness), kindness."

The KJV bible book of Galatians chapter 5 verse 22 with Greek inserts: "**Ὁ δὲ καρπὸς τοῦ πνεύματός ἐστιν ἀγάπη χαρά εἰρήνη μακροθυμία χρηστότης ἀγαθωσύνη πίστις, πραότης ἐγκράτεια κατὰ τῶν τοιούτων οὐκ ἔστιν νόμος**"

In the KJV bible book of Galatians chapter 5 verses 22-23: it states: "But the fruit of the Spirit is love, joy, peace, longsuffering, **gentleness**, goodness, faith, Meekness, temperance: against such there is no law."

SPIRITUAL TRILLIONAIRE:
Cherishing the Breath of Life while Simultaneously
Preparing for the Blow of Death!

CHILDREN OF THE MOST HIGH:
PRISTINE YOUTH AND FAMILY SOLUTIONS, LLC.
SONS AND DAUGHTERS OF THE MOST HIGH PUBLISHERS ®

OH, GRACIOUS MOST HIGH HEAVENLY FATHER, HOLY IS YOUR
NAME, YOUR WILL BE DONE NOW AND FOREVER!

So, a person who has **accepted the Lord Jesus Christ (Yashu'a Ha Mashiakh – Jesus the Messiah or Yehoshu'a – Yahayyu is Salvation or Yahayyu Saves) as their Savior, is in the Body of Christ** and has access to the **True Vine** (Yashu'a, Jesus**) Fruit of the Spirit of Positive Character-Building Essential** of "**Gentleness** – *Chrēstotēs (χρηστότης)*" through the daily practice of true-faith in the Most High Heavenly Father, a person can learn to overcome and resist the **1st of the 9 Deadly Venoms of the Desires of the great dragon, that old serpent called the devil and satan which deceiveth the whole world** known as "**Slothful**" by **being kind** to all life and by **being positively useful** every day.

2: The **2nd** of the **9** Deadly Venom of the Desires of the great dragon, that old serpent called the devil and satan which deceiveth the whole world is: **Wrath** which is the "KJV bible Hebrew Strong's Concordance#7110 word: (קֶצֶף) **Qetseph**) - indignation, sore, wrath from **qatsaph**; a splinter (as chipped off); figuratively, rage or strife -- foam, indignation, X sore, wrath. Be angry, displease, fret self, provoke to wrath come, be wroth, a primitive root; to crack off, i.e. (figuratively) burst out in rage -- (be) anger(-ry), displease, fret self, (provoke

115

SPIRITUAL TRILLIONAIRE:
Cherishing the Breath of Life while Simultaneously
Preparing for the Blow of Death!

OH, GRACIOUS MOST HIGH HEAVENLY FATHER, HOLY IS YOUR NAME, YOUR WILL BE DONE NOW AND FOREVER!

to) wrath (come), be wroth. Became very angry (1), become wrathful (1), enraged (1), furious (3), provoked (1), provoked him to wrath (1), provoked me to wrath (1), provoked to wrath (2), wrath (1), wrathful (1). Inordinate and uncontrolled feelings of hatred and anger. Wrath, in its purest form, presents with self-destructiveness, violence, and hate that may provoke feuds that can go on for thousands of years. Feelings of wrath can manifest in different ways, including impatience, revenge, and vigilantism." Frequent irritation over trifling matters is a sign of mental weakness.

This can be overcome by carefully developing its counterforce, the virtue of patience. Just as heat and light can be transferred into electricity, wrath can be transformed into positive spiritual energies. All vices, unwanted qualities and wrong actions stem from anger or wrath. When wrath has been controlled, all others die by themselves. Wrath gains strength with repetition, and by controlling your emotions instead of allowing your emotions to control you; one gradually strengthens the will. In the KJV bible book of Proverbs chapter 11 verse 23, it states: "The desire of the righteous is only good: but the expectation of the wicked is **wrath**."

SPIRITUAL TRILLIONAIRE:
Cherishing the Breath of Life while Simultaneously
Preparing for the Blow of Death!

CHILDREN OF THE MOST HIGH:
PRISTINE YOUTH AND FAMILY SOLUTIONS, LLC.
SONS AND DAUGHTERS OF THE MOST HIGH PUBLISHERS ®

OH, GRACIOUS MOST HIGH HEAVENLY FATHER, HOLY IS YOUR
NAME, YOUR WILL BE DONE NOW AND FOREVER!

The KJV bible book of Galatians chapter 5 verse 22 with Greek inserts:

"Ὁ δὲ καρπὸς τοῦ πνεύματός ἐστιν ἀγάπη χαρά εἰρήνη μακροθυμία χρηστότης ἀγαθωσύνη πίστις, πρᾳότης ἐγκράτεια κατὰ τῶν τοιούτων οὐκ ἔστιν νόμος"

In the KJV bible book of Galatians chapter 5 verses 22-23; it states: "But the fruit of the Spirit is love, joy, peace, **longsuffering**, gentleness, goodness, faith, Meekness, temperance: against such there is no law." In the "KJV bible Strong's Greek Concordance#3116, the word for: **Longsuffering – μακροθυμία** is **Makrothymía**, mak-roth-oo-mee'-ah; and means: longanimity, i.e. (objectively) forbearance or (subjectively) fortitude, **patience**, endurance, constancy, steadfastness, perseverance, longsuffering, slowness in avenging wrongs." By utilizing the **True Vine** (Yashu'a, Jesus) **Fruit of the Spirit of Positive Character-Building Essential** of "**longsuffering**" in action through the daily practice of true-faith in the Most High Heavenly Father, a person can learn to overcome and resist the **2nd of the 9 Deadly Venoms of the Desires of the great dragon, that old serpent called the devil and satan which deceiveth the whole world** known as "**Wrath**".

117

SPIRITUAL TRILLIONAIRE:
Cherishing the Breath of Life while Simultaneously
Preparing for the Blow of Death!

CHILDREN OF THE MOST HIGH:
PRISTINE YOUTH AND FAMILY SOLUTIONS, LLC.
SONS AND DAUGHTERS OF THE MOST HIGH PUBLISHERS ®

OH, GRACIOUS MOST HIGH HEAVENLY FATHER, HOLY IS YOUR
NAME, YOUR WILL BE DONE NOW AND FOREVER!

This is accomplished by exercising **patience (Longsuffering –
μακροθυμία Makrothymía)** at all times, thereby, learning to
control the emotions inside of you rather than you allowing the
emotions inside of you to control you.

3: The **3rd** of the **9** Deadly Venom of the Desires of the great
dragon, that old serpent called the devil and satan which
deceiveth the whole world is: **Pride: (גֵּאָה Geah)**, is the "KJV
bible Hebrew Strong's Concordance#**1344** word: גֵּאָה **(Geah)** –
means: arrogance, pride: (Latin, **Superbia**), or **Hubris (**Greek),
is the original and most serious of the 9 Deadly Venoms of
Desires, and the source of all of the others. It is identified as
a desire to be more important or attractive than others, failing
to acknowledge the good work of others, and excessive love of
self especially holding self out of proper position toward the
Most High Heavenly Father. **The ego is the root of pride,
greed, jealousy, lust, hatred, racism, and wanting to control
or dominate other people and asserts "I" "instead of we and
us."** The KJV bible Greek Strong's Concordance#1473 word
for "**I**" is: ἐγώ **ego. Control** of the "**Creative Garden of Will**"
which is "**the mind**" and annihilation of the **ego** are the essence
of all spiritual and emotional disciplines necessary on the path
of obtaining positive spiritual health and positive spiritual
wealth.

SPIRITUAL TRILLIONAIRE:
Cherishing the Breath of Life while Simultaneously
Preparing for the Blow of Death!

CHILDREN OF THE MOST HIGH:
PRISTINE YOUTH AND FAMILY SOLUTIONS, LLC.
SONS AND DAUGHTERS OF THE MOST HIGH PUBLISHERS ®

OH, GRACIOUS MOST HIGH HEAVENLY FATHER, HOLY IS YOUR
NAME, YOUR WILL BE DONE NOW AND FOREVER!

Obtaining positive spiritual health and positive spiritual wealth requires a person to work diligently and intentionally on a daily basis to eradicate the ego and to convert that energy into obedient service to the Most High Heavenly Father's will only. In the KJV bible book of Proverbs chapter 16 verse 18, it states that: "**Pride** goeth before destruction, and a haughty spirit before a fall."

The KJV bible book of Galatians chapter 5 verse 22 with Greek inserts:

"Ὁ δὲ καρπὸς τοῦ πνεύματός ἐστιν ἀγάπη χαρά εἰρήνη μακροθυμία χρηστότης ἀγαθωσύνη πίστις, πραότης ἐγκράτεια κατὰ τῶν τοιούτων οὐκ ἔστιν νόμος"

In the KJV bible book of Galatians chapter 5 verses 22-23; it states: "But the fruit of the Spirit is love, joy, peace, longsuffering, gentleness, goodness, faith, **Meekness**, temperance: against such there is no law."

119

SPIRITUAL TRILLIONAIRE:
Cherishing the Breath of Life while Simultaneously
Preparing for the Blow of Death!

CHILDREN OF THE MOST HIGH:
PRISTINE YOUTH AND FAMILY SOLUTIONS, LLC.
SONS AND DAUGHTERS OF THE MOST HIGH PUBLISHERS ®

OH, GRACIOUS MOST HIGH HEAVENLY FATHER, HOLY IS YOUR
NAME, YOUR WILL BE DONE NOW AND FOREVER!

Meekness - πραότης Praiótēs, prah-ot'-ace; is KJV bible Strong's Greek Concordance#G4235; and means gentleness, mildness by implication, **humility**. By utilizing the **True Vine** (Yashu'a, Jesus) **Fruit of the Spirit of Positive Character-Building Essential** of "**Meekness**" in action through the daily practice of true-faith in the Most High Heavenly Father, a person can learn to overcome and resist the **3rd of the 9 Deadly Venoms of the Desires of the great dragon, that old serpent called the devil and satan which deceiveth the whole world** known as "**Pride**" by practicing **humility** (**Meekness - πραότης Praiótēs**) at all times.

4: The **4th** of the **9** Deadly Venom of the Desires of the great dragon, that old serpent called the devil and satan which deceiveth the whole world is: **Greed**: (הַוָּת **Havvah**), is the "KJV bible Hebrew Strong's Concordance#**1942** word: הַוָּת (**Havvah**): and means: chasm, destruction, calamities, craving, deadly, desire, greed. Very excessive or rapacious desire and pursuit of material possessions."

SPIRITUAL TRILLIONAIRE:
Cherishing the Breath of Life while Simultaneously
Preparing for the Blow of Death!

OH, GRACIOUS MOST HIGH HEAVENLY FATHER, HOLY IS YOUR
NAME, YOUR WILL BE DONE NOW AND FOREVER!

In the KJV bible book of Galatians chapter 5 verse 22 with
Greek inserts:

"Ὁ δὲ καρπὸς τοῦ πνεύματός ἐστιν ἀγάπη χαρά εἰρήνη
μακροθυμία χρηστότης ἀγαθωσύνη πίστις, πραότης
ἐγκράτεια κατὰ τῶν τοιούτων οὐκ ἔστιν νόμος"

In the KJV bible book of Galatians chapter 5 verses 22-23; it
states: "But the fruit of the Spirit is love, joy, peace,
longsuffering, gentleness, goodness, faith, Meekness,
temperance: against such there is no law."

"**Temperance** ἐγκράτεια **Enkráteia**, eng-krat'-i-ah; is the
"KJV Bible Greek Strong's Concordance#**1468**; and means:
self-control (especially continence): temperance. Self-control
(the virtue of one who masters his or her desires and passions,
esp. his sensual appetites)."

By utilizing the **True Vine** (Yashu'a, Jesus) **Fruit of the Spirit
of Positive Character-Building Essential** of "Temperance"
in action through the daily practice of true-faith in the Most
High Heavenly Father, a person can learn to overcome and
resist the **4th of the 9 Deadly Venoms of the Desires of the**

121

SPIRITUAL TRILLIONAIRE:
**Cherishing the Breath of Life while Simultaneously
Preparing for the Blow of Death!**

CHILDREN OF THE MOST HIGH:
PRISTINE YOUTH AND FAMILY SOLUTIONS, LLC.
SONS AND DAUGHTERS OF THE MOST HIGH PUBLISHERS ®

OH, GRACIOUS MOST HIGH HEAVENLY FATHER, HOLY IS YOUR
NAME, YOUR WILL BE DONE NOW AND FOREVER!

**great dragon, that old serpent called the devil and satan
which deceiveth the whole world** known as "**Greed**" can be
accomplished by learning and practicing self-control
(**Temperance ἐγκράτεια Enkráteia**) which is the virtue of one
who masters his or her desires and passions every day.

5: The **5th** of the **9** Deadly Venom of the Desires of the great
dragon, that old serpent called the devil and satan which
deceiveth the whole world is: **Lust**: is the "KJV bible Hebrew
Strong's Hebrew#8457 word: תַּזְנוּת (**Taznuth**): and means:
harlotries, harlotry, fornication, lust. It is an intense desire. It is
usually thought of as excessive sexual wants. However,
according to the original Greek language that the New
Testament Bible was revealed in, the word for: "**fornication**"
is "**Porneia**" and it does not mean to have sex before getting
married. Is there a correlation between the word **lust** in the KJV
bible book of John chapter 8 verse 44 and the word **fornication**
in the KJV bible book of John chapter 8 verse 41?

SPIRITUAL TRILLIONAIRE:
Cherishing the Breath of Life while Simultaneously
Preparing for the Blow of Death!

CHILDREN OF THE MOST HIGH:
PRISTINE YOUTH AND FAMILY SOLUTIONS, LLC.
SONS AND DAUGHTERS OF THE MOST HIGH PUBLISHERS ®

OH, GRACIOUS MOST HIGH HEAVENLY FATHER, HOLY IS YOUR
NAME, YOUR WILL BE DONE NOW AND FOREVER!

According to the "**KJV bible Greek Strong's Concordance,
the word fornication is #4202** is: "**Porneia**" –pronounced as;
Por-ne-ah-harlotry; idolatry; from **#4203** is: **Porneuo–
pronounced as; Porn-yoo-o-**indulge in unlawful lust; to act
like a harlot; which both words have their root and come from
#4203 is: "**Porne**" – pronounced as; **por-nay**-harlot, whore. In
the **KJV bible Greek Strong Concordance#1939**, the word
for "**Lust**" is: "**Epithumia**" "means a longing for something
that is forbidden; to desire greatly; strong desire; carnal desires.

The **KJV bible Greek Strong's Concordance# 4202** word for
"**Fornication**" is: "**porneia**" and has it root meaning in **#4203**
is: "**porne**" – **pronounced as; por-nay**-harlot, whore. What is
the first word that comes to your mind when you say "**por-ne
(por-nay)**" – pronounced as; **por-nay**?" That's right,
"**pornography**"! So, there is a very clear correlation between
the word **lust** "**epithumia**" in the KJV bible book of John
chapter 8 verse 44 and the KJV Greek Strong's Concordance
word for "**porneia**" for the word fornication in the KJV book
of John chapter 8 verse 41.

SPIRITUAL TRILLIONAIRE:
Cherishing the Breath of Life while Simultaneously
Preparing for the Blow of Death!

CHILDREN OF THE MOST HIGH:
PRISTINE YOUTH AND FAMILY SOLUTIONS. LLC.
SONS AND DAUGHTERS OF THE MOST HIGH PUBLISHERS ®

OH, GRACIOUS MOST HIGH HEAVENLY FATHER, HOLY IS YOUR
NAME, YOUR WILL BE DONE NOW AND FOREVER!

The KJV book of Galatians chapter 5 verse 22 with Greek inserts:

"Ὁ δὲ καρπὸς τοῦ πνεύματός ἐστιν ἀγάπη χαρά εἰρήνη μακροθυμία χρηστότης ἀγαθωσύνη πίστις, πραότης ἐγκράτεια κατὰ τῶν τοιούτων οὐκ ἔστιν νόμος"

The KJV book of Galatians chapter 5 verses 22-23; it states: "But the fruit of the Spirit is **love**, joy, peace, longsuffering, gentleness, goodness, faith, Meekness, temperance: against such there is no law."

Love – "ἀγάπη Agápē, ag-ah'-pay; from KJV bible Strong's Greek #G25**;** means: love, i.e. affection or benevolence; specially (plural) a love-feast:—(feast of) charity(-ably), dear, love. Affection, good will, love, benevolence, brotherly love, love feasts." By utilizing the **True Vine (**Yashu'a, Jesus**) Fruit of the Spirit of Positive Character-Building Essential** of "**Love– ἀγάπη Agápē**)" in action through the daily practice of true-faith in the Most High Heavenly Father, a person can learn to overcome and resist the **5th of the 9 Deadly Venoms of the Desires of the great dragon, that old serpent called the devil**

124

SPIRITUAL TRILLIONAIRE:
Cherishing the Breath of Life while Simultaneously
Preparing for the Blow of Death!

OH, GRACIOUS MOST HIGH HEAVENLY FATHER, HOLY IS YOUR
NAME, YOUR WILL BE DONE NOW AND FOREVER!

and satan which deceiveth the whole world known as "**Lust**". This occurs by expressing divine love for the Most High Heavenly Father and by loving the Messiah Yashu'a (Jesus) to overcome the longing for something that is forbidden according to the commandments of the Most High every day.

6: The **6th** of the **9** Deadly Venom of the Desires of the great dragon, that old serpent called the devil and satan which deceiveth the whole world is: **Hopeless-Fear- Disobedience:** In the New KJV bible book of Jeremiah chapter 18 verse 12; it states: "And they said, that is **hopeless (יָאַשׁ** *Ya'ash*)! **the "KJV bible Hebrew Strong's Concordance#2976.** יָאַשׁ *Ya'ash* means: **no hope**, **despair**, and **desperate**. So, we will walk according to our own plans, and everyone will obey the dictates of his evil heart." Which is the willful act of **disobedience** to the Most High in action. In the KJV bible book of Hebrews chapter 2 verse 2; it states: "For if the word spoken by angels was steadfast, and every transgression and **disobedience** is the word: παρακοή *Parakoē* which is **the KJV bible Strong's Greek Concordance#3876** received a just recompence of reward. The word for "**disobedience**"

SPIRITUAL TRILLIONAIRE:
Cherishing the Breath of Life while Simultaneously
Preparing for the Blow of Death!

CHILDREN OF THE MOST HIGH:
PRISTINE YOUTH AND FAMILY SOLUTIONS, LLC.
SONS AND DAUGHTERS OF THE MOST HIGH PUBLISHERS ®

OH, GRACIOUS MOST HIGH HEAVENLY FATHER, HOLY IS YOUR
NAME, YOUR WILL BE DONE NOW AND FOREVER!

Is **(παρακοή *Parakoē*),** and means: unwillingness to hear; disobedience, to refuse to hear, pay no regard to, disobey."

In the KJV bible book of 2ⁿᵈ Timothy chapter 1 verse 7; it states: "For God hath not given us the spirit of **fear** (which is the KJV bible Strong's Greek **Concordance# 1167** word; δειλία D*eilia*) **but** of power, and of love, and of a sound mind." The word **δειλία Deilia** means: timidity, **fearfulness**, cowardice. So, **hopeless-fear-disobedience** can exist in a person or people who disobey the Most High and who lack true-faith in the Most High. Without obedience to the Most High and true-faith in the Most High, a child of the Most High spirit becomes toxic, which may lead to mental, physical, emotional and spiritual unhealthiness. **Real fear is the lack of true-faith in the Most High Heavenly Father!**

The KJV bible book of Galatians chapter 5 verse 22 (KJV with Greek inserts):

"Ὁ δὲ καρπὸς τοῦ πνεύματός ἐστιν ἀγάπη χαρά εἰρήνη μακροθυμία χρηστότης ἀγαθωσύνη πίστις, πραότης ἐγκράτεια κατὰ τῶν τοιούτων οὐκ ἔστιν νόμος"

SPIRITUAL TRILLIONAIRE:
Cherishing the Breath of Life while Simultaneously
Preparing for the Blow of Death!

CHILDREN OF THE MOST HIGH:
PRISTINE YOUTH AND FAMILY SOLUTIONS, LLC.
SONS AND DAUGHTERS OF THE MOST HIGH PUBLISHERS ®

OH, GRACIOUS MOST HIGH HEAVENLY FATHER, HOLY IS YOUR
NAME, YOUR WILL BE DONE NOW AND FOREVER!

The KJV bible book of Galatians chapter 5 verses 22-23; it states: "But the fruit of the Spirit is love, joy, peace, longsuffering, gentleness, goodness, **faith**, Meekness, temperance: against such there is no law." "**Faith - πίστις Pístis**, pis'-tis; is from the KJV bible Greek Strong's Concordance#**3982**; and means: persuasion, i.e. credence; moral conviction (of religious truth, or the truthfulness of God or a religious teacher), especially reliance upon Christ for salvation; abstractly, constancy in such profession; by extension, the system of religious (Gospel) truth itself:— assurance, belief, believe, faith, fidelity." By utilizing the **True Vine** (Yashu'a, Jesus) **Fruit of the Spirit of Positive Character-Building Essential** of "**Faith**" in action through the daily practice of true-faith in the Most High Heavenly Father, a person can learn to overcome and resist the **6th of the 9 Deadly Venoms of the Desires of the great dragon, that old serpent called the devil and satan which deceiveth the whole world** known as "**Hopeless-Fear-Disobedience**" by acquiring and practicing **true-faith** (**Faith - πίστις Pístis**) in the Most High Heavenly Father through the Messiah Yashu'a (Jesus) every day.

127

SPIRITUAL TRILLIONAIRE:
Cherishing the Breath of Life while Simultaneously
Preparing for the Blow of Death!

CHILDREN OF THE MOST HIGH:
PRISTINE YOUTH AND FAMILY SOLUTIONS, LLC.
SONS AND DAUGHTERS OF THE MOST HIGH PUBLISHERS ®

OH, GRACIOUS MOST HIGH HEAVENLY FATHER, HOLY IS YOUR
NAME, YOUR WILL BE DONE NOW AND FOREVER!

"Hopeless-Fear-Disobedience" is rooted in a lack of true-faith in the Most High Heavenly Father.

7: The **7th** of the **9** Deadly Venom of the Desires of the great dragon, that old serpent called the devil and satan which deceiveth the whole world is: **Lying**: which is the "KJV bible Hebrew Strong's Concordance# **8267** word שֶׁקֶר **Sā·qer**: and means: 1) lie, deception, disappointment, falsehood 1a) deception (what deceives or disappoints or betrays one) 1b) deceit, fraud, wrong 1b1) fraudulently, wrongfully (as adverb) 1c) falsehood (injurious in testimony) 1c1) testify falsehood, false oath, swear falsely 1d) falsity (of false or self-deceived prophets) 1e) lie, falsehood (in general) 1e1) false tongue 1f) in vain." In the KJV bible book of Proverbs chapter 6 verses 16-19; it states: "These six *things* doth the LORD hate: yea, seven *are* an abomination unto him: A proud look, **a lying tongue**, and hands that shed innocent blood, a heart that deviseth wicked imaginations, feet that be swift in running to mischief, **a false witness *that* speaketh lies**, and he that soweth discord among brethren."

128

SPIRITUAL TRILLIONAIRE:
Cherishing the Breath of Life while Simultaneously
Preparing for the Blow of Death!

CHILDREN OF THE MOST HIGH:
PRISTINE YOUTH AND FAMILY SOLUTIONS, LLC.
SONS AND DAUGHTERS OF THE MOST HIGH PUBLISHERS &

OH, GRACIOUS MOST HIGH HEAVENLY FATHER, HOLY IS YOUR
NAME, YOUR WILL BE DONE NOW AND FOREVER!

In the KJV bible book of Galatians chapter 5 verse 22 with Greek inserts):

"Ὁ δὲ καρπὸς τοῦ πνεύματός ἐστιν ἀγάπη χαρά εἰρήνη μακροθυμία χρηστότης ἀγαθωσύνη πίστις, πραότης ἐγκράτεια κατὰ τῶν τοιούτων οὐκ ἔστιν νόμος"

In the KJV bible book of Galatians chapter 5 verse 22-23; it states: "But the fruit of the Spirit is love, joy, **peace**, longsuffering, gentleness, goodness, faith, Meekness, temperance: against such there is no law." **"Peace – εἰρήνη Eirēnē**, i-ray'-nay; from the KJV bible Greek Strong's Concordance#1515 is defined as: probably from a primary verb εἴρω eírō (to join); peace (literally or figuratively); by implication, prosperity: —one, peace, quietness, rest, + set at one again. A state of national tranquility, exemption from the rage and havoc of war, peace between individuals, i.e. harmony, concord, security, safety, prosperity, felicity, (because peace and harmony make and keep things safe and prosperous); of the Messiah's peace, the way that leads to peace (salvation), the blessed state of **devout and upright** men after death."

129

SPIRITUAL TRILLIONAIRE:
Cherishing the Breath of Life while Simultaneously
Preparing for the Blow of Death!

CHILDREN OF THE MOST HIGH:
PRISTINE YOUTH AND FAMILY SOLUTIONS. LLC.
SONS AND DAUGHTERS OF THE MOST HIGH PUBLISHERS &

OH, GRACIOUS MOST HIGH HEAVENLY FATHER, HOLY IS YOUR
NAME, YOUR WILL BE DONE NOW AND FOREVER!

By utilizing the **True Vine** (Yashu'a, Jesus) **Fruit of the Spirit of Positive Character-Building Essential** of "Peace" in action through the daily practice of true-faith in the Most High Heavenly Father, a person can learn to overcome and resist the **7th of the 9 Deadly Venoms of the Desires of the great dragon, that old serpent called the devil and satan which deceiveth the whole world** known as "**Lying**" by learning and practicing being **peaceful, devout and upright (Peace – εἰρήνη Eirḗnē)** every day.

8: The **8th** of the **9** Deadly Venom of the Desires of the great dragon, that old serpent called the devil and satan which deceiveth the whole world is: **Heinous Murder (Shedding of innocent blood):** which is the "KJV bible Hebrew Strong's Concordance#2026 word: הָרַג **Harag**: and means: to kill, slay, destroyed (1), kill me as you killed (1), kill me at once (1), killed (58), killing (3), kills (2), murdered (2), murderer (1), murderers (1), occurs (1), slain (16), slaughter (1), slay (14), slayer (2), slays (2), slew (11), smitten (1), surely kill (1).

SPIRITUAL TRILLIONAIRE:
Cherishing the Breath of Life while Simultaneously
Preparing for the Blow of Death!

CHILDREN OF THE MOST HIGH:
PRISTINE YOUTH AND FAMILY SOLUTIONS, LLC.
SONS AND DAUGHTERS OF THE MOST HIGH PUBLISHERS ®

OH, GRACIOUS MOST HIGH HEAVENLY FATHER, HOLY IS YOUR
NAME, YOUR WILL BE DONE NOW AND FOREVER!

According to the Online American Heritage Dictionary (2019), **Heinous** is defined as: wicked; abominable. In the KJV bible book of Proverbs chapter 6 verses 16-19; it states: "These six *things* doth the LORD hate: yea, seven *are* an abomination unto him: A proud look, a lying tongue, and **hands that shed innocent blood**, a heart that deviseth wicked imaginations, feet that be swift in running to mischief, a false witness *that* speaketh lies, and he that soweth discord among brethren." **In the KJV bible book of 1ˢᵗ John chapter 3 verse 12, it states: "Not as Cain, [who] was of that wicked one, and slew his brother. And wherefore slew he him? Because his own works were evil, and his brother's righteous."**

In the KJV bible book of Galatians chapter 5 verse 22 with Greek inserts):

"Ὁ δὲ καρπὸς τοῦ πνεύματός ἐστιν ἀγάπη χαρά εἰρήνη μακροθυμία χρηστότης ἀγαθωσύνη πίστις, πρᾳότης ἐγκράτεια κατὰ τῶν τοιούτων οὐκ ἔστιν νόμος"

SPIRITUAL TRILLIONAIRE:
Cherishing the Breath of Life while Simultaneously
Preparing for the Blow of Death!

CHILDREN OF THE MOST HIGH:
PRISTINE YOUTH AND FAMILY SOLUTIONS, LLC.
SONS AND DAUGHTERS OF THE MOST HIGH PUBLISHERS ®

OH, GRACIOUS MOST HIGH HEAVENLY FATHER, HOLY IS YOUR
NAME, YOUR WILL BE DONE NOW AND FOREVER!

In the KJV bible book of Galatians chapter 5 verses 22-23; it states: "But the fruit of the Spirit is love, **joy**, peace, longsuffering, gentleness, goodness, faith, Meekness, temperance: against such there is no law."

"Joy – χαρά Chará, Khar-ah'; from the KJV bible Strong's Greek Concordance#G5463; cheerfulness, i.e. calm delight:— gladness, × greatly, (X be exceeding) joy(-ful, -fully, -fulness, -ous). Joy, gladness, the joy received from you, the cause or occasion of joy, of persons who are one's joy. According to *"The will to kill: Making sense of senseless murder (2018),"* over 90% of all **Heinous Murder**s were committed by people who were not **joyful, but were very angry or enraged**. By utilizing the **True Vine** (Yashu'a, Jesus) **Fruit of the Spirit of Positive Character-Building Essential** of "Joy" in action through the daily practice of true-faith in the Most High Heavenly Father, a person can learn to overcome and resist the **8th of the 9 Deadly Venoms of the Desires of the great dragon, that old serpent called the devil and satan which deceiveth the whole world** known as "**Heinous Murder**" by learning and practicing being happy inside, **cheerful, calm** and **delightful (Joy – χαρά Chará, Khar-ah')** every day.

132

SPIRITUAL TRILLIONAIRE:
Cherishing the Breath of Life while Simultaneously
Preparing for the Blow of Death!

CHILDREN OF THE MOST HIGH:
PRISTINE YOUTH AND FAMILY SOLUTIONS, LLC.
SONS AND DAUGHTERS OF THE MOST HIGH PUBLISHERS &

OH, GRACIOUS MOST HIGH HEAVENLY FATHER, HOLY IS YOUR
NAME, YOUR WILL BE DONE NOW AND FOREVER!

9: The **9th** of the **9** Deadly Venom of the Desires of the great dragon, that old serpent called the devil and satan which deceiveth the whole world is: **Wickedness** which is the "KJV Bible Hebrew Strong's Concordance#**7563** word: רָשָׁע **(Rasha)**: means: evil (1), evil man (1), evil men (1), guilty (3), man (1), offender (1), ungodly (1), wicked (228), wicked man (21), wicked men (2), wicked one (1), wicked ones (3)." **According to the bible, are people born wicked? Yes, wicked people or the devil's children just like the children of the Most High start out as babies.** In the KJV bible book of Psalms chapter 58 verses 3-5; it states: "The **wicked** רָשָׁע **Rasha are estranged from the womb: they go astray as soon as they be born, speaking lies. Their poison is like the poison of a serpent: they are like the deaf** adder **(venomous serpent) that stoppeth her ear; Which will not hearken to the voice of charmers, charming never so wisely.**"

133

SPIRITUAL TRILLIONAIRE:
Cherishing the Breath of Life while Simultaneously
Preparing for the Blow of Death!

CHILDREN OF THE MOST HIGH:
PRISTINE YOUTH AND FAMILY SOLUTIONS, LLC.
SONS AND DAUGHTERS OF THE MOST HIGH PUBLISHERS ®

OH, GRACIOUS MOST HIGH HEAVENLY FATHER, HOLY IS YOUR
NAME, YOUR WILL BE DONE NOW AND FOREVER!

In the KJV bible book of Proverbs chapter 6 verses 16-19; it states: "These six *things* doth the LORD hate: yea, seven *are* an abomination unto him: A proud look, a lying tongue, and hands that shed innocent blood, a heart that deviseth **wicked** imaginations, feet that be swift in running to mischief, a false witness *that* speaketh lies, and he that soweth discord among brethren." Yashu'a (Jesus) said in the KJV bible book of John chapter 8 verse 44; the Messiah Yashu'a (Jesus) said: "Ye are of *your* father the devil, and the lusts of your father ye will do. He was a murderer from the beginning, and abode not in the truth, because there is no truth in him. When he speaketh a lie, he speaketh of his own: for he is a liar, and the father of it."

SPIRITUAL TRILLIONAIRE:
Cherishing the Breath of Life while Simultaneously
Preparing for the Blow of Death!

CHILDREN OF THE MOST HIGH:
PRISTINE YOUTH AND FAMILY SOLUTIONS, LLC.
SONS AND DAUGHTERS OF THE MOST HIGH PUBLISHERS ®

OH, GRACIOUS MOST HIGH HEAVENLY FATHER, HOLY IS YOUR
NAME, YOUR WILL BE DONE NOW AND FOREVER!

Wickedness and a lack of knowing can also lead to many people seeking evil spirits or unclean spirits, and opening themselves up to receive evil or unclean spirits through venues such as: playing with or interacting with **Quija boards**, consulting **tarot cards**, participating in **seances**, **consulting familiar spirits, sexual acts with person or people who do not have our best interest**, **practicing all forms of instructions or all forms of teaching that are potentially harmful to us physically, mentally, spiritually, emotionally, and financially, and all harmful forms of intoxication that can be lethal to our health**.

According to Rev. Dr. A. J. Varmah (2004), "a **Quija Board** is a device consisting of a board inscribed with the alphabet and other characters. It enables you to communicate with non-physical entities and your own higher or lower self. It is used to communicate with people on the other side, but in reality, it invokes evil spirits by the way it is designed, for it has been put together by demons in human form who were and are in communication with certain powerful disembodied spirits of 6 "ether and ghost. Nowadays it is being called the talking board "instead of Ouija board, though it looks very similar to what the

SPIRITUAL TRILLIONAIRE:
**Cherishing the Breath of Life while Simultaneously
Preparing for the Blow of Death!**

 **CHILDREN OF THE MOST HIGH:**
PRISTINE YOUTH AND FAMILY SOLUTIONS, LLC.
SONS AND DAUGHTERS OF THE MOST HIGH PUBLISHERS ®

OH, GRACIOUS MOST HIGH HEAVENLY FATHER, HOLY IS YOUR
NAME, YOUR WILL BE DONE NOW AND FOREVER!

Ouija board looks like. What most people who play with Ouija boards and Tarots don't know is that once you play with the board you are opened forever, for unlike a vortex which closes and opens at appointed times, a Ouija board opens and remains opened. You are like a shell, and all types of beings can walk in and out of you, because you have opened up the doors to other dimensions by tearing a hole in the very fiber of your Etheric self, thus any type of being good or evil can walk through which opens the doors forever. So, think about it before engaging in these practices. The Ouija board is an alphabet board with a pointer used for various forms of divination and/or spirit contact. The modern Ouija board dates back to Greece where divination was done with a table that moved on wheels to point to signs, which were interpreted as revelations from the "unseen world." The **rolling table** was used through the nineteenth century. Other such devices were used by the Romans as early as the third century A.D., and the thirteenth century by the Mongols. Some Native Americans "used "**squdilate** boards" to find missing objects and person, and obtain spiritual information."

SPIRITUAL TRILLIONAIRE:
**Cherishing the Breath of Life while Simultaneously
Preparing for the Blow of Death!**

CHILDREN OF THE MOST HIGH:
PRISTINE YOUTH AND FAMILY SOLUTIONS, LLC.
SONS AND DAUGHTERS OF THE MOST HIGH PUBLISHERS ®

OH, GRACIOUS MOST HIGH HEAVENLY FATHER, HOLY IS YOUR NAME, YOUR WILL BE DONE NOW AND FOREVER!

"In 1853 the **planchette** came into use in Europe and the Ouija enjoyed enormous popularity during and after World War I, when many people were desperate to communicate with loved ones killed in the war and Spiritualism was in a revival. The modern occult origin of this "**parlor game**" is specifically designed to contact the spirit world. Its recent development began with prominent French spiritualist, **M. Planchette** in 1853 and in 1899 was bought by William Fuld, an inventor interested in **spiritism**. In **1966** Fuld, considered the modern "father" of the Ouija board, sold his patent to **Parker Brothers**. Although Parker Brothers keep sales figures confidential, the board has sold over **20-25 million sets**. The board puts one in contact with the spirit world and as a result, it should be considered anything but a game. It continues to be marketed as a game, just to make a dollar and gain a soul. Many so-called famous mediums began their trade by experimentation with the Ouija board and what they came in contact with are demons. Participants believe they are contacting a departed loved one or someone from the past, who has information. It usually starts out as innocent fun and then can lead to addiction. The force behind the board is demonic. Demonic forces are actually deceiving the one who is desperately asking questions."

SPIRITUAL TRILLIONAIRE:
**Cherishing the Breath of Life while Simultaneously
Preparing for the Blow of Death!**

CHILDREN OF THE MOST HIGH:
PRISTINE YOUTH AND FAMILY SOLUTIONS, LLC.
SONS AND DAUGHTERS OF THE MOST HIGH PUBLISHERS

OH, GRACIOUS MOST HIGH HEAVENLY FATHER, HOLY IS YOUR NAME, YOUR WILL BE DONE NOW AND FOREVER!

"It should come as no surprise that nine out of ten times the answer happens to be what the person wants to hear. It could be a family member or someone talking for them saying they are ok in the hereafter. Once contact is established, Satan lures the victim into other occult activities (Varmah, 2004)." Knowing how a person or people utilize power, why a person or people utilize power the way that they do, and knowing the source of that power are indicators of whether or not it is **wickedness or malevolent or whether it is benevolent** from the Most High Heavenly Father.

The KJV bible book of Galatians chapter 5 verse 22 with Greek inserts:

"Ὁ δὲ καρπὸς τοῦ πνεύματός ἐστιν ἀγάπη χαρά εἰρήνη μακροθυμία χρηστότης ἀγαθωσύνη πίστις, πραότης ἐγκράτεια κατὰ τῶν τοιούτων οὐκ ἔστιν νόμος"

The KJV bible book of Galatians chapter 5 verses 22-23; it states: "But the fruit of the Spirit is love, joy, peace, longsuffering, gentleness, **goodness**, faith, Meekness, temperance: against such there is no law."

138

SPIRITUAL TRILLIONAIRE:
Cherishing the Breath of Life while Simultaneously
Preparing for the Blow of Death!

CHILDREN OF THE MOST HIGH:
PRISTINE YOUTH AND FAMILY SOLUTIONS, LLC.
SONS AND DAUGHTERS OF THE MOST HIGH PUBLISHERS ®

OH, GRACIOUS MOST HIGH HEAVENLY FATHER, HOLY IS YOUR
NAME, YOUR WILL BE DONE NOW AND FOREVER!

"**Goodness** is the KJV bible Greek Strong's Concordance#18 word: ἀγαθωσύνη **Agathōsýnē**, ag-ath-o-soo'-nay; from goodness and means uprightness of heart and life, kindness, i.e. virtue or beneficence." By utilizing the **True Vine (**Yashu'a, Jesus**) Fruit of the Spirit of Positive Character-Building Essential** of "**Goodness**" in action through the daily practice of true-faith in the Most High Heavenly Father, a person can learn to overcome and resist the **9th of the 9 Deadly Venoms of the Desires of the great dragon, that old serpent called the devil and satan which deceiveth the whole world** known as "**Wickedness**," by learning and practicing goodness, uprightness of heart and life, kindness, and the virtue of beneficence (**Goodness - ἀγαθωσύνη Agathōsýnē**) every day.

~OH, MOST HIGH HEAVENLY FATHER, LET YOUR DIVINE
MERCY BE BESTOWED ON US. AMEN~

139

SPIRITUAL TRILLIONAIRE:
**Cherishing the Breath of Life while Simultaneously
Preparing for the Blow of Death!**

CHILDREN OF THE MOST HIGH:
PRISTINE YOUTH AND FAMILY SOLUTIONS, LLC.
SONS AND DAUGHTERS OF THE MOST HIGH PUBLISHERS

OH, GRACIOUS MOST HIGH HEAVENLY FATHER, HOLY IS YOUR
NAME, YOUR WILL BE DONE NOW AND FOREVER!

Chapter 5: What is the True Vine (Yashu'a, Jesus) Art of Spiritual Warfare?

~OH, MOST HIGH HEAVENLY FATHER, YOU HAVE
POWER OVER ALL THINGS. CONTINUE TO GUIDE US TO
BE ON YOUR PATH OF RIGHTEOUSNESS AND TO
ETERNALLY STAY ON YOUR PATH OF RIGHTEOUSNESS
AMEN~

SPIRITUAL TRILLIONAIRE:
Cherishing the Breath of Life while Simultaneously
Preparing for the Blow of Death!

CHILDREN OF THE MOST HIGH:
PRISTINE YOUTH AND FAMILY SOLUTIONS, LLC.
SONS AND DAUGHTERS OF THE MOST HIGH PUBLISHERS ®

OH, GRACIOUS MOST HIGH HEAVENLY FATHER, HOLY IS YOUR
NAME, YOUR WILL BE DONE NOW AND FOREVER!

What is the True Vine (Yashu'a, Jesus) Art of Spiritual Warfare?

The True Vine (Yashu'a, Jesus) Art of Spiritual Warfare is: A disciplined, waging of mental, spiritual and emotional war skill that is attained by rigorous study and practice of the Doctrine of the Most High that was taught by the True Vine (Yashu'a, Jesus) against all wickedness. Without a foe a soldier never knows his or her strength, and the **True Vine (Yashu'a, Jesus) Mind** must be developed by the exercise of experience, evidence, reason, strength, and the willingness to change over time. So, aspiring Spiritual Trillionaires become aware that the carnal nature is a foe that the children of the Most High Heavenly Father must fight. In order to overcome the foe of the carnal nature, a child of the Most High must decrease and the Messiah Yashu'a (Jesus) must increase in them as the strength of him manifest. Those of us who are successful in this battle will regain our lost eternal heritage; but we must do it in a conflict that cannot be told in words!

141

SPIRITUAL TRILLIONAIRE:
Cherishing the Breath of Life while Simultaneously
Preparing for the Blow of Death!

CHILDREN OF THE MOST HIGH:
PRISTINE YOUTH AND FAMILY SOLUTIONS, LLC.
SONS AND DAUGHTERS OF THE MOST HIGH PUBLISHERS ®

OH, GRACIOUS MOST HIGH HEAVENLY FATHER, HOLY IS YOUR
NAME, YOUR WILL BE DONE NOW AND FOREVER!

Earlier in the book, you mentioned True-Prayer Supplication, what is True-Prayer Supplication?

True-Prayer Supplication occurs through the combination of spoken words from a sincere heart and intentionally, concentrated mind that is focused on the Most High only, and through the daily internal practicing of meditation. This occurs by us willingly, allowing the Most High's words and laws to be placed in our hearts and in our minds. When this occurs, it puts our minds in alignment with the "**Will**" of the Most High as stated in the KJV bible book of Hebrews chapter 8 verse 10; it states: "For this is the covenant that I will make with the house of Israel after those days, saith the Lord; I will put my laws into their mind, and write them in their hearts: and I will be to them a God, and they shall be to me a people." Thus, when we pray the Most High's words and obey the Most High's laws that are placed in our hearts and minds, the Most High's "**Will**", becomes our will. Our True-Prayer Supplications must be directed through the portion of the Most High that exists in us as stated in the KJV bible book of John chapter 1 verses 1-5.

SPIRITUAL TRILLIONAIRE:
Cherishing the Breath of Life while Simultaneously
Preparing for the Blow of Death!

CHILDREN OF THE MOST HIGH:
PRISTINE YOUTH AND FAMILY SOLUTIONS, LLC.
SONS AND DAUGHTERS OF THE MOST HIGH PUBLISHERS ®

OH, GRACIOUS MOST HIGH HEAVENLY FATHER, HOLY IS YOUR
NAME, YOUR WILL BE DONE NOW AND FOREVER!

However, this should not ever be misinterpreted as praying to yourself as the Most High (that would be BLASPHEMY!). In the KJV bible book of John chapter 1 verses 1-5; it states: "In the beginning was the Word, and the Word was with God, and the Word was God. The same was in the beginning with God. All things were made by him; and without him was not anything made that was made. In him was life (**breath of life from the Lord God**); and the life (**from the Lord God made people into living souls**) was the light (**Neshamaw Khayyeem** נשמה חיים - **Divine Breath of Life**) of men (human beings). And the light (**portion of the Most High that exists in every person**) shineth in darkness (**is inside the body of every person**); and the darkness (**the body and the mind in many people lack of the knowledge of how a portion of the Most High exists in every person**) comprehended it not." So, there is a portion of the Most High Heavenly Father which is a: "**Spiritual Majesty**" that exists in each person that is dormant in many of us. Remember: **Spiritual Majesty** is a portion of the Most High that exists in each person which is usually not allowed to function in our lives due to many of us living most days according to other people plans of how they want us to utilize our limited time, places and worldly things and other

143

SPIRITUAL TRILLIONAIRE:
Cherishing the Breath of Life while Simultaneously
Preparing for the Blow of Death!

CHILDREN OF THE MOST HIGH:
PRISTINE YOUTH AND FAMILY SOLUTIONS, LLC.
SONS AND DAUGHTERS OF THE MOST HIGH PUBLISHERS ®

OH, GRACIOUS MOST HIGH HEAVENLY FATHER, HOLY IS YOUR
NAME, YOUR WILL BE DONE NOW AND FOREVER!

people plans for our lives that may not have our best interest; rather than becoming aware of the Most High's pre-ordained plan for each of our lives and learning how to best, only live by the "**Will**" and commandments of the Most High. **Spiritual Majesty** is an inner quality that when it is intentionally organized and directed towards positive accomplishments it activates our higher potential that helps us to conquer adverse situations. Also, when our **Spiritual Majesty** is intentionally organized and directed towards positive accomplishments, it activates the ability to create positive life achievements that afford us the opportunity to get more out of life by sacrificing through our works in a positive healthy manner to give more to life. So, the most important aspect of True-Prayer Supplication as it relates to the acquisition of positive spiritual health and positive spiritual wealth is that the Most High Heavenly Father's "**Will**" be done!

In the KJV bible book of Mathew chapter 6 verses 9-10; Yashu'a (Jesus) said: "After this manner therefore pray ye: Our Father which art in heaven, hallowed (Holy) be thy name. Thy kingdom come. Thy will be done in earth, as it is in heaven."

SPIRITUAL TRILLIONAIRE:
**Cherishing the Breath of Life while Simultaneously
Preparing for the Blow of Death!**

CHILDREN OF THE MOST HIGH:
PRISTINE YOUTH AND FAMILY SOLUTIONS, LLC.
SONS AND DAUGHTERS OF THE MOST HIGH PUBLISHERS ®

OH, GRACIOUS MOST HIGH HEAVENLY FATHER, HOLY IS YOUR
NAME, YOUR WILL BE DONE NOW AND FOREVER!

In the KJV bible book of Luke chapter 22 verse 42, Yashu'a (Jesus) said: "Father, if thou be willing, remove this cup from me: nevertheless, not my will, but thine, be done." "During his earthly life, he offered prayers and appeals with loud cries and tears to the one who was able to save him from death, and he was heard because of his reverence, KJV Hebrews 5:7."

Earlier in the book, you mentioned True-Faith, what is True-Faith? True-Faith is unshakable moral conviction of the truth and trust in the Most High Heavenly Father, the Messiah Yashu'a (Jesus), the Most High Heavenly Father's Angelic-Beings who are Messengers of the Most High, that are sent to certain members of humanity to teach us how to obey the Most High's laws, and how to learn and teach the Most High's Doctrine. This is essential in order for the Most High's "**Will**" to be done through us, around us, and seen to members of humanity through our works. As aspiring Spiritual Trillionaires, we are willing instruments that are utilized by the Most High, to only do the Most High Heavenly Father's "**Will**" on earth as it is in **heaven** (the word "**heaven**" is the KJV bible Greek Strong's Concordance#3772 word: οὐρανός *ouranos*. **Ouranos** is the **Greek word** for the **English word "Orion"** in reference to the Orion Star Constellation.

145

SPIRITUAL TRILLIONAIRE:
Cherishing the Breath of Life while Simultaneously
Preparing for the Blow of Death!

CHILDREN OF THE MOST HIGH:
PRISTINE YOUTH AND FAMILY SOLUTIONS, LLC.
SONS AND DAUGHTERS OF THE MOST HIGH PUBLISHERS ®

OH, GRACIOUS MOST HIGH HEAVENLY FATHER, HOLY IS YOUR
NAME, YOUR WILL BE DONE NOW AND FOREVER!

Not to be mistaken for the Kingdom of God. Heaven (Ouranos) is in the Kingdom of God. In the **KJV bible book of Job chapter 9 verse 9**; it states: "Which maketh **Arcturus, Orion**, and **Pleiades**, and the **chambers of the south**." These are Star Constellations created by the Most High Heavenly Father. That's why in the KJV bible book of John chapter 14 verse 2; Yashu'a (Jesus) said: "In my Father's house [**throughout the boundless universes** and **outside the boundless universes**] are many mansions (the KJV bible Greek Strong's Concordance word for **"mansions"** is the word: μονή monē which means: a staying, abiding, dwelling, abode): if it were not so, I would have told you. I go to prepare a place for you.

What do you mean when you say: "outside the boundless universes?"

We mean that **Existence predates Creation**. In order for the Most High Heavenly Father to have **created the boundless universes, the Most High Heavenly Father had to exist before the creation of all that was created.** The Most High Heavenly Father is the **Creator of all creators** and **existed**

146

SPIRITUAL TRILLIONAIRE:
Cherishing the Breath of Life while Simultaneously
Preparing for the Blow of Death!

CHILDREN OF THE MOST HIGH:
PRISTINE YOUTH AND FAMILY SOLUTIONS, LLC.
SONS AND DAUGHTERS OF THE MOST HIGH PUBLISHERS ®

OH, GRACIOUS MOST HIGH HEAVENLY FATHER, HOLY IS YOUR
NAME, YOUR WILL BE DONE NOW AND FOREVER!

outside of creation during the time that the **sum of things** or that which **adds up to something** were being created.

Also, True-Faith must be grounded in substantiated facts that are strongly supported through, evidence, experience and reason.

As it relates to True-Faith, what questions do the Children of the Most High Pristine Youth and Family Solution, LLC. recommend that people who do not believe that there is a heaven or hell, or that the True Vine (Yashu'a, Jesus) ever existed, or that a man named Jesus Christ ever walked the face of the earth, may need to consider?

147

SPIRITUAL TRILLIONAIRE:
**Cherishing the Breath of Life while Simultaneously
Preparing for the Blow of Death!**

CHILDREN OF THE MOST HIGH:
PRISTINE YOUTH AND FAMILY SOLUTIONS, LLC.
SONS AND DAUGHTERS OF THE MOST HIGH PUBLISHERS ®

OH, GRACIOUS MOST HIGH HEAVENLY FATHER, HOLY IS YOUR
NAME, YOUR WILL BE DONE NOW AND FOREVER!

The Children of the Most High Pristine Youth and Family Solution, LLC. ask that each reader may need to consider the following:

In the KJV bible book of John chapter 14 verse 6; Yashu'a (Jesus), stated: "I am the way, the truth, and the life: no man cometh unto the Father, but by me."

1). If this verse is true, are you willing to jeopardize your eternal spiritual future after you take your last physical breath because you ignored the KJV bible book of John chapter 14 verse 6?

2). Can you afford to be wrong in your decision making of whether or not you accept Yashu'a (Jesus) as the way, the truth, and the life back **to the Most High Heavenly Father**? In the KJV bible book of Revelation chapter 20 verse 15; it states: "And whosoever was not found written in the book of life was cast into the lake of fire."

SPIRITUAL TRILLIONAIRE:
**Cherishing the Breath of Life while Simultaneously
Preparing for the Blow of Death!**

CHILDREN OF THE MOST HIGH:
PRISTINE YOUTH AND FAMILY SOLUTIONS, LLC.
SONS AND DAUGHTERS OF THE MOST HIGH PUBLISHERS ®

OH, GRACIOUS MOST HIGH HEAVENLY FATHER, HOLY IS YOUR
NAME, YOUR WILL BE DONE NOW AND FOREVER!

3). If heaven, hell or the lake of fire really exists, can you afford to be wrong in your decision making of whether or not you accept Yashu'a (Jesus) as the way, the truth, and the life back **to the Most High Heavenly Father**?

Does a person choose to come to Yashu'a (Jesus)? Or is a person led to Yashu'a (Jesus) by the Most High Heavenly Father and chosen by Yashu'a (Jesus)?

According the KJV bible book of John chapter 6 verse 44; Yashu'a (Jesus) said: "No man (the KJV bible Greek Strong's Concordance #3762 word for **"no man" is: οὐδείς oudeís, oo-dice'; from G3761 and G1520; and means: no one, nothing, not even one (man, woman or thing), i.e. none, nobody, nothing: any**) can come to me, except the Father which hath sent me draw him: and I will raise him up at the last day." According the KJV bible book of John chapter 15 verse 16; Yashu'a (Jesus) said: "Ye have not chosen me, but I have chosen you, and ordained you, that ye should go and bring forth fruit, and [that] your fruit should remain: that whatsoever ye shall ask of the Father in my name, he may give it you."

SPIRITUAL TRILLIONAIRE:
Cherishing the Breath of Life while Simultaneously
Preparing for the Blow of Death!

CHILDREN OF THE MOST HIGH:
PRISTINE YOUTH AND FAMILY SOLUTIONS, LLC.
SONS AND DAUGHTERS OF THE MOST HIGH PUBLISHERS ®

OH, GRACIOUS MOST HIGH HEAVENLY FATHER, HOLY IS YOUR
NAME, YOUR WILL BE DONE NOW AND FOREVER!

In the KJV bible book of John chapter 14 verse 14; Yashu'a (Jesus) said: "If ye shall ask any thing in my name, I will do [it]."

What is the original Judean/Galilean birth name of the Messiah whose translated name is called Jesus? Jesus original Judean/Galilean birth name was and is: **"Yashu'a" (Judean) or Yasu' (Galilean) in the Aramic/Hebrew and Galilean languages that he spoke.**

Yashu'a (Jesus) also did not come in his own name nor did he ever claim his name as being **Holy**. Yashu'a came in the name of "**the Most High Heavenly Father**" (ELYOWN עֶלְיוֹן ELYOWN עֶלְיוֹן EL אֵל).

In the KJV bible book of John chapter 5 verse 43; Yashu'a (Jesus) said: "I am come in my Father's name, and ye receive me not: if another shall come in his own name (the "I" principle), him ye will receive. **Yashu'a (Je-ho-shu-a**, Jesus) said that the Most High Heavenly One's name is **Holy** in the KJV bible book of Mathew chapter 6 verse 9; Yashu'a (Jesus) stated: "After this manner therefore pray ye: Our Father

SPIRITUAL TRILLIONAIRE:
Cherishing the Breath of Life while Simultaneously
Preparing for the Blow of Death!

CHILDREN OF THE MOST HIGH:
PRISTINE YOUTH AND FAMILY SOLUTIONS, LLC.
SONS AND DAUGHTERS OF THE MOST HIGH PUBLISHERS ®

OH, GRACIOUS MOST HIGH HEAVENLY FATHER, HOLY IS YOUR
NAME, YOUR WILL BE DONE NOW AND FOREVER!

which art in heaven, "Hallowed be" is the KJV bible Greek
Strong Concordance#37 word: "Hagiazo" – pronounced as
hag-ee-ad' zo; and it means HOLY). So, Yashu'a (Jesus) said
that: "the Most High Heavenly Father's Name is HOLY!"

**What do I need to know if I presently pray in the name of
Jesus or if I want to pray in the name of Jesus?**

**By all means, please pray in whatever name or names works
best for you.** However, if you choose to pray in the name of
Jesus according to the New Testament of the bible, please know
that the name "**Jesus**" is the translated English name in the
"**KJV bible Greek Strong's Concrdance#2424** as: "Iēsous,
Ἰησοῦς" and means: **Jesus = "Jehovah is salvation"**. Ἰησοῦς
Iēsoûs, pronounced as: "ee-ay-sooce'"; of Hebrew origin
**KJV bible Hebrew Strong's Concrdance#3091 יְהוֹשׁוּעַ,
Yĕhowshuwa`**); Jesus (i.e. **Je-ho-shu-a**), the name of our Lord
and two (three) other Israelites:—Jesus. When **Yehoshu'a** is
translated in the modern Hebrew language, it translates as
Yahayyu Saves or simply **Joshua**. As it relates to the Greek
name: "**Iēsous, Ἰησοῦς**" "**Ie**" means "**Hail**" and "**Sous**" means
"**Zeus**" – **head of all Greek and all Roman Gods**."

151

SPIRITUAL TRILLIONAIRE:
Cherishing the Breath of Life while Simultaneously
Preparing for the Blow of Death!

CHILDREN OF THE MOST HIGH:
PRISTINE YOUTH AND FAMILY SOLUTIONS, LLC.
SONS AND DAUGHTERS OF THE MOST HIGH PUBLISHERS ®

OH, GRACIOUS MOST HIGH HEAVENLY FATHER, HOLY IS YOUR
NAME, YOUR WILL BE DONE NOW AND FOREVER!

Unterman, Thames and Hudson (1991) in "Dictionary of Jewish lore & legend" state: "So, **Yahusha** is English for the Hebrew name of the Messiah (anointed King of Israel) and Jesus is the name of the Greek "good man" or Chistos. It is that simple. __But what does "Iesous" mean in Greek__. It has no meaning in Hebrew; as it is not a Hebrew word. In Greek, "**Iesous**" literally translated means "**Hail Zeus**". The name "**Jesus**" didn't even exist until the 4th Century and was a later derivative of the late Latin **Isus**. It is known that the Greek name endings with **sus, seus,** and **sous were attached by the Greeks to names and geographical areas as means to give honor to their supreme deity, Zeus.**"

Defaming The Messiah

"IESOUS" = Hail ZEUS
"JESUS" = Hail ZEUS

Source - Dictionary of
Christian Lore and Legend

SPIRITUAL TRILLIONAIRE:
Cherishing the Breath of Life while Simultaneously
Preparing for the Blow of Death!

CHILDREN OF THE MOST HIGH:
PRISTINE YOUTH AND FAMILY SOLUTIONS, LLC.
SONS AND DAUGHTERS OF THE MOST HIGH PUBLISHERS ®

OH, GRACIOUS MOST HIGH HEAVENLY FATHER, HOLY IS YOUR
NAME, YOUR WILL BE DONE NOW AND FOREVER!

According to: "**The Origin of Christianity**" by **A.B. Traina**, "The name of the true Messiah, **Jahshuwah (Jehoshua)**, being Hebrew, was objectionable to the Greeks and Romans, who hated the Judeans (Jews), and so it was deleted from the records, and a new name inserted. Jahshuwah (Jehoshua) was thus replaced by **Ie-Sous (hail Zeus)**, now known to us as **Jesus**. **We see in historical documents that the name "Jesus" did not even come into existence until the 1500's when the letter "J" was introduced into our English language.** So, the name "Jesus" is only around 500 years old! The Greek "**Iesus**" comes from the name **Zeus**, the ruling God in the Greek pantheon. "Je*sus*" is a transliteration of a Latin name only ONE letter off "Ioe*sus*" pronounced **hey-sus** - which has no meaning in Hebrew, but in Latin it means "**Hail Zeus**". If Yahusha's name had been transliterated into our language; it would have been *Joshua*."

According to Dr. Henry Clifford Kinley in "**the Gospel of The Kingdom True Names and Title**", Ohio 1931; "**It is simply amazing to think that all these years, hundreds of years, mankind has been calling the Saviour by the wrong name**!! **It's hard to give up the name of Jesus because it's so deeply**

SPIRITUAL TRILLIONAIRE:
Cherishing the Breath of Life while Simultaneously
Preparing for the Blow of Death!

CHILDREN OF THE MOST HIGH:
PRISTINE YOUTH AND FAMILY SOLUTIONS, LLC.
SONS AND DAUGHTERS OF THE MOST HIGH PUBLISHERS ®

OH, GRACIOUS MOST HIGH HEAVENLY FATHER, HOLY IS YOUR
NAME, YOUR WILL BE DONE NOW AND FOREVER!

ingrained in us and much has been said and done in that name. In the 1611 KJV bible New Testament, the name **Yahusha** appeared originally wherever the Messiah was spoken of **Yahusha** means "**Yahuah is Salvation**". Later the **Messiah's name was replaced with Iesus (Greek) which later in the 1500's it became Jesus starting with the new English letter "J"** which was introduced at that time. Further, the Greek "**Iesus**" comes from the name **Zeus**, the ruling God in the Greek pantheon."

So, as it relates to the aforementioned, pray in whatever name or names works best for you.

According to the KJV bible book of Hebrews chapter 5 verses 5-10; Yashu'a (Jesus) was after the Order of Melchizedek as was Moses and Abraham for **Yashu'a (Jesus) is called the first and the last and everything we** (the Children of the Most High: Pristine Youth and Family Solutions, LLC.) do, **we do it in the name of the first and the last who came in the name of the Most High Heavenly Father.**

154

SPIRITUAL TRILLIONAIRE:
Cherishing the Breath of Life while Simultaneously
Preparing for the Blow of Death!

CHILDREN OF THE MOST HIGH:
PRISTINE YOUTH AND FAMILY SOLUTIONS, LLC.
SONS AND DAUGHTERS OF THE MOST HIGH PUBLISHERS

OH, GRACIOUS MOST HIGH HEAVENLY FATHER, HOLY IS YOUR
NAME, YOUR WILL BE DONE NOW AND FOREVER!

In the KJV bible book of Hebrews chapter 5 verses 5-10; it states that: "So, also Christ glorified not himself to be made a high priest; but he that said unto him, thou art my Son, today have I begotten thee. As he saith also in another place, Thou art a priest for ever after the order of Melchizedek **who in the days of his flesh, when he had offered up prayers and supplications with strong crying and tears unto him that was able to save him from death, and was heard in that he feared**; Though he were a Son, yet learned he obedience by the things which he suffered; And being made perfect, he became the author of eternal salvation unto all them that obey him; called of God a high priest after the order of Melchizedek."

155

SPIRITUAL TRILLIONAIRE:
**Cherishing the Breath of Life while Simultaneously
Preparing for the Blow of Death!**

CHILDREN OF THE MOST HIGH:
PRISTINE YOUTH AND FAMILY SOLUTIONS. LLC.
SONS AND DAUGHTERS OF THE MOST HIGH PUBLISHERS ®

OH, GRACIOUS MOST HIGH HEAVENLY FATHER, HOLY IS YOUR
NAME, YOUR WILL BE DONE NOW AND FOREVER!

As it relates to the True Vine (Yashu'a, Jesus) Art of Spiritual Warfare, of what the Children of the Most High Pristine Youth and Family Solutions, LLC. refer to as the: 9X9 True Vine (Yashu'a, Jesus) B.A.-K.A.-R.E. Sequential Order of Learning Habits of Success. **Why does the names we use in True-Prayer Supplication matter?**

If we call on the wrong names during prayer, we can unintentionally invoke malevolent spirits of the angels (messengers) of the dragon and/or the dragon, that old serpent called the devil and satan which can result in our prayers not being answered, and can result in those malevolent spirits or spiritual vampires working against us mentally, physically, spiritually, emotionally, financially, professionally and socially in the societies where we reside in on the planet earth.

SPIRITUAL TRILLIONAIRE:
Cherishing the Breath of Life while Simultaneously
Preparing for the Blow of Death!

CHILDREN OF THE MOST HIGH:
PRISTINE YOUTH AND FAMILY SOLUTIONS, LLC.
SONS AND DAUGHTERS OF THE MOST HIGH PUBLISHERS ®

OH, GRACIOUS MOST HIGH HEAVENLY FATHER, HOLY IS YOUR
NAME, YOUR WILL BE DONE NOW AND FOREVER!

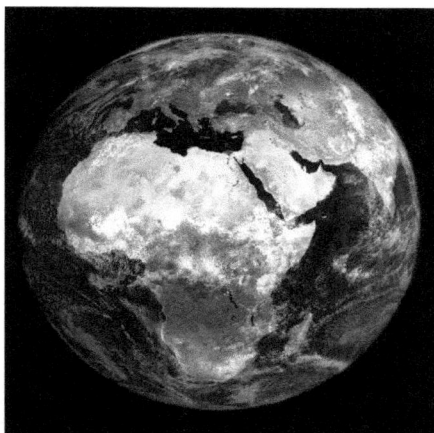

Now that you know what the biblical names such as: the **Most High** (**Elyown** עֶלְיוֹן **El** אֵל) or **YaHuHi** (the creative force and source of will), the Real Messiah who **we** (the Children of the Most High: Pristine Youth and Family Solutions, LLC.) **refer to** in his original Galilean/Judean Aramaic (Hebrew) language birth name **Yasu'a** (يسوع) or **Yashu'a** (ישוע) meaning "Savior" also spelled Yeshua or Yehoshu'a, **Issa** or **Isa** in Ashuric Syriac (Arabic), or **Yehoshu'a** in the Hebrew language which translates as **Yahayyu Saves** or simply **Joshua**, are names to be considered for those who choose to engage in True-Prayer Supplication.

157

SPIRITUAL TRILLIONAIRE:
**Cherishing the Breath of Life while Simultaneously
Preparing for the Blow of Death!**

CHILDREN OF THE MOST HIGH:
PRISTINE YOUTH AND FAMILY SOLUTIONS, LLC.
SONS AND DAUGHTERS OF THE MOST HIGH PUBLISHERS ®

OH, GRACIOUS MOST HIGH HEAVENLY FATHER, HOLY IS YOUR
NAME, YOUR WILL BE DONE NOW AND FOREVER!

The aforementioned information is essential to know and practice for those who seek to acquire, maintain or sustain positive spiritual health and positive spiritual wealth.

~OH, MOST HIGH HEAVENLY FATHER, PLEASE ENDOW
PORTIONS OF YOUR KNOWLEDGE UPON THE CHILDREN
OF THE MOST HIGH ONLY ACCORDING TO YOUR WILL
NOW AND FOREVER. AMEN~

SPIRITUAL TRILLIONAIRE:
Cherishing the Breath of Life while Simultaneously
Preparing for the Blow of Death!

CHILDREN OF THE MOST HIGH:
PRISTINE YOUTH AND FAMILY SOLUTIONS, LLC.
SONS AND DAUGHTERS OF THE MOST HIGH PUBLISHERS &

OH, GRACIOUS MOST HIGH HEAVENLY FATHER, HOLY IS YOUR
NAME, YOUR WILL BE DONE NOW AND FOREVER!

Chapter 6: Is there a difference between Spirit, Soul, Gin, Jinn, and Sin?

~OH MOST HIGH HEAVENLY FATHER, WE ETERNALLY
SEEK REFUGE IN YOU FROM THE GREAT DRAGON,
THAT OLD SERPENT CALLED THE DEVIL AND SATAN
AND HIS FALLEN ANGELS (MESSENGERS) HELPERS,
AND HIS CHILDREN! PLEASE PROTECT US FROM ALL
EVIL, ALL HARM, ALL DISEASES, AND FROM ALL THAT
IS DISAGREEABLE AND WICKED IN YOUR EYESIGHT,
NOW AND FOREVER. AMEN~

SPIRITUAL TRILLIONAIRE:
Cherishing the Breath of Life while Simultaneously
Preparing for the Blow of Death!

CHILDREN OF THE MOST HIGH:
PRISTINE YOUTH AND FAMILY SOLUTIONS, LLC.
SONS AND DAUGHTERS OF THE MOST HIGH PUBLISHERS ®

OH, GRACIOUS MOST HIGH HEAVENLY FATHER, HOLY IS YOUR
NAME, YOUR WILL BE DONE NOW AND FOREVER!

What is the Latin origin of the word spirit?

The origin of the word **spirit** comes from the Latin **spiritus** which means *"breath, breath of God, inspiration"*; **spirare**, the Latin from Old Roman, *"to breathe"*. In Spanish, which is derived from Latin, the word **"spirit"** is: espiritu (alma) soul; (mente) intelligence, wit; according to the Simon & Schuster's International Spanish-English Dictionary English-Spanish (Gámez, 1973).

The American Heritage Larousse Spanish Dictionary Spanish word for **soul** is **alma** which is defined as: the spiritual element of the human being from where comprehension, memory and will come from; b: What strengthens something; c: Principle part of a person or individual; central part void, solid of something (Dubois-Charlier, 1986). As you can see from the Spanish definitions, they call spirit, soul and soul, spirit and mente for mind.

SPIRITUAL TRILLIONAIRE:
Cherishing the Breath of Life while Simultaneously
Preparing for the Blow of Death!

CHILDREN OF THE MOST HIGH:
PRISTINE YOUTH AND FAMILY SOLUTIONS, LLC.
SONS AND DAUGHTERS OF THE MOST HIGH PUBLISHERS ®

OH, GRACIOUS MOST HIGH HEAVENLY FATHER, HOLY IS YOUR
NAME, YOUR WILL BE DONE NOW AND FOREVER!

Is there a connection between the Yehovah (LORD) Elohiym (God), spirit, soul, healthy and unhealthy breathing in the KJV bible book of: Genesis chapter 2 verse 7?

ז וַיִּיצֶר יְהוָה אֱלֹהִים אֶת־הָאָדָם עָפָר מִן־הָאֲדָמָה וַיִּפַּח בְּאַפָּיו
נִשְׁמַת חַיִּים וַיְהִי הָאָדָם לְנֶפֶשׁ חַיָּה

And the LORD יְהוָה *<Yehovah> God* אֱלֹהִים *<'elohiym> formed* יֵצֶר *<yatsar> man* אָדָם *<'adam> of the dust* עָפָר *< 'aphar> of Nm <min> the ground* אֲדָמָה *<'adamah>, and breathed* נָפַח *<naphach> into his nostrils* אַף *<'aph> the breath* נְשָׁמָה *<neshamah> of life* חַי *<chay>; and man* אָדָם *<'adam> became a living* חַי *<chay> soul* נֶפֶשׁ *<nephesh>.*

The KJV bible book of Genesis chapter 2 verse 7; states: "And the Lord God formed man of the dust of the ground, and breathed into his nostrils the breath of life; and man became a living soul." So, according to the above verse, the connection occurred when the Yehovah (LORD) Elohiym (God) breathed the **Khay** or **Hayy (Neshamaw Khayyeem** נְשָׁמָה חַיִּים - Divine Breath of Life) into the nostrils of Adam (man) and Adam became a **Nephesh Khay** which in the Aramic (Hebrew) language, **Nephesh** is "Spirit".

SPIRITUAL TRILLIONAIRE:
Cherishing the Breath of Life while Simultaneously
Preparing for the Blow of Death!

CHILDREN OF THE MOST HIGH:
PRISTINE YOUTH AND FAMILY SOLUTIONS, LLC.
SONS AND DAUGHTERS OF THE MOST HIGH PUBLISHERS ®

OH, GRACIOUS MOST HIGH HEAVENLY FATHER, HOLY IS YOUR
NAME, YOUR WILL BE DONE NOW AND FOREVER!

Why is it so confusing for some people to understand the difference between spirit, soul and mind as it is utilized in many translations of the bible?

It is so confusing for some people to understand the difference between spirit and soul as it is utilized in many translations of the bible **because sometimes the words: spirit, soul, and mind are translated as the same word in the various English translations.**

In some places in the English translations of the bible as shown in the previous verse, the word soul is translated for spirit in one place, **soul** in another place, and **mind, soul, spirit** in other bible verses such as in the KJV bible book of Genesis chapter 1 verse 2 as seen on the next page with Hebrew inserts. This creates confusion in the minds of people who may not have reached the point of growth to begin their in-depth research into the letters and words in the original languages that the 1st Testament (Old Testament) and 2nd Testament (New Testament) of the Bible where revealed in.

SPIRITUAL TRILLIONAIRE:
Cherishing the Breath of Life while Simultaneously
Preparing for the Blow of Death!

CHILDREN OF THE MOST HIGH:
PRISTINE YOUTH AND FAMILY SOLUTIONS, LLC.
SONS AND DAUGHTERS OF THE MOST HIGH PUBLISHERS ®

OH, GRACIOUS MOST HIGH HEAVENLY FATHER, HOLY IS YOUR NAME, YOUR WILL BE DONE NOW AND FOREVER!

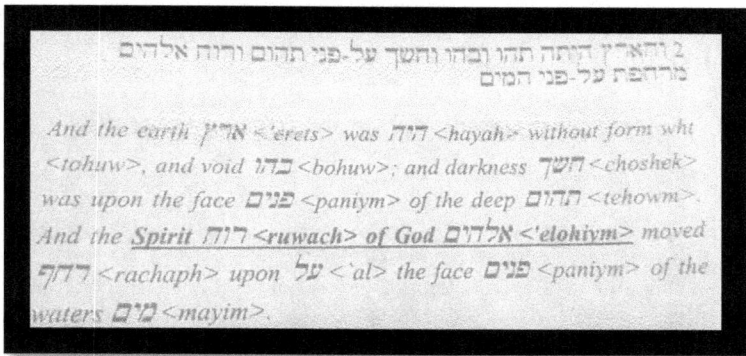

And the earth אֶרֶץ <'erets> was הָיָה <hayah> without form wht <tohuw>, and void בֹּהוּ <bohuw>; and darkness חֹשֶׁךְ <choshek> was upon the face פָּנִים <paniym> of the deep תְהוֹם <tehowm>. And the **Spirit** רוּחַ <ruwach> of God אֱלֹהִים <'elohiym> moved רָחַף <rachaph> upon עַל <'al> the face פָּנִים <paniym> of the waters מַיִם <mayim>.

Therefore, as it relates to positive spiritual health and positive spiritual wealth, it is important to know that the breath of life from the Yehovah (LORD) Elohiym (God) is from a **healthy** spirit, and when the lungs become sick, it may come from an **unhealthy "Pneuma πνεῦμα (Spirit)"**. The original Greek word for **"Spirit"** is *"Pneuma"* (**pronounced as: pnyoo' - mah)**" which is the root word for **Pneumonia**. Some places that sell alcohol, **refer to alcohol as "spirits"**.

In Ashuric/Syriac (Arabic) language, the word used for one classification of demons is **"Jinn."** In English, there is an alcohol beverage called: **"Gin." "Jinn"** and **"Gin"** is

SPIRITUAL TRILLIONAIRE:
Cherishing the Breath of Life while Simultaneously
Preparing for the Blow of Death!

CHILDREN OF THE MOST HIGH:
PRISTINE YOUTH AND FAMILY SOLUTIONS, LLC.
SONS AND DAUGHTERS OF THE MOST HIGH PUBLISHERS ®

OH, GRACIOUS MOST HIGH HEAVENLY FATHER, HOLY IS YOUR
NAME, YOUR WILL BE DONE NOW AND FOREVER!

phonetically the same sounding word and there is a saying that goes like this: "If you drink **Gin**, you will **Sin**."

The word: *"sin"* "(is the KJV bible Hebrew Strong's Concordance#2403 word: *chatta'ath* – Pronunciation khat·tä·ä' חַטָּאת occurs **448** times in **389** verses, and Strong's Number 2403 matches the Hebrew חַטָּאת (chatta'ath), which occurs 296 times in 272 verses in the Hebrew concordance in the King James Version of the bible and **means: "an offence (sometimes habitual sinfulness), and its penalty, occasion, sacrifice, or expiation; also (concretely) an offender:— punishment (of sin), purifying(-fication for sin), sin(-ner, offering)."**

164

SPIRITUAL TRILLIONAIRE:
**Cherishing the Breath of Life while Simultaneously
Preparing for the Blow of Death!**

CHILDREN OF THE MOST HIGH:
PRISTINE YOUTH AND FAMILY SOLUTIONS, LLC.
SONS AND DAUGHTERS OF THE MOST HIGH PUBLISHERS ®

OH, GRACIOUS MOST HIGH HEAVENLY FATHER, HOLY IS YOUR
NAME, YOUR WILL BE DONE NOW AND FOREVER!

Some places that sell alcohol, utilize marketing billboards like
the ones below:

JINN, GIN AND SIN MAY RHYME, IF YOU SURRENDER TO THESE, YOU MAY WASTE MUCH UNRECYCLABLE TIME!

Cherishing the Breath of Life while Simultaneously Preparing for the Blow of Death!

CHILDREN OF THE MOST HIGH:
PRISTINE YOUTH AND FAMILY SOLUTIONS, LLC.
SONS AND DAUGHTERS OF THE MOST HIGH PUBLISHERS ®

OH, GRACIOUS MOST HIGH HEAVENLY FATHER, HOLY IS YOUR NAME, YOUR WILL BE DONE NOW AND FOREVER!

SPIRITUAL TRILLIONAIRE:
Cherishing the Breath of Life while Simultaneously
Preparing for the Blow of Death!

CHILDREN OF THE MOST HIGH:
PRISTINE YOUTH AND FAMILY SOLUTIONS, LLC.
SONS AND DAUGHTERS OF THE MOST HIGH PUBLISHERS

OH, GRACIOUS MOST HIGH HEAVENLY FATHER, HOLY IS YOUR
NAME, YOUR WILL BE DONE NOW AND FOREVER!

The root word of: "in-**tox-i-c**ation" is *toxic*. The symbol for toxic is:

Toxic means *poison*. So, when a person drinks or takes in various *spirits* (alcohol) it could lead to a person making negative decisions, injuries or death. According to the bible, becoming intoxicated from drinking alcohol is a sin. List some King James Bible verses that teach us to be sober:

The KJV bible book of 1st Peter chapter 5 verse 8; states: "**Be sober**, be vigilant; because your adversary the devil, as a roaring lion, walketh about, seeking whom he may devour."

167

SPIRITUAL TRILLIONAIRE:
Cherishing the Breath of Life while Simultaneously
Preparing for the Blow of Death!

CHILDREN OF THE MOST HIGH:
PRISTINE YOUTH AND FAMILY SOLUTIONS, LLC.
SONS AND DAUGHTERS OF THE MOST HIGH PUBLISHERS ®

OH, GRACIOUS MOST HIGH HEAVENLY FATHER, HOLY IS YOUR
NAME, YOUR WILL BE DONE NOW AND FOREVER!

The KJV bible book of Romans chapter 14 verse 21; states: "[It
is] good neither to eat flesh, nor to drink wine, nor [anything]
whereby thy brother stumbled, or is offended, or is made weak."

The KJV bible book of Proverbs chapter 20 verse 1; states:
"**Wine [is] a mocker, strong drink [is] raging: and
whosoever is deceived thereby is not wise**."

The KJV bible book of Galatians chapter 5 verse 21; states:
"Envyings, murders, **drunkenness**, reviling, and such like: of
the which I tell you before, as I have also told [you] in time past,
that they which do such things shall not inherit the kingdom of
God."

The KJV bible book of 1st Corinthians chapter 6 verse 10; it
states: "Nor thieves, nor covetous, **nor drunkards**, nor revilers,
nor extortioners, **shall inherit the kingdom of God**."

The KJV bible book of Isaiah chapter 5 verse 11; states: "**Woe
unto them that rise up early in the morning, [that] they may
follow strong drink; that continue until night, [till] wine
inflame them**!"

168

SPIRITUAL TRILLIONAIRE:
Cherishing the Breath of Life while Simultaneously
Preparing for the Blow of Death!

CHILDREN OF THE MOST HIGH:
PRISTINE YOUTH AND FAMILY SOLUTIONS, LLC.
SONS AND DAUGHTERS OF THE MOST HIGH PUBLISHERS ®

OH, GRACIOUS MOST HIGH HEAVENLY FATHER, HOLY IS YOUR
NAME, YOUR WILL BE DONE NOW AND FOREVER!

The KJV bible book of Proverbs chapter 23 verses 20; states: "**Be not among winebibbers**; among riotous eaters of flesh."

The KJV bible book of Hosea chapter 4 verse 11; states: "**Whoredom and wine and new wine take away the heart**."

So, according to the aforementioned KJV bible verses, **abstaining from alcohol intoxication** is essential for those who seek to acquire, maintain or sustain positive spiritual health and positive spiritual wealth.

How does the KJV bible define the word "sin?"

According to the KJV bible book of Psalms chapter 51 verses 1-2; it states: "[To the chief Musician, A Psalm of David, when Nathan the prophet came unto him, after he had gone in to Bathsheba.] Have mercy upon me, O God, according to thy lovingkindness: according unto the multitude of thy tender mercies blot out my transgressions. Wash me thoroughly from mine iniquity, and cleanse me from my **sin**."

169

SPIRITUAL TRILLIONAIRE:
**Cherishing the Breath of Life while Simultaneously
Preparing for the Blow of Death!**

CHILDREN OF THE MOST HIGH:
PRISTINE YOUTH AND FAMILY SOLUTIONS, LLC.
SONS AND DAUGHTERS OF THE MOST HIGH PUBLISHERS ®

OH, GRACIOUS MOST HIGH HEAVENLY FATHER, HOLY IS YOUR
NAME, YOUR WILL BE DONE NOW AND FOREVER!

In the KJV bible book of Psalms chapter 51 verse 2, the word "sin" in the "**KJV bible Hebrew Strong's Concordance #2403 word:** חַטָּאת **chatta'ath**, which means: an offence (sometimes habitual sinfulness), sin, sinful, sin offering, condition of sin, guilt of sin, punishment for sin, purification from sins of ceremonial uncleanness, and its penalty, occasion, sacrifice, or expiation; also (concretely) an offender:— punishment (of sin), purifying (-fication for sin), sin (-ner, offering)."

הַחַטָּאָה — (1) f. of the word חֹטֵא *a sinner* f., or *sinful*, Am. 9:8.

(2) i. q. חַטָּאת — (*a*) *sin*, Ex. 34:7. — (*b*) *penalty of sin* (like חַטָּאת No. 3), Isa. 5:18.

חַטָּאָה constr. חַטַּאת plur. חַטָּאוֹת f. ["*a miss, misstep, slip with the foot*, Pro. 13:6"].

(1) *sin*, Ex. 28:9; Isa. 6:27, etc. ["Rarely for the habit of sinning, *sinfulness*, Prov. 14:34; Isa. 3:9."] Also applied to that by which any one sins, e.g. idols, Hos. 10:8; Deut. 9:21; comp. 2 Ki. 13:2, *water of sin*, i. e. of expiation or purifying, Num. 8:7.

(2) *a sin offering*, Levit. 6:18, 23; as to its difference from אָשָׁם see that word.

(3) *penalty*, Lam. 3:39; Zec. 14:19; hence *calamity, misfortune*, Isa. 40:2; Prov. 10:16 (opp. to חַיִּים). [Is not this last sense wholly needless? and would not its introduction utterly mar the sense of the passages referred to in support of it?]

170

SPIRITUAL TRILLIONAIRE:
Cherishing the Breath of Life while Simultaneously
Preparing for the Blow of Death!

CHILDREN OF THE MOST HIGH:
PRISTINE YOUTH AND FAMILY SOLUTIONS, LLC.
SONS AND DAUGHTERS OF THE MOST HIGH PUBLISHERS ®

OH, GRACIOUS MOST HIGH HEAVENLY FATHER, HOLY IS YOUR
NAME, YOUR WILL BE DONE NOW AND FOREVER!

According to the KJV bible book of 1st John chapter 1 verse 9; it states: "If we confess our **sins**, he is faithful and just to forgive us our **sins**, and to cleanse us from all unrighteousness." In the KJV bible book of 1st John chapter 1 verses 9, the word "**sins**" in the "**KJV bible Greek Strong's Concordance #266 word: ἁμαρτία hamartia,** which means: to be without a share in, to miss the mark, to err, be mistaken to miss or wander from the path of uprightness and honor, to do or go wrong, to wander from the law of God, violate God's law, sin that which is done wrong, sin, an offence, a violation of the divine law in thought or in act collectively, the complex or aggregate of sins committed either by a single person or by many"

SPIRITUAL TRILLIONAIRE:
Cherishing the Breath of Life while Simultaneously
Preparing for the Blow of Death!

CHILDREN OF THE MOST HIGH:
PRISTINE YOUTH AND FAMILY SOLUTIONS, LLC.
SONS AND DAUGHTERS OF THE MOST HIGH PUBLISHERS ®

OH, GRACIOUS MOST HIGH HEAVENLY FATHER, HOLY IS YOUR NAME, YOUR WILL BE DONE NOW AND FOREVER!

According to the KJV bible book of Genesis chapter 4 verse 7; it states:

"If (אִם 'im) thou doest well (יָטַב yatab) shalt thou not be accepted (שְׂאֵת sě'eth) and if thou doest not well (יָטַב yatab) <u>sin</u> (חַטָּאת chatta'ath) lieth (רָבַץ rabats) at the door (פֶּתַח pethach) And unto thee shall be his desire (תְּשׁוּקָה tĕshuwqah) and thou shalt rule (מָשַׁל mashal) over him."

In the KJV bible book of Genesis chapter 4 verse 7, the word "sin" in the **KJV bible Hebrew Strong's Concordance #2403 word: חַטָּאת chatta'ath**, which means: an offence (sometimes habitual sinfulness), sin, sinful, sin offering, condition of sin, guilt of sin, punishment for sin, purification from sins of ceremonial uncleanness, and its penalty, occasion, sacrifice, or expiation; also (concretely) an offender:—punishment (of sin), purifying(-fication for sin), sin(-ner, offering).

In the KJV bible book of Genesis chapter 4 verse 5 with Hebrew inserts; it states:

5: וְאֶל־קַיִן וְאֶל־מִנְחָתוֹ לֹא שָׁעָה וַיִּחַר לְקַיִן מְאֹד וַיִּפְּלוּ פָּנָיו

172

SPIRITUAL TRILLIONAIRE:
Cherishing the Breath of Life while Simultaneously
Preparing for the Blow of Death!

CHILDREN OF THE MOST HIGH:
PRISTINE YOUTH AND FAMILY SOLUTIONS, LLC.
SONS AND DAUGHTERS OF THE MOST HIGH PUBLISHERS ®

OH, GRACIOUS MOST HIGH HEAVENLY FATHER, HOLY IS YOUR
NAME, YOUR WILL BE DONE NOW AND FOREVER!

"But unto Cain and to his offering he had not respect. And Cain was very <u>wroth</u> (the word "wroth" is the KJV bible **Hebrew Strong's Concordance#2734** חָרָה **charah, which means:** to be very angry, to glow or grow warm; figuratively (usually) to blaze up, of anger, zeal, jealousy: —be angry, burn, be displeased, × earnestly, fret self, grieve, be (wax) hot, be incensed, kindle, × very, be wroth." **his <u>countenance</u> (paniym** – Pronunciation pä·nēm') fell, and is defined as: "when a person face frowns when they don't get their way," and then he became **wroth or very angry.**

173

SPIRITUAL TRILLIONAIRE:
Cherishing the Breath of Life while Simultaneously
Preparing for the Blow of Death!

CHILDREN OF THE MOST HIGH:
PRISTINE YOUTH AND FAMILY SOLUTIONS, LLC.
SONS AND DAUGHTERS OF THE MOST HIGH PUBLISHERS ®

OH, GRACIOUS MOST HIGH HEAVENLY FATHER, HOLY IS YOUR
NAME, YOUR WILL BE DONE NOW AND FOREVER!

So, according to the previous verses, we learn that when Cain was disrespectful to the Yehovah (LORD) and he did not get his way, **he became very angry**, and it led to him committing the *sin* of killing his brother Abel in the KJV bible book of Genesis chapter 4 verse 8. Anger and alcohol can impair the prefrontal lobe of the brain which is responsible for making sound decisions and can negatively affect the body (Hendricks, Bore, Aslinia, & Morriss, 2013). Therefore; the aforementioned KJV bible verses teach us that, "**Sin**" "lays and waits at the door" for the essence (soul) of people in hopes that **the great dragon**, that **old serpent** called the **devil** and **satan** and **his angels (Jinn)** can seduce people to commit "**Sin**". Cain's encounter with "**Sin**" is a warning and sign for those who seek to acquire, maintain or sustain positive spiritual health and positive spiritual wealth; that the **devil** and **his angels (Jinn)** will do everything in their power to sway members of humanity from being on the path back to the Most High. **For Example:** the **devil** and **his angels (Jinn)** can plant a negative thought in our minds via news media or person, place or thing, and a person may unfortunately act on that negative thought which could lead to that person's life and the lives of those closest to him or her being in ruins.

SPIRITUAL TRILLIONAIRE:
Cherishing the Breath of Life while Simultaneously
Preparing for the Blow of Death!

CHILDREN OF THE MOST HIGH:
PRISTINE YOUTH AND FAMILY SOLUTIONS, LLC.
SONS AND DAUGHTERS OF THE MOST HIGH PUBLISHERS ®

OH, GRACIOUS MOST HIGH HEAVENLY FATHER, HOLY IS YOUR
NAME, YOUR WILL BE DONE NOW AND FOREVER!

How does the American Heritage Dictionary define the word "sin?"

The American Heritage Dictionary defines the word "sin" as:
sin [1] (sĭn) *n.*
1. A transgression of a religious or moral law, especially when deliberate.
2. *Theology*
a. Deliberate disobedience to the known will of God.
b. A condition of estrangement from God resulting from such disobedience.
3. Something regarded as being shameful, deplorable, or utterly wrong.
intr.v. **sinned, sin·ning, sins**

To violate a religious or moral law.
Idioms:
live in sin
To cohabit in a sexual relationship without being married.
as sin

Completely or extremely: *He is guilty as sin.*

175

SPIRITUAL TRILLIONAIRE:
Cherishing the Breath of Life while Simultaneously
Preparing for the Blow of Death!

CHILDREN OF THE MOST HIGH:
PRISTINE YOUTH AND FAMILY SOLUTIONS, LLC.
SONS AND DAUGHTERS OF THE MOST HIGH PUBLISHERS ®

OH, GRACIOUS MOST HIGH HEAVENLY FATHER, HOLY IS YOUR
NAME, YOUR WILL BE DONE NOW AND FOREVER!

[Middle English *sinne*, from Old English *synn*; see **es-** in the Appendix of Indo-European roots.]

SPIRITUAL TRILLIONAIRE:
Cherishing the Breath of Life while Simultaneously
Preparing for the Blow of Death!

CHILDREN OF THE MOST HIGH:
PRISTINE YOUTH AND FAMILY SOLUTIONS, LLC.
SONS AND DAUGHTERS OF THE MOST HIGH PUBLISHERS ®

OH, GRACIOUS MOST HIGH HEAVENLY FATHER, HOLY IS YOUR
NAME, YOUR WILL BE DONE NOW AND FOREVER!

According to the KJV bible book of Genesis chapter 1 verse
2; what is soul? Is there a difference between soul and
spirit? What is the difference between spirit and soul?

The KJV bible book of Genesis chapter 1 verse 2 with
Hebrew inserts:

And the earth אֶרֶץ <'erets> was הָיָה <hayah> without form wht
<tohuw>, and void בֹּהוּ <bohuw>; and darkness חֹשֶׁךְ <choshek>
was upon the face פָּנִים <paniym> of the deep תְּהוֹם <tehowm>.
And the Spirit רוּחַ <ruwach> of God אֱלֹהִים <'elohiym> moved
רָחַף <rachaph> upon עַל <al> the face פָּנִים <paniym> of the
waters מַיִם <mayim>.

SPIRITUAL TRILLIONAIRE:
**Cherishing the Breath of Life while Simultaneously
Preparing for the Blow of Death!**

CHILDREN OF THE MOST HIGH:
PRISTINE YOUTH AND FAMILY SOLUTIONS, LLC.
SONS AND DAUGHTERS OF THE MOST HIGH PUBLISHERS ®

OH, GRACIOUS MOST HIGH HEAVENLY FATHER, HOLY IS YOUR
NAME, YOUR WILL BE DONE NOW AND FOREVER!

The word "Soul" is:

rooakh (רוח) in Hebrew or ruwh (رُوح) in

Arabic

(نفس)

The word "Spirit" is "nafs" in

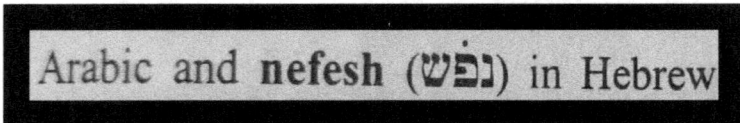

Arabic and **nefesh** (נפֶשׁ) in Hebrew

SPIRITUAL TRILLIONAIRE:
**Cherishing the Breath of Life while Simultaneously
Preparing for the Blow of Death!**

CHILDREN OF THE MOST HIGH:
PRISTINE YOUTH AND FAMILY SOLUTIONS, LLC.
SONS AND DAUGHTERS OF THE MOST HIGH PUBLISHERS ®

OH, GRACIOUS MOST HIGH HEAVENLY FATHER, HOLY IS YOUR
NAME, YOUR WILL BE DONE NOW AND FOREVER!

Let's further examine the word **ruwh** (روح) in Arabic from the root **raaha** (راح), which means: *"it was violently windy"*.

Other derivatives are:

reeh	ريح	(n.) wind, fart, smell, odor
rayyah	ريح	(adj.) a gentle wind
ruwh	روح	(n.) breath of life, soul
al ruwhul quwdus	الريح القدوس	(n.) the holy soul

And in Hebrew the root of **ruwach** (רוח) means, *"to blow, breathe."*

SPIRITUAL TRILLIONAIRE:
**Cherishing the Breath of Life while Simultaneously
Preparing for the Blow of Death!**

CHILDREN OF THE MOST HIGH:
PRISTINE YOUTH AND FAMILY SOLUTIONS, LLC.
SONS AND DAUGHTERS OF THE MOST HIGH PUBLISHERS ®

OH, GRACIOUS MOST HIGH HEAVENLY FATHER, HOLY IS YOUR
NAME, YOUR WILL BE DONE NOW AND FOREVER!

Other derivatives are:

Ruwach	(רוּחַ)	*mind, spirit, wind.*
Ruwach	(רוּחַ)	*wind, by resemblance breath, a sensible (or even violent) exhalation; life, anger, unsubstantiality;* ***a region in the sky;*** *by resemblance spirit, but only of a rational being (its expression and functions): air, anger, blast, breath, cool, courage, mind, quarter, side, spirit, tempest, vain,* ***(whirl wind).***

Is there a difference between soul and spirit? Yes.

What is the difference between spirit and soul?

SPIRITUAL TRILLIONAIRE:
Cherishing the Breath of Life while Simultaneously
Preparing for the Blow of Death!

OH, GRACIOUS MOST HIGH HEAVENLY FATHER, HOLY IS YOUR
NAME, YOUR WILL BE DONE NOW AND FOREVER!

In the King James Bible Greek Strong's Concordance #4151, is the word: "**Pneuma πνεῦμα (Spirit)**". The original Greek word for "**Spirit**" is "***Pneuma***" (pronounced as: pnyoo' - mah); meaning: a movement of air (a gentle blast), of the wind, hence the wind itself; breath of nostrils or mouth.

In the King James Bible Greek Strong's Concordance #5590, the word: **Soul** is: ψυχή psyché, pronounced as psoo-khay'; meaning:

1. Soul, Life Mind;
2. the breath of life
3. the vital force which animates the body and shows itself in breathing
4. of animals
5. of men or human beings

1. life

2. that in which there is life
    1. a living being, a living soul

181

SPIRITUAL TRILLIONAIRE:
Cherishing the Breath of Life while Simultaneously
Preparing for the Blow of Death!

CHILDREN OF THE MOST HIGH:
PRISTINE YOUTH AND FAMILY SOLUTIONS, LLC.
SONS AND DAUGHTERS OF THE MOST HIGH PUBLISHERS ®

OH, GRACIOUS MOST HIGH HEAVENLY FATHER, HOLY IS YOUR
NAME, YOUR WILL BE DONE NOW AND FOREVER!

3. the seat of the feelings, desires, affections, aversions (our heart, soul etc.).

4. The (human) soul in so far as it is constituted that by the right use of the aids offered it by God it can attain its highest end and secure eternal blessedness, the soul regarded as a moral being designed for everlasting life.

5. The soul as an essence which differs from the body and is not dissolved by death (distinguished from other parts of the body).

As you can see from the aforementioned KJV bible book of Genesis chapter 1 verse 2 with Hebrew inserts, in the KJV bible Hebrew Strong's Concordance, the Aramic (Hebrew) word **"Rooakh"** (**Ruwh** in Arabic and **soul** in English) is translated in English as **"spirit"**, and Hebrew word **"Nefesh"** (**spirit**) is translated for the word **"soul"**. So, an in-depth research of the **Original Aramic** (Hebrew) words **Rooakh (soul)** and **Nefesh** (**spirit**) in the **Aramaic** (Hebrew) language would clear up the confusion of the mistranslation of these two words that are so frequently used interchangeably.

SPIRITUAL TRILLIONAIRE:
Cherishing the Breath of Life while Simultaneously
Preparing for the Blow of Death!

CHILDREN OF THE MOST HIGH:
PRISTINE YOUTH AND FAMILY SOLUTIONS, LLC.
SONS AND DAUGHTERS OF THE MOST HIGH PUBLISHERS ®

OH, GRACIOUS MOST HIGH HEAVENLY FATHER, HOLY IS YOUR
NAME, YOUR WILL BE DONE NOW AND FOREVER!

The physical body is the shell for the spirit and the soul. The spirit is the shell for the soul. The spirit is the life body, and the soul is the emotionally **etheric** body. The soul (**emotional body**) allows a person the ability to respond emotionally to needs of humanity in a way that reflects moral integrity. The soul is the essence that connects the mind or mental flow to the spiritual world. The etheric body is ether. Ether is a combination of all existing gases of nature or in other words, your soul (**etheric body**) is energy.

Why is it important to take the time to research our English translations of the bible, word by word in the original languages (Tongues, KJV bible book of Acts chapter 2 verses 7-8) they were revealed in?

That is an excellent question! The Messiah Yashu'a (Jesus) said in the KJV bible book of Matthews chapter 24 verses 4-5; states: "Take heed (*βλέπω blepō*, is the KJV bible Greek Strong's Concordance #991word: βλέπω **blepō**, which means *be aware of) that no man* (τις **tis**, is the KJV bible Greek Strong's Concordance #5100 word: τις **tis**, which means **any one, inclusive of all people regardless of gender**) deceive

SPIRITUAL TRILLIONAIRE:
**Cherishing the Breath of Life while Simultaneously
Preparing for the Blow of Death!**

**OH, GRACIOUS MOST HIGH HEAVENLY FATHER, HOLY IS YOUR
NAME, YOUR WILL BE DONE NOW AND FOREVER!**

you." The Messiah Yashu'a (Jesus) also said in the KJV bible book of John chapter 8 verse 32;

"And ye shall know the truth, and the truth shall make you free." "**Ye shall know**" (γινώσκω **ginōskō**, is the KJV bible Greek Strong's Concordance #1097word: γινώσκω **ginōskō**, which means **to know**, **understand**, **perceive**). The word "**translation**" means the act or process of translating, especially from one language into another. So, in order to ensure that sincere-hearted people who have accepted the real Messiah Yashu'a (Jesus) as their Savior are **not being deceived** by modern day mistranslations of the bible, and to ensure that they **know the truth**; we must make the time to do intense, evidence-based, non-bias, rigorous research into the original languages that the bible and other scriptures were revealed in. This process can begin for a person by utilizing 21st century free online Hebrew and Greek Languages Strong's Concordances, Lexicons, http://www.eliyah.com/lexicon.html, and **free cell phone Bible Hub KJV Strong's Exhaustive Concordance of the Bible app**.

SPIRITUAL TRILLIONAIRE:
Cherishing the Breath of Life while Simultaneously
Preparing for the Blow of Death!

CHILDREN OF THE MOST HIGH:
PRISTINE YOUTH AND FAMILY SOLUTIONS, LLC.
SONS AND DAUGHTERS OF THE MOST HIGH PUBLISHERS ®

OH, GRACIOUS MOST HIGH HEAVENLY FATHER, HOLY IS YOUR
NAME, YOUR WILL BE DONE NOW AND FOREVER!

This on-going process of studying the bible and other scriptures, word by word in the original languages they were revealed in, may help prevent the sincere-hearted truth seeker from being capable of being deceived by mistranslations, blind faith, and nonconfirmed beliefs with no substantiated facts.

In the KJV bible book of 2nd Timothy chapter 2 verse 15; it states: "**Study to shew thyself approved unto God**, a workman that needeth not to be ashamed, rightly dividing the word of truth,"

According to the Children of the Most High: Pristine Youth and Family Solutions, LLC., the most beneficial bible study consists of studying the bible, word by word in the original languages it was revealed in to be capable of receiving the original message and original messages that were sent to members of humanity for guidance. This book utilizes the King James Version (KJV) of the Bible verses. Why? According to www.christiantoday.com, the King James Version of the Bible is the most widely used English translation in the world (Ong, 2016).

SPIRITUAL TRILLIONAIRE:
Cherishing the Breath of Life while Simultaneously
Preparing for the Blow of Death!

CHILDREN OF THE MOST HIGH:
PRISTINE YOUTH AND FAMILY SOLUTIONS, LLC.
SONS AND DAUGHTERS OF THE MOST HIGH PUBLISHERS ®

OH, GRACIOUS MOST HIGH HEAVENLY FATHER, HOLY IS YOUR
NAME, YOUR WILL BE DONE NOW AND FOREVER!

Therefore, the Children of the Most High: Pristine Youth and Family Solutions, LLC. utilize the Hebrew-Greek Key Word Study King James Version of the Bible and Strong's Concordance to start with the English translation, in the process of researching the original words and meanings from the original languages that the Bible was revealed in. This ensures that all readers receive the original message or messages and information that the Elohiym (God) intended for members of humanity to receive, and this also helps to eliminate misinformation.

So, for many of us that read and speak English only, we must remember that the English language, the Greek language, the Latin Language, and may other languages did not exist when the 1st Testament (the Old Testament) was revealed and the English language did not exist when the 2nd Testament (the New Testament) was revealed.

SPIRITUAL TRILLIONAIRE:
Cherishing the Breath of Life while Simultaneously
Preparing for the Blow of Death!

CHILDREN OF THE MOST HIGH:
PRISTINE YOUTH AND FAMILY SOLUTIONS, LLC.
SONS AND DAUGHTERS OF THE MOST HIGH PUBLISHERS ®

OH, GRACIOUS MOST HIGH HEAVENLY FATHER, HOLY IS YOUR
NAME, YOUR WILL BE DONE NOW AND FOREVER!

Yashu'a (Jesus) said in the KJV bible book of John chapter 8 verse 32; "Ye (you) shall know the truth and the truth shall make you free, (however, this only applies to those who take the time to learn the Most High's truth, accept it and apply it in all that they do)." Yashu'a (Jesus) also said in the KJV bible book of John chapter 13 verse 20: "Verily, verily, I say unto you, he that receiveth whomsoever I send receiveth me; and he that receiveth me receiveth him that sent me."

What does the word "Genesis" mean?

The translated word "**Genesis**" is from the **Greek word GHEN-NAY-SIS** meaning: "the very beginning." **Why would an Aramic/Hebrew bible have translated Greek names for their chapters if those translated chapters were not influenced by the Greeks? And is it possible that the Greek influences on an Aramic/Hebrew bible, may have been inclusive of some bias?**

The word "Genesis" is **Ghen'nay-Sis**, from **Genos, Ghen-Os**, meaning: **particular kind or kindred**; **Gennao** means: "**To Procreate**" of a father by extension of a mother, the word

SPIRITUAL TRILLIONAIRE:
Cherishing the Breath of Life while Simultaneously
Preparing for the Blow of Death!

CHILDREN OF THE MOST HIGH:
PRISTINE YOUTH AND FAMILY SOLUTIONS, LLC.
SONS AND DAUGHTERS OF THE MOST HIGH PUBLISHERS ®

OH, GRACIOUS MOST HIGH HEAVENLY FATHER, HOLY IS YOUR
NAME, YOUR WILL BE DONE NOW AND FOREVER!

Genealogia and **Genealogeo** means: "Tracing by Generations", making **Genesis a book of Generations**.

In the KJV book of the bible **Genesis chapter 2 verse 4**; it states with Hebrew inserts:

אֵלֶּה תוֹלְדוֹת הַשָּׁמַיִם וְהָאָרֶץ בְּהִבָּרְאָם בְּיוֹם עֲשׂוֹת יְהוָה אֱלֹהִים אֶרֶץ 2:4
וְשָׁמָיִם:

"These אֵלֶּה 'el-leh are <u>the generations תוֹלְדוֹת towlĕdah of the heavens שָׁמַיִם shamayim and of the earth אֶרֶץ 'erets</u> when they were created בָּרָא bara' (Khalaq) in the day יוֹם yowm that the **Yĕhovah** יְהוָה LORD **Elohiym** אֱלֹהִים God made עָשָׂה 'asah the earth אֶרֶץ 'erets and the heavens שָׁמַיִם shamayim." The **Aramic/Hebrew** word: "תוֹלְדוֹת *towlĕdah*" is the KJV bible Hebrew Strong's Concordance **#8435**, and it means: birth, descendants, results, proceedings, generations, genealogies, account of men and their descendants, genealogical list of one's descendants, one's contemporaries, course of history (of creation etc.), begetting in reference to replenishment, not creation; of the generations or births of the heavens and the earth.

188

SPIRITUAL TRILLIONAIRE:
Cherishing the Breath of Life while Simultaneously
Preparing for the Blow of Death!

CHILDREN OF THE MOST HIGH:
PRISTINE YOUTH AND FAMILY SOLUTIONS, LLC.
SONS AND DAUGHTERS OF THE MOST HIGH PUBLISHERS ®

OH, GRACIOUS MOST HIGH HEAVENLY FATHER, HOLY IS YOUR
NAME, YOUR WILL BE DONE NOW AND FOREVER!

תּוֹלְדֹת f. pl. (from the root יָלַד)—(1) *genera-tions, families, races,* Nu. 1:20, seqq. לְתוֹלְדֹתָם according to their races, Gen. 10:32; 25:13; Exod. 6:16. Hence סֵפֶר תּוֹלְדֹת genealogy, pedigree, Gen. 5:1. As a very large portion of the most ancient Oriental history consists of genealogies, it means—

(2) *history,* properly of families. Gen. 6:9, אֵלֶּה תּוֹלְדֹת נֹחַ "this is the history of Noah." Genesis 37:2; and thus also applied to the *origin* of other things. Gen. 2:4, " this is the origin of the heaven and earth." (Compare יָחַשׂ and Syr. ܫܲܪܒܬܐ family, genealogy, history.)

What is the difference between the **original Aramic/Hebrew** words: **Barashiyth** or **Barasheeth** or **Rashiyth** or **Ray-Sheeth** and **Khalaqa**?

The Original Aramic (Hebrew) name of the 1st Book of the Bible is: "**Barashiyth**" sometimes spelled: "**Rashiyth or Ray-Sheeth**" and in Aramic/Hebrew, it means: "**Re-Create, Pro-Create, Re-Construction, not to be confused with the original Aramic/Hebrew word: "Khalaqa**" which means **creation or creation period**. In the **Ashuric Syriac (Arabic)**, the word: "**Khalaq**" means **to create**.

SPIRITUAL TRILLIONAIRE:
Cherishing the Breath of Life while Simultaneously Preparing for the Blow of Death!

CHILDREN OF THE MOST HIGH:
PRISTINE YOUTH AND FAMILY SOLUTIONS, LLC.
SONS AND DAUGHTERS OF THE MOST HIGH PUBLISHERS ®

OH, GRACIOUS MOST HIGH HEAVENLY FATHER, HOLY IS YOUR
NAME, YOUR WILL BE DONE NOW AND FOREVER!

In the **Aramic/Hebrew** language, the word: "**Genesis**" is "**Barashiyth** or **Barasheeth**" is from the root word: "**Bara**" and means: "To **re**construct or **re**construction" not to be confused with the **original Aramic/Hebrew word: "Khalaqa"** which means **creation or creation period**.

Barasheeth (בראשית) Comes From The Root Word Roshe (ראש)

Meaning *"The Head, Beginning, Captain, Chief, First, Forefront"*.

In the KJV bible book of Proverbs chapter 8 verse 23 with Hebrew inserts; it states:

8:23 מֵעוֹלָם נִסַּכְתִּי מֵרֹאשׁ מִקַּדְמֵי־אָרֶץ׃

"I was set up נָסַךְ **nacak** from everlasting עוֹלָם `**owlam** from the **beginning** רֹאשׁ **ro'she** or ever קֶדֶם **qedem** the earth אָרֶץ **'erets** was."

190

SPIRITUAL TRILLIONAIRE:
**Cherishing the Breath of Life while Simultaneously
Preparing for the Blow of Death!**

CHILDREN OF THE MOST HIGH:
PRISTINE YOUTH AND FAMILY SOLUTIONS, LLC.
SONS AND DAUGHTERS OF THE MOST HIGH PUBLISHERS ®

OH, GRACIOUS MOST HIGH HEAVENLY FATHER, HOLY IS YOUR
NAME, YOUR WILL BE DONE NOW AND FOREVER!

In the English language, the prefix: "**Re**" means to do again in comparison from the original Aramic (Hebrew) name of the 1st Book of the Bible is: "**Barashiyth**" from the root word: **Bara** which means: "**Re-construction**" and does not mean "**Khalaqa**", which is the **original Aramic/Hebrew** word that means **creation or creation period**.

In the KJV bible book of Genesis chapter 1 verse 28 with Hebrew inserts; it states:

1:28 וַיְבָרֶךְ אֹתָם אֱלֹהִים וַיֹּאמֶר לָהֶם אֱלֹהִים פְּרוּ וּרְבוּ וּמִלְאוּ אֶת־הָאָרֶץ וְכִבְשֻׁהָ וּרְדוּ בִּדְגַת הַיָּם וּבְעוֹף הַשָּׁמַיִם וּבְכָל־חַיָּה הָרֹמֶשֶׂת עַל־הָאָרֶץ׃

"And **Elohiym** אֱלֹהִים God blessed them בָּרַךְ **barak** and **Elohiym** אֱלֹהִים God said אָמַר **'amar** unto them, be fruitful פָּרָה **parah** and multiply רָבָה **rabah** and **replenish** מָלֵא **maw-lay'** the earth אֶרֶץ **'erets** and subdue it כָּבַשׁ **kabash** and have dominion רָדָה **radah** over the fish דָּגָה **dagah** of the sea יָם **yam** and over the fowl עוֹף **'owph** of the air שָׁמַיִם **shamayim** and over every living thing חַי **khay or chay** that moveth רָמַשׂ **ramas** upon the earth אֶרֶץ **'erets**."

191

SPIRITUAL TRILLIONAIRE:
Cherishing the Breath of Life while Simultaneously
Preparing for the Blow of Death!

CHILDREN OF THE MOST HIGH:
PRISTINE YOUTH AND FAMILY SOLUTIONS, LLC.
SONS AND DAUGHTERS OF THE MOST HIGH PUBLISHERS ®

OH, GRACIOUS MOST HIGH HEAVENLY FATHER, HOLY IS YOUR
NAME, YOUR WILL BE DONE NOW AND FOREVER!

"And God blessed them, and God said unto them, be fruitful, and multiply, and "**re-plenish**" the earth, and subdue it: and have dominion over the fish of the sea, and over the fowl of the air, and over every living thing that moveth upon the earth."

The Aramic/Hebrew word used for **re-plenish** in the King James Version of the bible is the word is: "**MAW-LAY**" which means to **Re-Plenish** or **Re-Fill**: **For example:** If you were at a restaurant and you had a very good tasting lemonade that you drank up, you may ask the waiter or waitress if you can have a **Re-fill** on your lemonade. You can't **re-fill** or **re-plenish** something that was not already once filled or plenish. According to the KJV bible book of Genesis chapter 1 verse 28, Adam and Eve had to **re-fill** or **re-plenish** the earth (Genesis 1:28).

So, according to the aforementioned KJV bible verse, the biblical Adam and Eve; contrary to what many have been taught and continue to teach and preach; the biblical Adam and Eve were not the first people on the planet earth and nowhere in the KJV bible book of Genesis Chapter 1 does it state that Adam

SPIRITUAL TRILLIONAIRE:
Cherishing the Breath of Life while Simultaneously
Preparing for the Blow of Death!

CHILDREN OF THE MOST HIGH:
PRISTINE YOUTH AND FAMILY SOLUTIONS, LLC.
SONS AND DAUGHTERS OF THE MOST HIGH PUBLISHERS ®

OH, GRACIOUS MOST HIGH HEAVENLY FATHER, HOLY IS YOUR
NAME, YOUR WILL BE DONE NOW AND FOREVER!

and Eve were the first people on the planet. So, where did that concept come from?

It came from a lack of understanding, misinterpretation and mistranslation of the book of Genesis from the Aramic/Hebrew into the English language. **Another point**: You have **Adam, Eve, Cain** and **Abel. Cain** kills **Abel**; that leaves **Adam, Eve** and **Cain** which **= 3 people**; so, **who was Cain worried about who might slay or kill him in the KJV bible book of Genesis chapter 4 verse 14 if there was no one else on the planet other than him and his parents?** Where did the beings that Cain was worried about who might kill him **and who were already living in the land of Nod come from if there was no one else on the planet? And where did Cain get his wife in the KJV bible book of Genesis chapter 4 verse 17 if there was no one else on the planet? ANSWER**: The great dragon, that old serpent, called the devil and satan and his angels (messengers) were the original inhabitants of the Land of Nod. The KJV bible book of Revelation chapter 12 verses 7-9; states: "And there was war in heaven: Michael and his angels fought against the dragon; and the dragon fought and his angels, and prevailed not; neither was their place found any more in heaven.

193

SPIRITUAL TRILLIONAIRE:
Cherishing the Breath of Life while Simultaneously
Preparing for the Blow of Death!

CHILDREN OF THE MOST HIGH:
PRISTINE YOUTH AND FAMILY SOLUTIONS, LLC.
SONS AND DAUGHTERS OF THE MOST HIGH PUBLISHERS ®

OH, GRACIOUS MOST HIGH HEAVENLY FATHER, HOLY IS YOUR
NAME, YOUR WILL BE DONE NOW AND FOREVER!

And the great dragon was cast out, that old serpent, called the
Devil, and Satan, which deceiveth the whole world: he was cast
out **into the earth, and his angels were cast out with him**.''

**So, in the KJV bible book of Genesis Chapter 1 verse 1, is
God singular or plural?**

**KJV bible book of Genesis Chapter 1 verse 1 with Hebrew
inserts; it states: 1:1** בְּרֵאשִׁית בָּרָא אֱלֹהִים אֵת הַשָּׁמַיִם וְאֵת הָאָרֶץ:

In the beginning רֵאשִׁית re'shiyth God (**KJV bible Hebrew
Strong's Concordance#430**) אֱלֹהִים 'elohiym created בָּרָא
bara' (Khalaq) the heaven שָׁמַיִם shamayim and אֵת 'eth the
earth אֶרֶץ 'erets.

In the KJV bible book of Genesis Chapter 1 verse 1, the
original Aramic/Hebrew plural word "Elohiym" was
translated into the **English singular word: "God"**. According
to the "King James Bible Hebrew Strong's Concordance: **#430
"Elohiym"** (God) is the **original Aramic/Hebrew word**:
אֱלֹהִים, Phonetic Spelling: (El-o-heem'), is a **Plural** word that
means: (1), Gods (204), great (2), judges (3), mighty (2), rulers

194

SPIRITUAL TRILLIONAIRE:
**Cherishing the Breath of Life while Simultaneously
Preparing for the Blow of Death!**

CHILDREN OF THE MOST HIGH:
PRISTINE YOUTH AND FAMILY SOLUTIONS, LLC.
SONS AND DAUGHTERS OF THE MOST HIGH PUBLISHERS ®

OH, GRACIOUS MOST HIGH HEAVENLY FATHER, HOLY IS YOUR
NAME, YOUR WILL BE DONE NOW AND FOREVER!

(1), shrine* (1). **plural in number**. a. rulers, judges, either as divine representatives at sacred places or as reflecting divine majesty and power: b. divine ones, superhuman beings."

As the aforementioned reflects, **the correct translation** of Genesis Chapter 1 verse 1 **would be**: In the beginning, the **Gods** created the heavens and the earth. **Those** or **these beings**; "**Gods**" are part of the Most High Heavenly Father's Guardian-Angelic Hosts.

It is one of the Children of the Most High: Pristine Youth and Family Solutions, LLC. greatest hopes that members of humanity will now be aware that by studying the scriptures in the languages that they were revealed in, it can empower the sincere-hearted person by them being able to receive the original messages in the scriptures that he or she was intended to receive. In KJV bible book of Psalms chapter 82 verse 1 with Hebrew inserts; it states:

82:1 מִזְמוֹר לְאָסָף אֱלֹהִים נִצָּב בַּעֲדַת־אֵל בְּקֶרֶב אֱלֹהִים יִשְׁפֹּט:

God (KJV bible Hebrew Strong's Concordance#430 אֱלֹהִים **'Elohiym**, plural) standeth in the congregation

195

SPIRITUAL TRILLIONAIRE:
**Cherishing the Breath of Life while Simultaneously
Preparing for the Blow of Death!**

CHILDREN OF THE MOST HIGH:
PRISTINE YOUTH AND FAMILY SOLUTIONS, LLC.
SONS AND DAUGHTERS OF THE MOST HIGH PUBLISHERS ®

OH, GRACIOUS MOST HIGH HEAVENLY FATHER, HOLY IS YOUR
NAME, YOUR WILL BE DONE NOW AND FOREVER!

עֵדָה `edah of the mighty אֵל 'el he judgeth שָׁפַט shaphat among קֶרֶב qereb the gods (KJV bible Hebrew Strong's Concordance#430 אֱלֹהִים 'elohiym, plural).

In the previous KJV bible book of Psalms chapter 82 verse 1, the Aramic/Hebrew word for "God" and "gods" is the same Aramic/Hebrew word: "**Elohiym אֱלֹהִים**" it states: "**God**" standeth in the congregation of the mighty; he judgeth among the "**gods**" (being that the words "**God**" and "**gods**" in this verse is translated from the exact same original Aramic/Hebrew word: "**Elohiym אֱלֹהִים**"; let's look at this word in the Aramic/Hebrew language. The KJV bible Hebrew Strong's Concordance#430 word for "**God**" and "**gods**" is "**Elohiym**" which is a plural. **The truth is that there are no lower-case letters in the Hebrew language, so everywhere you see a small "g"; it is incorrect and may lead the sincere-hearted truth seeker astray.** The **Thayer Greek Lexicon** equivalent to the Aramic/Hebrew "**Elohiym**" (Gods) is Theos (Gods) as used in KJV bible book of John chapter 10 verse 34. **Also, there are no lower-case letters in the Greek language, so everywhere you see a small "g"; it is incorrect and may lead the sincere-hearted truth seeker astray.**

196

SPIRITUAL TRILLIONAIRE:
Cherishing the Breath of Life while Simultaneously
Preparing for the Blow of Death!

CHILDREN OF THE MOST HIGH:
PRISTINE YOUTH AND FAMILY SOLUTIONS, LLC.
SONS AND DAUGHTERS OF THE MOST HIGH PUBLISHERS ®

OH, GRACIOUS MOST HIGH HEAVENLY FATHER, HOLY IS YOUR
NAME, YOUR WILL BE DONE NOW AND FOREVER!

Did the words "God, Lord and Jesus" exist in the original Aramic Language of the Bible?

As many of us read the English translations of the bible, it is critical to our growth that we remember that the 1st Testament called **the "Old Testament was revealed in the Aramic language at a time when the English language, the Greek language and the Latin Language did not exist.**

This means that in the original Aramic language, that words such as: **God, GOD, god, Lord, LORD GOD, Christ,** and **Jesus** did not exist. **However, even though the name Jesus did not and does not exist in the original Aramic or modern Hebrew language, the name: "Yashu'a" did exist, and Lower-case letters do not exist in the Aramic (Hebrew) and Greek languages of the bible.**

SPIRITUAL TRILLIONAIRE:
**Cherishing the Breath of Life while Simultaneously
Preparing for the Blow of Death!**

CHILDREN OF THE MOST HIGH:
PRISTINE YOUTH AND FAMILY SOLUTIONS, LLC.
SONS AND DAUGHTERS OF THE MOST HIGH PUBLISHERS ®

OH, GRACIOUS MOST HIGH HEAVENLY FATHER, HOLY IS YOUR
NAME, YOUR WILL BE DONE NOW AND FOREVER!

Why does this matter? This matters' because you cannot be spiritually healthy or attain positive spiritual health and positive spiritual wealth while being infected by the **Deadly Venoms of Lying and Wickedness** which are the root causes of intentional **real lies (realized)** misinterpretations of the original languages that the bible was revealed in. This also matters to sincere-hearted people who only want to learn the non-bias original messages that are in the original language that the bible was revealed in. This is necessary, in an effort to acquire the original messages that the Elohiym (God) intended on us receiving before the original biblical scriptures, were translated hundreds or more times differently than in the original languages they were revealed in. This also matters to the real followers of **Yashu'a Ha Mashiakh (Jesus the Messiah)** because he said in the KJV bible book of John chapter 8 verse 32: "And ye shall know the truth, and the truth shall make you free." "**Ye shall know**" (γινώσκω **ginōskō,** is KJV bible Greek Strong's Concordance#1097 word: γινώσκω **ginōskō,** which means **to know, understand, perceive**).

The word "**translation**" means the act or process of translating, especially from one language into another. So, in order to

198

SPIRITUAL TRILLIONAIRE:
Cherishing the Breath of Life while Simultaneously
Preparing for the Blow of Death!

CHILDREN OF THE MOST HIGH:
PRISTINE YOUTH AND FAMILY SOLUTIONS, LLC.
SONS AND DAUGHTERS OF THE MOST HIGH PUBLISHERS ®

OH, GRACIOUS MOST HIGH HEAVENLY FATHER, HOLY IS YOUR
NAME, YOUR WILL BE DONE NOW AND FOREVER!

ensure that sincere-hearted people who have accepted the real Messiah Yashu'a (Jesus) as their Savior are **not being <u>deceived</u>** by modern day mistranslations of the bible, and to ensure that they **<u>know the truth</u>**; we must make the time to do intense, evidence-based, non-bias, rigorous research into the original languages that the bible and other scriptures were revealed in. In other words, sincere-hearted people who have accepted the real Messiah Yashu'a (Jesus) as their Savior have to study the bible from a **Messiah con<u>scio</u>usness** and **Spirit of the Messiah Yashu'a** (Jesus) **<u>scien</u>ce** of the seen and unseen perspective in order **<u>to know</u> <u>the truth that will make you free</u>**. According to the Online American Heritage Dictionary (2019), science is defined as:

sci·ence - (sī'əns)
[From Middle English, knowledge, learning, from Old French, from Latin *scientia*, from *sciēn, scient-*, present participle of *scīre*, <u>to know</u>; from the root word **scio** – <u>**to know**</u>;

*n.***1. a.** The observation, identification, description, experimental investigation, and theoretical explanation of phenomena: *new advances in science and technology.*

SPIRITUAL TRILLIONAIRE:
**Cherishing the Breath of Life while Simultaneously
Preparing for the Blow of Death!**

CHILDREN OF THE MOST HIGH:
PRISTINE YOUTH AND FAMILY SOLUTIONS, LLC.
SONS AND DAUGHTERS OF THE MOST HIGH PUBLISHERS ®

OH, GRACIOUS MOST HIGH HEAVENLY FATHER, HOLY IS YOUR
NAME, YOUR WILL BE DONE NOW AND FOREVER!

b. Such activities restricted to a class of natural phenomena: *the science of astronomy.*

2. A systematic method or body of knowledge in a given area: *the science of marketing.*

3. *Archaic* Knowledge, especially that gained through experience.

According to the Latdict, Latin dictionary and grammar resources (2016), **SCIO** is defined as a: verb: **know**, **understand;** So, according to the aforementioned, sincere-hearted people who have accepted the real Messiah Yashu'a (Jesus) as their Savior have to study the bible from a **Messiah** con**scio**usness and **Spirit of the Messiah Yashu'a** (Jesus) **scien**ce of the seen and unseen perspective in order **to know the truth that will make you free**.

Now, members of humanity have an opportunity to utilize the Hebrew-Greek Key Word Study King James Version of the Bible and Strong's Concordance to research the bible, word by word in the original languages they were revealed in.

200

SPIRITUAL TRILLIONAIRE:
**Cherishing the Breath of Life while Simultaneously
Preparing for the Blow of Death!**

CHILDREN OF THE MOST HIGH:
PRISTINE YOUTH AND FAMILY SOLUTIONS, LLC.
SONS AND DAUGHTERS OF THE MOST HIGH PUBLISHERS

OH, GRACIOUS MOST HIGH HEAVENLY FATHER, HOLY IS YOUR
NAME, YOUR WILL BE DONE NOW AND FOREVER!

This may lead to members of humanity learning and knowing the truth that will make them free just as the Messiah Yashu'a (Jesus) said that it would. This process is essential for those who seek to acquire, maintain or sustain positive spiritual health and positive spiritual wealth on the path to becoming a Spiritual Trillionaire.

~OH, MOST HIGH HEAVENLY FATHER, PLEASE GUIDE
US TO LEARN, KNOW AND APPLY YOUR KINGDOM
DOCTRINE KNOWLEDGE IN ALL THAT YOU ALLOW US TO
DO IN A MANNER THAT ONLY REFLECTS YOUR WILL
BEING DONE, NOW AND FOREVER. AMEN~

SPIRITUAL TRILLIONAIRE:
Cherishing the Breath of Life while Simultaneously
Preparing for the Blow of Death!

CHILDREN OF THE MOST HIGH:
PRISTINE YOUTH AND FAMILY SOLUTIONS, LLC.
SONS AND DAUGHTERS OF THE MOST HIGH PUBLISHERS

OH, GRACIOUS MOST HIGH HEAVENLY FATHER, HOLY IS YOUR
NAME, YOUR WILL BE DONE NOW AND FOREVER!

Chapter 7: What is a Spiritual Trillionaire?

~OH, MOST HIGH HEAVENLY FATHER, PLEASE GUIDE
US TO WORK TO ACQUIRE, MAINTAIN AND SUSTAIN
POSITIVE SPIRITUAL HEALTH AND POSITIVE SPIRITUAL
WEALTH ONLY IN ACCORDANCE TO WHAT THAT MEANS
TO YOU, NOW AND FOREVER. AMEN~

SPIRITUAL TRILLIONAIRE:
Cherishing the Breath of Life while Simultaneously
Preparing for the Blow of Death!

CHILDREN OF THE MOST HIGH:
PRISTINE YOUTH AND FAMILY SOLUTIONS, LLC.
SONS AND DAUGHTERS OF THE MOST HIGH PUBLISHERS ®

OH, GRACIOUS MOST HIGH HEAVENLY FATHER, HOLY IS YOUR
NAME, YOUR WILL BE DONE NOW AND FOREVER!

What is a Spiritual Trillionaire?

In the "King James Bible Greek Strong's Concordance #4151 is the word for "**spirit**" which is: "**Pneuma πνεῦμα (Spirit)**". The original Greek word for "**Spirit**" is "*Pneuma*" (pronounced as: pnyoo' - mah); means: a movement of air (a gentle blast), of the wind, hence the wind itself; breath of nostrils or mouth. In the **original Aramic/Hebrew**, the word: "**Nefesh**, pronounced as: **Neh-Fesh**, means: "**spirit**", and in the **original Aramic/Hebrew** word: "**Rooahk**, pronounce as **Roo-Akh**, means: **Soul**."

SPIRITUAL TRILLIONAIRE:
Cherishing the Breath of Life while Simultaneously
Preparing for the Blow of Death!

CHILDREN OF THE MOST HIGH:
PRISTINE YOUTH AND FAMILY SOLUTIONS, LLC.
SONS AND DAUGHTERS OF THE MOST HIGH PUBLISHERS ®

OH, GRACIOUS MOST HIGH HEAVENLY FATHER, HOLY IS YOUR
NAME, YOUR WILL BE DONE NOW AND FOREVER!

However, in the English translation of the KJV of the bible and other bibles, spirit, soul and mind are sometimes utilized interchangeably like in the KJV of the bible book of Genesis chapter 1 verse 2 and Genesis chapter 2 verse 7 as seen below with Hebrew inserts:

The KJV bible book of Genesis chapter 1 verse 2 with Hebrew inserts:

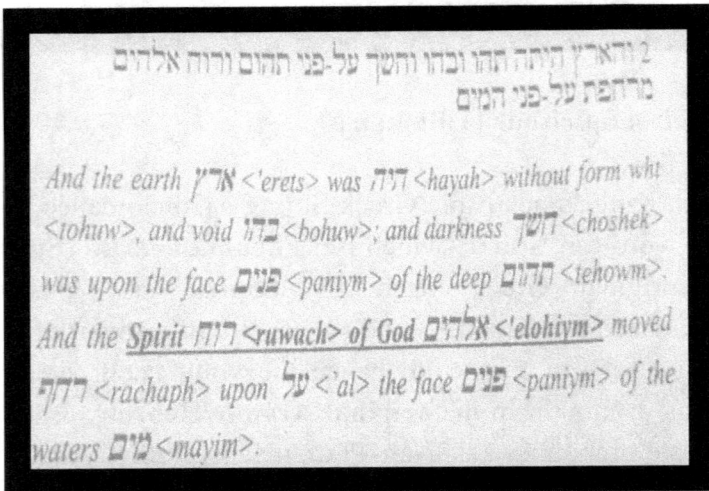

And the earth ץֶרֶא <'erets> was הָיָה <hayah> without form wht <tohuw>, and void וּהֹב <bohuw>; and darkness ךֶשֹׁח <choshek> was upon the face םיִנָפ <paniym> of the deep םוֹהְת <tehowm>. And the Spirit ַחוּר <ruwach> of God םיִהֹלֱא <'elohiym> moved ףַחָר <rachaph> upon לַע <'al> the face םיִנָפ <paniym> of the waters םִיַמ <mayim>.

SPIRITUAL TRILLIONAIRE:
**Cherishing the Breath of Life while Simultaneously
Preparing for the Blow of Death!**

CHILDREN OF THE MOST HIGH:
PRISTINE YOUTH AND FAMILY SOLUTIONS, LLC.
SONS AND DAUGHTERS OF THE MOST HIGH PUBLISHERS ®

OH, GRACIOUS MOST HIGH HEAVENLY FATHER, HOLY IS YOUR
NAME, YOUR WILL BE DONE NOW AND FOREVER!

The KJV bible book of Genesis chapter 2 verse 7 with Hebrew inserts:

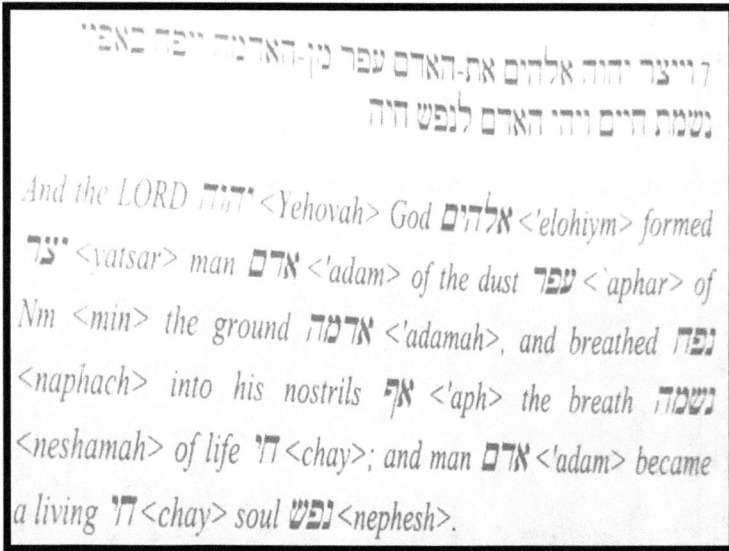

In the KJV bible book of Genesis chapter 1 verse 2; it states: "And the earth was without form, and void; and darkness was upon the face of the deep. And the Spirit of God moved upon the face of the waters."

CHILDREN OF THE MOST HIGH:
PRISTINE YOUTH AND FAMILY SOLUTIONS, LLC.
SONS AND DAUGHTERS OF THE MOST HIGH PUBLISHERS ®

OH, GRACIOUS MOST HIGH HEAVENLY FATHER, HOLY IS YOUR NAME, YOUR WILL BE DONE NOW AND FOREVER!

In the KJV bible book of Genesis chapter 2 verse 7; it states: "And the Lord God formed man of the dust of the ground, and breathed into his nostrils the breath of life; and man became a living soul." So, according to the previous verses, the connection occurred when the Yehovah (LORD) Elohiym (God) breathed the **Khay** or **Hayy (Neshamaw Khayyeem** נשמה חיים - Divine Breath of Life) into the nostrils of Adam (man) and Adam became a **Nephesh Khay** which in the Aramic (Hebrew) language, **Nephesh** is "**Spirit**".

SPIRITUAL TRILLIONAIRE:
Cherishing the Breath of Life while Simultaneously
Preparing for the Blow of Death!

CHILDREN OF THE MOST HIGH:
PRISTINE YOUTH AND FAMILY SOLUTIONS, LLC.
SONS AND DAUGHTERS OF THE MOST HIGH PUBLISHERS ®

OH, GRACIOUS MOST HIGH HEAVENLY FATHER, HOLY IS YOUR
NAME, YOUR WILL BE DONE NOW AND FOREVER!

According to the Online American Heritage Dictionary (2019),
trillionaire is defined as:

trill·lion·aire - (trĭll′yə-nâr', trĭll′yə-nâr′)

n. A person whose wealth amounts to at least a trillion dollars,
pounds, or the equivalent in other currency.

So, according to the Children of the Most High: Pristine Youth
and Family Solutions, LLC., **A Spiritual Trillionaire is a
being who utilizes all of their Neshamaw Khayyeem
(נשמה חיים - Divine Breath of Life) - to be 100% mentally,
spiritually, emotionally and physically devout and obedient
to the Most High Heavenly Father with Unshakable True-
Faith and Divine-Love for the Most High Heavenly Father
only; and one who loves the Messiah Yashu'a (Jesus) and
have accepted the Messiah Yashu'a (Jesus) as their personal
Savior! A Spiritual Trillionaire also: only obeys the
commandments of the Most High, only has positive
intentions and only is an obedient vessel of the Most High
Heavenly Father's "Will" being done through them by way
of their True Vine "Yashu'a" (Jesus) good works.**

207

SPIRITUAL TRILLIONAIRE:
Cherishing the Breath of Life while Simultaneously
Preparing for the Blow of Death!

CHILDREN OF THE MOST HIGH:
PRISTINE YOUTH AND FAMILY SOLUTIONS, LLC.
SONS AND DAUGHTERS OF THE MOST HIGH PUBLISHERS ®

OH, GRACIOUS MOST HIGH HEAVENLY FATHER, HOLY IS YOUR
NAME, YOUR WILL BE DONE NOW AND FOREVER!

This makes our hearts pure so that the Most High Heavenly Father's "Will", will be done on earth as it is in heaven. This way of thinking, loving and doing removes all mental, spiritual and emotional potential barriers that a person may knowingly or unknowingly have; which allows our hearts to be prepared for the Most High to divide the disagreeable from agreeable in our hearts! **The Most High is the Watcher of what is in the heart!**

According the Messiah Yashu'a (Jesus), through obedience to the Most High, and by accepting him as our Savior; this leads to receiving eternal life after we take our last breath!

This is why the Messiah Yashu'a (Jesus) said in the "KJV bible book of Mark chapter 8 verse 36; it states: "For what shall it profit a man (the word for "**man**" in this verse is the KJV bible Greek Strong's Concordance #444 word ἄνθρωπος anthropos, **pronounced as: ä'n-thrō-pos**), which means **a human being, whether male or female generically, to include all human individuals.**), if he **(or she)** shall gain the whole **(the KJV bible Greek Strong's Concordance word for the phrase:**

SPIRITUAL TRILLIONAIRE:
Cherishing the Breath of Life while Simultaneously
Preparing for the Blow of Death!

CHILDREN OF THE MOST HIGH:
PRISTINE YOUTH AND FAMILY SOLUTIONS, LLC.
SONS AND DAUGHTERS OF THE MOST HIGH PUBLISHERS ®

OH, GRACIOUS MOST HIGH HEAVENLY FATHER, HOLY IS YOUR
NAME, YOUR WILL BE DONE NOW AND FOREVER!

"<u>the whole</u>" is: ὅλος hólos, hol'-os; which means "whole"
or "all") world, and lose his own soul?"

So, according the Messiah Yashu'a (Jesus), all of the wealth of
the world cannot afford to buy 1 human soul which makes
becoming a **Spiritual Trillionaire** *invaluable* (of inestimable
value; priceless). Thus, by becoming a **P.A.S.S.I.O.N.A.T.E.
P.A.T.H.F.I.N.D.E.R.** (**P**ositive, **A**ttitude, **S**miling, **S**eeker,
Improving, **O**ptimistically, **N**ow, **A**ctively, **T**hriving,
Efficiently, - **P**ersevering, **A**greeably, **T**hankful, **H**appy,
Faithful, **I**nspired, **N**oble, **D**evoted, **E**mpowered, **R**esiliency)
on the path through the Messiah Yashu'a (Jesus) to get back to
the Most High, a person has an opportunity to acquire, maintain
and sustain positive spiritual health and positive spiritual
wealth! According to Dr. Leaf, "when health invades your
body, your mind and spirit are next (Leah, 2009, p.139)."

Is it possible to become a Spiritual Trillionaire?

Some may say: "it is **impossible** to become a Spiritual
Trillionaire," right? The Children of the Most High: Pristine
Youth and Family Solutions, LLC. merely ask; does the word:

209

SPIRITUAL TRILLIONAIRE:
Cherishing the Breath of Life while Simultaneously
Preparing for the Blow of Death!

CHILDREN OF THE MOST HIGH:
PRISTINE YOUTH AND FAMILY SOLUTIONS, LLC.
SONS AND DAUGHTERS OF THE MOST HIGH PUBLISHERS ®

OH, GRACIOUS MOST HIGH HEAVENLY FATHER, HOLY IS YOUR
NAME, YOUR WILL BE DONE NOW AND FOREVER!

Im-possible spell **I'm-possible**? In the KJV bible book of Matthew Chapter 19 verse 26 the Messiah Yashu'a (Jesus) said: **"With men this is impossible, with God, all things are possible."** According to the KJV bible, is money evil? Or is the love of money evil? In the KJV bible book of 1st Timothy chapter 6 verse 10, it states: "For ***the love of money*** is the root of all evil: which while some coveted after, they have erred from the faith, and pierced themselves through with many sorrows." So, instead of loving money, consider what Mr. Gibran said: **"I love you, my brothers and sisters, whoever you are. You and I are all children of one faith, for the diverse paths of religion are fingers of the loving hand of one Supreme Being, a hand extended to all offering completeness of spirit to all, eager to receive all,** (Gibran, 1964, p.14)."

210

SPIRITUAL TRILLIONAIRE:
Cherishing the Breath of Life while Simultaneously
Preparing for the Blow of Death!

OH, GRACIOUS MOST HIGH HEAVENLY FATHER, HOLY IS YOUR
NAME, YOUR WILL BE DONE NOW AND FOREVER!

Why does becoming a Spiritual Trillionaire matter?

Becoming a Spiritual Trillionaire may or may not matter to some people depending on what they value. However, becoming a Spiritual Trillionaire would only matter to the children of the Most High who want to **utilize all of their Neshamaw Khayyeem (** נשמה חיים **- Divine Breath of Life) - to be 100% mentally, spiritually, emotionally and physically devout and obedient to the Most High Heavenly Father with Unshakable True-Faith and Divine-Love for the Most High Heavenly Father only; and who loves the Messiah Yashu'a (Jesus) and has accepted the Messiah Yashu'a (Jesus) as their personal Savior, and all who are loving and are peacemakers at heart!** Also, becoming a Spiritual Trillionaire would only matter to the children of the Most High who only obeys the commandments of the Most High, only has positive intentions and only is an obedient vessel of the Most High's "Will" being done through them through their True Vine "Yashu'a" (Jesus) good works.

SPIRITUAL TRILLIONAIRE:
Cherishing the Breath of Life while Simultaneously
Preparing for the Blow of Death!

CHILDREN OF THE MOST HIGH:
PRISTINE YOUTH AND FAMILY SOLUTIONS, LLC.
SONS AND DAUGHTERS OF THE MOST HIGH PUBLISHERS ®

OH, GRACIOUS MOST HIGH HEAVENLY FATHER, HOLY IS YOUR
NAME, YOUR WILL BE DONE NOW AND FOREVER!

How can a person receive the holy spirit? And is this a mandatory step to becoming a Spiritual Trillionaire?

A child of the Most High must first become aware of what they value the most. If a child of the Most High values spiritual growth aspiration, according to the bible, a person must be born again. In the KJV bible book of John chapter 3 verses 3-9; Yashu'a (Jesus) said: "Verily, verily, I say unto thee, except a man [person] be born again, he [a person] cannot see the kingdom of God.

SPIRITUAL TRILLIONAIRE:
**Cherishing the Breath of Life while Simultaneously
Preparing for the Blow of Death!**

CHILDREN OF THE MOST HIGH:
PRISTINE YOUTH AND FAMILY SOLUTIONS, LLC.
SONS AND DAUGHTERS OF THE MOST HIGH PUBLISHERS ®

**OH, GRACIOUS MOST HIGH HEAVENLY FATHER, HOLY IS YOUR
NAME, YOUR WILL BE DONE NOW AND FOREVER!**

"Nicodemus saith unto him, how can a man **[person]** be born when he **[a person]** is old? can he **[a person]** enter the second time into his mother's womb, and be born? Yashu'a said: "Verily, verily, I say unto thee, except a man **[person]** be born of water and of the Spirit, **[a person]** cannot enter into the kingdom of God. That which is born of the flesh is flesh; and that which is born of the Spirit is spirit. Marvel not that I said unto thee, Ye must be born again. The wind bloweth where it listeth, and thou hearest the sound thereof, but canst not tell whence it cometh, and whither it goeth: so is every one that is born of the Spirit."

In the KJV bible book of Romans chapter 10 verses 9-10; it states: "That if thou shalt confess with thy mouth the Lord Jesus, and shalt believe in thine heart that God hath raised him from the dead, thou shalt be saved. For with the heart **[of a person]** believeth unto righteousness; and with the mouth confession is made unto salvation."

213

SPIRITUAL TRILLIONAIRE:
Cherishing the Breath of Life while Simultaneously
Preparing for the Blow of Death!

CHILDREN OF THE MOST HIGH:
PRISTINE YOUTH AND FAMILY SOLUTIONS, LLC.
SONS AND DAUGHTERS OF THE MOST HIGH PUBLISHERS ®

OH, GRACIOUS MOST HIGH HEAVENLY FATHER, HOLY IS YOUR
NAME, YOUR WILL BE DONE NOW AND FOREVER!

Receiving the holy spirit is a mandatory step to becoming a Spiritual Trillionaire. The aforementioned verses gives' a person some insight into being born again. However, there is a plethora of additional lifelong works that a person has to do on themselves as they grow spiritually. Meaning, you have to rid yourself of everything that you think is right so that the holy spirit can access your temple (body). In the KJV bible book of 1st Corinthians chapter 6 verses 19-20; it states: "What? know ye not that your body is the temple of the Holy Ghost which is in you, which ye have of God, and ye are not your own? For ye are bought with a price: therefore, glorify God in your body, and in your spirit, which are God's." In the KJV bible book of 1st Corinthians chapter 3 verses 16-17; it states: "Know ye not that ye are the temple of God, and that the Spirit of God dwelleth in you? If any [person] defile the temple of God, [that person] shall God destroy; for the temple of God is holy, which temple ye are."

> **YOUR BODY IS YOUR FRIEND, SO, DON'T TREAT IT LIKE AN ENEMY!**

SPIRITUAL TRILLIONAIRE:
Cherishing the Breath of Life while Simultaneously
Preparing for the Blow of Death!

CHILDREN OF THE MOST HIGH:
PRISTINE YOUTH AND FAMILY SOLUTIONS, LLC.
SONS AND DAUGHTERS OF THE MOST HIGH PUBLISHERS ®

OH, GRACIOUS MOST HIGH HEAVENLY FATHER, HOLY IS YOUR
NAME, YOUR WILL BE DONE NOW AND FOREVER!

So, the holy spirit can only come into a clean temple (body). The holy spirit can only stay in a comfortable, purified temple (body). This means, a person who is contemplating rather or not they are ready to receive the holy spirit has to be willing to commit themselves to moment-to-moment work of eradicating negative habits, negative thinking, negative speaking, negative intentions, negative aspirations, negative actions, and unhealthy eating. If a person does not eradicate themselves of the above-mentioned negative attributes, **a holy (pure) spirit (pneuma, nephesh) cannot dwell inside an** impure mind, impure heart and impure body. Acquiring, maintaining and sustaining positive spiritual health and positive spiritual wealth requires active discipline exhibited moment to moment on a daily basis. It is a serious commitment of **discipline** that is required in order to keep your temple (body) purified mentally, spiritually, emotionally and physically. The Online American Heritage Dictionary (2019) defines **discipline** as:

"1. Training expected to produce a specific character or pattern of behavior, especially training that produces moral or mental improvement: was raised in the strictest discipline.

SPIRITUAL TRILLIONAIRE:
Cherishing the Breath of Life while Simultaneously
Preparing for the Blow of Death!

CHILDREN OF THE MOST HIGH:
PRISTINE YOUTH AND FAMILY SOLUTIONS, LLC.
SONS AND DAUGHTERS OF THE MOST HIGH PUBLISHERS ®

OH, GRACIOUS MOST HIGH HEAVENLY FATHER, HOLY IS YOUR
NAME, YOUR WILL BE DONE NOW AND FOREVER!

2. b. Controlled behavior resulting from disciplinary training; self-control."

The Children of the Most High Pristine Youth and Family Solutions, LLC. defines **discipline** as: **"doing what you need to do when it needs to be done whether you feel like doing it or not**." Some people may make the mistake of thinking that they can just cleanse their mind and spirit without cleansing their body (temple) from unhealthy eating and unhealthy drinking. Many people may make statements like:

"In my heart, I'm good and that's all that matters." "As long as I have God in my heart, that's all that matters." If that were the case, the Most High would put the truth in our hearts instead of in books and scriptures.

SPIRITUAL TRILLIONAIRE:
Cherishing the Breath of Life while Simultaneously
Preparing for the Blow of Death!

CHILDREN OF THE MOST HIGH:
PRISTINE YOUTH AND FAMILY SOLUTIONS, LLC.
SONS AND DAUGHTERS OF THE MOST HIGH PUBLISHERS ®

OH, GRACIOUS MOST HIGH HEAVENLY FATHER, HOLY IS YOUR
NAME, YOUR WILL BE DONE NOW AND FOREVER!

Why would the Most High put the truth in a book like the Torah, Bible or other scriptures or a book like the one you are reading right now, when the Most High could have just put the information in our hearts?

Because there is a part of becoming a Spiritual Trillionaire that is physical, that requires great discipline in order to not give into **the temptations of the 9 Deadly Venoms of the Desires of the dragon, that old serpent called the devil and satan that deceived the whole world**. The great discipline to not give into the temptations of the 9 Deadly Venoms is essential to overall potential spiritual growth success because the temptations cannot work on the soul, they can only work on the body. The body interprets the temptations for the soul. **For example:** As it relates to lusts, sometimes, the temptation is put on television through images of nudity in effort **to plant the thought in the mind** for the soul to interpret as lusts.

So, when a person receives the holy spirit, he or she transforms from a son or daughter of human beings to a child of the Most High and the holy spirit will reeducate your soul over time and substantiate what you learn as the Most High's truth through

217

SPIRITUAL TRILLIONAIRE:
**Cherishing the Breath of Life while Simultaneously
Preparing for the Blow of Death!**

CHILDREN OF THE MOST HIGH:
PRISTINE YOUTH AND FAMILY SOLUTIONS, LLC.
SONS AND DAUGHTERS OF THE MOST HIGH PUBLISHERS ®

OH, GRACIOUS MOST HIGH HEAVENLY FATHER, HOLY IS YOUR
NAME, YOUR WILL BE DONE NOW AND FOREVER!

evidence, reasoning and experience. Essentially, a person would have to make what the Children of the Most High: Pristine Youth and Family Solutions, LLC. refer to as a: **"True Vine "Yashu'a (Jesus) Conscious and Conscientious (C.A.C.) decision"** that will allow their mind to guide their brain to a Spiritual Trillionaire way of thinking. This decision process is also referred to by the Children of the Most High: Pristine Youth and Family Solutions, LLC. as: **"Choices, Actions, Consequences and Repercussions (C.A.C.A.R) through Potential Diversification and Overstanding."** Dr. Leah refers to this process as: "The Brain Does the Bidding of the Mind, Leah, 2013, p.32)."

What is Potential Diversification?

According to the Children of the Most High: Pristine Youth and Family Solutions, LLC., **"Potential Diversification** is having or showing the capacity to create a number of different concepts into something positive that will benefit you and others in the present and in the future. **Potential Diversification** is also having the ability to utilize your mental capacity to develop

218

SPIRITUAL TRILLIONAIRE:
Cherishing the Breath of Life while Simultaneously
Preparing for the Blow of Death!

CHILDREN OF THE MOST HIGH:
PRISTINE YOUTH AND FAMILY SOLUTIONS, LLC.
SONS AND DAUGHTERS OF THE MOST HIGH PUBLISHERS ®

OH, GRACIOUS MOST HIGH HEAVENLY FATHER, HOLY IS YOUR
NAME, YOUR WILL BE DONE NOW AND FOREVER!

resources and use them more efficiently or to reduce risks that may not lead to positive outcomes in your life."

What does the words: "Overstanding and Overstand" mean to the Children of the Most High: Pristine Youth and Family Solutions, LLC.? "Overstanding is mastering the comprehension of what is understood or what many may not have an understanding of."

Therefore, the Children of the Most High: Pristine Youth and Family Solution, LLC. define the word: "**Overstand**" as: having the ability by way of the Most High Heavenly Father to master the ability to clearly teach and explain the Most High's Scriptural knowledge from the original languages that the scriptures were revealed in; inclusive of teaching the children of the Most High how to study and research the Most High's scriptures in the original languages that they were revealed through the principles that the acronym "S.E.R.V.E." represent."

SPIRITUAL TRILLIONAIRE:
Cherishing the Breath of Life while Simultaneously
Preparing for the Blow of Death!

CHILDREN OF THE MOST HIGH:
PRISTINE YOUTH AND FAMILY SOLUTIONS, LLC.
SONS AND DAUGHTERS OF THE MOST HIGH PUBLISHERS ®

OH, GRACIOUS MOST HIGH HEAVENLY FATHER, HOLY IS YOUR
NAME, YOUR WILL BE DONE NOW AND FOREVER!

What do the acronyms of: S.E.R.V.E. represent to the Children of the Most High; Pristine Youth and Family Solution, LLC.?

The acronyms of: **S.E.R.V.E.** represents: **S**erving, **E**ducation, **R**esearching, **V**olunteering, and **E**ntrepreneurship. So, the values of **s**erving and volunteering, the process of receiving instruction through the reversal of mis-education, and the acquisition of Elohiym (God's) evidence-based **A.W.A.R.E.** (**A**ll **W**ise **A**bundant **R**ight **E**xact) knowledge. This occurs through novice, non-bias life-long researching. Also, the benefits of entrepreneurship education are instilled in youth and adult participants who learn and practice the potent 9x9 True

SPIRITUAL TRILLIONAIRE:
Cherishing the Breath of Life while Simultaneously
Preparing for the Blow of Death!

CHILDREN OF THE MOST HIGH:
PRISTINE YOUTH AND FAMILY SOLUTIONS, LLC.
SONS AND DAUGHTERS OF THE MOST HIGH PUBLISHERS &

OH, GRACIOUS MOST HIGH HEAVENLY FATHER, HOLY IS YOUR
NAME, YOUR WILL BE DONE NOW AND FOREVER!

Vine "Yashu'a (Jesus) B.A.-K.A.-R.E. Sequential Order of Learning Habits of Success Elohiym (God's) evidence-based **A.W.A.R.E. (All Wise Abundant Right Exact**) knowledge.

Define the word "education". According to Craft (1984), he noted that there are two different Latin roots of the English word "**education**." They are "**educare**," which means to train or to mold, and "**educere**," meaning to lead out or bring out. While the two meanings are quite different, they are both represented in the word "**education**." To educate' comes from 'educere': 'to bring out/draw out'. According to the Online American Heritage Dictionary (2019), education is: "The act or process of educating or being educated. The knowledge or skill obtained or developed by a learning process. A program of instruction of a specified kind or level: *driver education; a college education.* The field of study that is concerned with the pedagogy of teaching and learning. An instructive or enlightening experience: *Her work in an animal shelter was a real education.*"

SPIRITUAL TRILLIONAIRE:
Cherishing the Breath of Life while Simultaneously
Preparing for the Blow of Death!

CHILDREN OF THE MOST HIGH:
PRISTINE YOUTH AND FAMILY SOLUTIONS, LLC.
SONS AND DAUGHTERS OF THE MOST HIGH PUBLISHERS ®

OH, GRACIOUS MOST HIGH HEAVENLY FATHER, HOLY IS YOUR
NAME, YOUR WILL BE DONE NOW AND FOREVER!

How can becoming a Spiritual Trillionaire benefit youth
and adults personally, professionally and globally?

**Becoming a Spiritual Trillionaire may benefit youth and
adults personally, professionally and globally** who learn how
to activate the principles of **S.E.R.V.E.** (**S**erving, **E**ducation,
Researching, **V**olunteering, and **E**ntrepreneurship) through the
moment to moment living and intentional practicing of the
youth **True Vine** Yashu'a (Jesus) **D.A.I.L.Y.** (**D**evout,
Ambitus, **I**ncorruptible, **L**oving, **Y**outh, -
T.O.G.E.T.H.E.R.N.E.S.S. (**T**hrough, **O**beying, **G**od's,
Empowering, **T**rue, **H**ealing, **E**ternal, **R**enewing, **N**eeded,
Everlasting, **S**acred, **S**alvation) non-formal **education
essential elements of success, and the adults True Vine**
Yashu'a (Jesus) **T.O.G.E.T.H.E.R.N.E.S.S.** (**T**hrough,
Obeying, **G**od's, **E**mpowering, **T**rue, **H**ealing, **E**ternal,
Renewing, **N**eeded, **E**verlasting, **S**acred, **S**alvation) non-
formal **education essential elements of success.**

222

SPIRITUAL TRILLIONAIRE:
**Cherishing the Breath of Life while Simultaneously
Preparing for the Blow of Death!**

CHILDREN OF THE MOST HIGH:
PRISTINE YOUTH AND FAMILY SOLUTIONS, LLC.
SONS AND DAUGHTERS OF THE MOST HIGH PUBLISHERS ®

OH, GRACIOUS MOST HIGH HEAVENLY FATHER, HOLY IS YOUR NAME, YOUR WILL BE DONE NOW AND FOREVER!

The youth True Vine Yashu'a (Jesus) D.A.I.L.Y. T.O.G.E.T.H.E.R.N.E.S.S. non-formal education essential elements of success in action, utilizes the Messiah Yashu'a (Jesus) teachings which are reflected in the key elements of positive youth development, Cs' of positive youth development, and in the seven crucial Cs' of resiliency. The Children of the Most High: Pristine Youth and Family Solutions, LLC. teach youth and adults: how to create positive predetermined goals, how to define what success means to them, how to help them to define what happiness means to them, and how to learn to work together to begin the process of creating a world where all youth are happy, healthy, and balanced mentally, spiritually, physically, emotionally, financially, personally, professionally, and socially. Authors: Lyubomirsky, King, and Diener, (2005), suggest that: "happiness is associated with and precedes numerous successful outcomes, as well as behaviors paralleling success. Furthermore, the evidence suggests that positive affect is the hallmark of well-being and may be the cause of many of the desirable characteristics, resources, and successes correlated with happiness, (Lyubomirsky, King, & Diener, (2005).

SPIRITUAL TRILLIONAIRE:
Cherishing the Breath of Life while Simultaneously
Preparing for the Blow of Death!

OH, GRACIOUS MOST HIGH HEAVENLY FATHER, HOLY IS YOUR
NAME, YOUR WILL BE DONE NOW AND FOREVER!

As it relates to youth, the aforementioned matters for our youth to receive the protection from the Most High Heavenly Father from all harm during the pre-adult years of their life, in order to have an opportunity to become adults that will become inspired and empowered children of the Most High. By doing so, they will have an opportunity to pristinely make the world a safe and healthy place for all members of humanity. They will also have the opportunity to create a world that is ruled by Love and the "Will" of the Most High, void of negative emotions, greed, lusts and love of money.

According the Bible, this can only occur if our youth learn Elohiym (God's) knowledge and obey Elohiym (God's) laws. According to Hosea KJV 4:6, Elohiym (God) states: "**My people are destroyed for lack of knowledge**: because thou hast rejected knowledge, I will also reject thee, that thou shalt be no priest to me: **seeing thou hast forgotten the law of thy God, I will also forget thy children**."

So, in order to best prepare today's youth to survive until adulthood, they need to learn God's (Elohiym) knowledge and God's (Elohiym) laws to be eligible to receive God's (Elohiym)

SPIRITUAL TRILLIONAIRE:
Cherishing the Breath of Life while Simultaneously
Preparing for the Blow of Death!

CHILDREN OF THE MOST HIGH:
PRISTINE YOUTH AND FAMILY SOLUTIONS, LLC.
SONS AND DAUGHTERS OF THE MOST HIGH PUBLISHERS &

OH, GRACIOUS MOST HIGH HEAVENLY FATHER, HOLY IS YOUR
NAME, YOUR WILL BE DONE NOW AND FOREVER!

protection from all harm. Therefore, today's youth must be informed with God's (Elohiym) **A.W.A.R.E.** knowledge. How do you know? Because God's (Elohiym) knowledge is **All Wise Abundant Right Exact (A.W.A.R.E).** Therefore, God's (Elohiym) **A.W.A.R.E. Knowledge is** best to guide and protect all of the global children of the Most High from all harm. God's (Elohiym) **A.W.A.R.E. Knowledge** gives youth and any person the ability to develop the habit of positive or **right thinking** as oppose to **wrong thinking**. A person with **wrong knowledge** thinks negatively by having wrong **I. D. E. A. S.** (**I**mpure **D**esires **E**motionally **A**ctivated **S**equentially) or negative thoughts continuously, which leads to negative speaking, and negative actions. **Learning and obeying the laws of God (Elohiym) activates the will of God (Elohiym) in the mind which initiates all thoughts, and a person acts and speaks, as he or she thinks!**

In the KJV bible book of Hebrews chapter 8 verse 10; it states: "For this is the covenant that I will make with the house of Israel after those days, saith the Lord; I will put my laws into their mind, and write them in their hearts: and I will be to them a God, and they shall be to me a people."

225

SPIRITUAL TRILLIONAIRE:
Cherishing the Breath of Life while Simultaneously
Preparing for the Blow of Death!

CHILDREN OF THE MOST HIGH:
PRISTINE YOUTH AND FAMILY SOLUTIONS, LLC.
SONS AND DAUGHTERS OF THE MOST HIGH PUBLISHERS ®

OH, GRACIOUS MOST HIGH HEAVENLY FATHER, HOLY IS YOUR
NAME, YOUR WILL BE DONE NOW AND FOREVER!

In the KJV bible book of Revelation chapter 22 verse 14; it states: "Blessed are they that do his commandments, that they may have right to the tree of life, and may enter in through the gates into the city."

In summary of this section, God's (Elohiym) A.W.A.R.E. knowledge is the **best knowledge** for our youth to receive God's (Elohiym) protection to help ensure that our youth will become the future positive leaders of tomorrow, today!

How can becoming a Spiritual Trillionaire improve the overall well-being of members of humanity?

Becoming a Spiritual Trillionaire may improve the overall well-being of members of humanity through the invaluableness of sincere-hearted repentance to the Most High for all of their unforgiven sins, the acceptance of the Messiah Yashu'a (Jesus), and by assisting members of humanity in their endeavors of achieving and sustaining life-long success. Thereby; inspiring and empowering all children of the Most High to pristinely make the world a safe and healthy place for all members of humanity.

SPIRITUAL TRILLIONAIRE:
Cherishing the Breath of Life while Simultaneously
Preparing for the Blow of Death!

CHILDREN OF THE MOST HIGH:
PRISTINE YOUTH AND FAMILY SOLUTIONS, LLC.
SONS AND DAUGHTERS OF THE MOST HIGH PUBLISHERS *

OH, GRACIOUS MOST HIGH HEAVENLY FATHER, HOLY IS YOUR
NAME, YOUR WILL BE DONE NOW AND FOREVER!

Which may lead to the children of the Most High creating a world that is ruled by **Love** and the "**Will**" of the Most High, void of negative emotions, greed, lusts and love of money. By doing so, this may improve the overall well-being of members of humanity.

Can becoming a Spiritual Trillionaire increase a person's economic earning potential?

Yes, because in the process of becoming a Spiritual Trillionaire, a person learns what governs this physical realm that we live and exist in. **What governs this physical realm that we live and exist in? Cause and Effect governs this physical realm that we live and exist in.** Also, a person learns what law governs this universe. **What law governs this universe? The law of "change" governs this universe.** Learning how to strategically make sound financial decisions and how create economic growth for oneself and others, requires an overstanding of the significance of cause, effect, change, and the doctrine of the Most High as it relates to a person learning how to best increase their personal economic earning potential.

SPIRITUAL TRILLIONAIRE:
**Cherishing the Breath of Life while Simultaneously
Preparing for the Blow of Death!**

CHILDREN OF THE MOST HIGH:
PRISTINE YOUTH AND FAMILY SOLUTIONS, LLC.
SONS AND DAUGHTERS OF THE MOST HIGH PUBLISHERS ®

OH, GRACIOUS MOST HIGH HEAVENLY FATHER, HOLY IS YOUR
NAME, YOUR WILL BE DONE NOW AND FOREVER!

This is also essential as it relates to underserved underrepresented members of humanity achieving and sustaining positive **social economic mobility**.

According to Duncan (2018), "Socioeconomic mobility in the United States refers to the upward or downward movement of Americans from one social class or economic level to another, through job changes, inheritance, marriage, connections, tax changes, innovation, illegal activities, hard work, lobbying, health changes or other factors."

How can we create a world that is ruled by love and not ruled by negative emotions, greed, lust and love of money?

We can create a world that is ruled by love and not ruled by negative emotions, greed, lust and love of money by: loving the Most High Heavenly Father with all of our heart, all of our soul, all of our spirit, all of our mind, all of our body, and being loving to our local, state, national and international neighbors as much as we love ourselves, and as much as we love our personal loved ones.

SPIRITUAL TRILLIONAIRE:
Cherishing the Breath of Life while Simultaneously
Preparing for the Blow of Death!

CHILDREN OF THE MOST HIGH:
PRISTINE YOUTH AND FAMILY SOLUTIONS, LLC.
SONS AND DAUGHTERS OF THE MOST HIGH PUBLISHERS ®

OH, GRACIOUS MOST HIGH HEAVENLY FATHER, HOLY IS YOUR
NAME, YOUR WILL BE DONE NOW AND FOREVER!

Also, in order to truly create a world that is ruled by love and not ruled by negative emotions, greed, lust and love of money, each person has to willingly decide to eternally commit their entire life and future existence to obeying the Most High Heavenly Father, doing the Most High Heavenly Father's **"Will"** only, and accepts the Real Messiah Yashu'a (Jesus) as their Savior. In doing so, the **"Will"** of the Most High Heavenly Father will be activated in their minds, which will inspire and initiate all their thoughts and all of their actions.

Also, they will have the ability to initiate the spiritual (**which is unseen physically**) within themselves to utilize the dominion given to them through the True Vine Spirits of the Messiah. The True Vine Spirits of the Messiah "Yashu'a (Jesus) are from the Most High as part of the essential preparation of the minds, spirits, souls and hearts of all members of humanity who are willing to change, before "Thy Kingdom comes to earth as it is in heaven." This process occurs through the children of the Most High utilizing their inborn gifts from the Most High to consciously, conscientiously and physically to do their preordained work on earth, in designated geographical areas at

SPIRITUAL TRILLIONAIRE:
Cherishing the Breath of Life while Simultaneously
Preparing for the Blow of Death!

CHILDREN OF THE MOST HIGH:
PRISTINE YOUTH AND FAMILY SOLUTIONS, LLC.
SONS AND DAUGHTERS OF THE MOST HIGH PUBLISHERS ®

OH, GRACIOUS MOST HIGH HEAVENLY FATHER, HOLY IS YOUR
NAME, YOUR WILL BE DONE NOW AND FOREVER!

different times and in different ways throughout their lives, where the Most High has given them dominion over.

Their anointed areas or inborn gifts from the Most High, gives them dominion over their areas of responsibility, which can be any skill in action that helps to uplift humanity and upkeep the preservation of the planet earth in a manner that reflects the Most High's "**Will**" being done on earth as it is in heaven.

In the KJV bible book of Luke chapter 17 verses 20-21; it states: "And when he [Yashu'a, Jesus] was demanded of the Pharisees, when the kingdom of God should come, [Yashu'a, Jesus] answered them and said, "The kingdom of God cometh not with observation: Neither shall they say, Lo here! or, lo there! for, behold, the kingdom of God is within you."

In the KJV bible book of James chapter 1 verse 17; it states: "Every good gift and every perfect gift is from above, and cometh down from the Father of lights, with whom is no variableness, neither shadow of turning." In the KJV bible book of John chapter 14 verse 17; it states: "[Even] the Spirit of truth; whom the world cannot receive, because it seeth him not,

SPIRITUAL TRILLIONAIRE:
Cherishing the Breath of Life while Simultaneously Preparing for the Blow of Death!

CHILDREN OF THE MOST HIGH:
PRISTINE YOUTH AND FAMILY SOLUTIONS, LLC.
SONS AND DAUGHTERS OF THE MOST HIGH PUBLISHERS

OH, GRACIOUS MOST HIGH HEAVENLY FATHER, HOLY IS YOUR
NAME, YOUR WILL BE DONE NOW AND FOREVER!

neither knoweth him: but ye know him; for he dwelleth with you, and shall be in you."

In the KJV bible book of Proverbs chapter 18 verse 16; it states: A [person's] gift maketh room for [them], and bringeth [a person] before great [people].

In the KJV bible book of Genesis chapter 1 verse 26; it states with Hebrew inserts:

וַיֹּאמֶר אֱלֹהִים נַעֲשֶׂה אָדָם בְּצַלְמֵנוּ כִּדְמוּתֵנוּ וְיִרְדּוּ בִדְגַת הַיָּם וּבְעוֹף 1:26
הַשָּׁמַיִם וּבַבְּהֵמָה וּבְכָל־הָאָרֶץ וּבְכָל־הָרֶמֶשׂ הָרֹמֵשׂ עַל־הָאָרֶץ:

"And God אֱלֹהִים 'elohiym said אָמַר 'amar Let us make עָשָׂה `asah man (according to the KJV bible book Hebrew Strong's Concordance# 120, the word for "**man**" is the word "**adam**" **which in this verse is in reference to human beings**, not just a single person. אָדָם 'adam, aw-dam'; **means human beings (not just an individual), the species and can also be in reference to a person**); in our image צֶלֶם tselem after our likeness דְּמוּת děmuwth and let **them** have **dominion** רָדָה radah over the fish דָּגָה dagah of the sea יָם yam and over the fowl עוֹף

231

SPIRITUAL TRILLIONAIRE:
**Cherishing the Breath of Life while Simultaneously
Preparing for the Blow of Death!**

CHILDREN OF THE MOST HIGH:
PRISTINE YOUTH AND FAMILY SOLUTIONS, LLC.
SONS AND DAUGHTERS OF THE MOST HIGH PUBLISHERS ®

OH, GRACIOUS MOST HIGH HEAVENLY FATHER, HOLY IS YOUR
NAME, YOUR WILL BE DONE NOW AND FOREVER!

'owph) of the air שָׁמַיִם shamayim and over the cattle בְּהֵמָה bĕhemah and over all the earth אֶרֶץ 'erets and over every creeping thing רֶמֶשׂ remes that creepeth רָמַשׂ ramas upon the earth אֶרֶץ 'erets."

The KJV bible book of Genesis chapter 1 verse 26; it states: "And God said, Let us make man in our image, after our likeness: and let them have dominion over the fish of the sea, and over the fowl of the air, and over the cattle, and over all the earth, and over every creeping thing that creepeth upon the earth." In order for members of humanity to sustain a world that is ruled by love and not ruled by negative emotions, greed, lust and love of money, we must practice the following on a daily basis:

♥ Be or become an avid practitioner of "Self-Care".

♥ Become aware of your agreeable passion, purpose and inborn gifts from the Most High and put them into action by activating your will to awaken the potential that resides in you and in each person. This is known to the Children of the Most High: Pristine Youth and

232

SPIRITUAL TRILLIONAIRE:
**Cherishing the Breath of Life while Simultaneously
Preparing for the Blow of Death!**

CHILDREN OF THE MOST HIGH:
PRISTINE YOUTH AND FAMILY SOLUTIONS, LLC.
SONS AND DAUGHTERS OF THE MOST HIGH PUBLISHERS

OH, GRACIOUS MOST HIGH HEAVENLY FATHER, HOLY IS YOUR
NAME, YOUR WILL BE DONE NOW AND FOREVER!

♥ Family Solutions, LLC. as your Spiritual Majesty. This is essential in order to continuously create solutions to critical issues that exists amongst members of humanity by putting creativity into action vs giving in to wasted potential distractions.

♥ Wasted potential distractions are the persons, places, things, issues and life situations that for one reason or another **leads to wasting time**. Another thing that all of the money and all of the wealth in the world cannot buy is time! We cannot recycle wasted time. Unfortunately, some people allow those distractions to become the reasons that they live an entire lifetime without working diligently to develop their potential.

♥ Overcome the 9 Deadly Venoms of the Desires of the great dragon, that old serpent called satan and the devil that deceived the whole world.

Overcoming the 9 Deadly Venoms of the Desires of the great dragon, that old serpent called satan and the devil that deceived the whole world, and teaching others how to do so may help

SPIRITUAL TRILLIONAIRE:
**Cherishing the Breath of Life while Simultaneously
Preparing for the Blow of Death!**

CHILDREN OF THE MOST HIGH:
PRISTINE YOUTH AND FAMILY SOLUTIONS, LLC.
SONS AND DAUGHTERS OF THE MOST HIGH PUBLISHERS ®

OH, GRACIOUS MOST HIGH HEAVENLY FATHER, HOLY IS YOUR
NAME, YOUR WILL BE DONE NOW AND FOREVER!

members of humanity to become the best practitioners of focusing on our similarities while simultaneously not dwelling on our differences. That prevents us from creating global peace. We have to learn how to disagree without being disagreeable towards one another.

How is it possible for married, faith-based believing couples, to focus on their similarities while simultaneously not dwelling on their differences if they have different beliefs?

For example: Mrs. Fatimah Muhammad married Mr. John Christian and Mrs. Muhammad wants their two children to practice peace-ship at the Mosque of Allah, and Mr. Christian wants their three children to practice wor-ship at the Church of the Lord and Savior Jesus Christ each Sunday. However, on Sundays, Mrs. Fatimah Muhammad only wants to attend the Mosque of Allah with her entire family and does not want to attend the Church of the Lord and Savior Jesus Christ on Sundays. Mr. John Christian only wants to attend the Church of the Lord and Savior Jesus Christ with his entire family on Sundays and does not want to attend the Mosque of Allah.

SPIRITUAL TRILLIONAIRE:
Cherishing the Breath of Life while Simultaneously
Preparing for the Blow of Death!

CHILDREN OF THE MOST HIGH:
PRISTINE YOUTH AND FAMILY SOLUTIONS, LLC.
SONS AND DAUGHTERS OF THE MOST HIGH PUBLISHERS ®

OH, GRACIOUS MOST HIGH HEAVENLY FATHER, HOLY IS YOUR
NAME, YOUR WILL BE DONE NOW AND FOREVER!

Both loving parents don't want their children to experience inconsistency on Sundays as it relates to the attending the Mosque of Allah or the Church of the Lord and Savior Jesus Christ with their entire family.

The situation has become so stressful for both parents that they are contemplating getting a divorce and their children are suffering psychologically and emotionally because they don't want their family torn apart due to their parents' potential divorce. Mrs. Muhammad thinks her husband teachings are wrong and extremely different than what she believes, and Mr. Christian thinks his wife's teachings are wrong and extremely different than what he believes. So, one day, their 19 years old son, Malachi took the time to do an in-depth study into his mom's Mosque of Allah's teachings and dad's Church of the Lord and Savior Jesus Christ's teachings to inquire if they had similarities rather than differences that may be able to prevent his parents for getting a divorce.

SPIRITUAL TRILLIONAIRE:
Cherishing the Breath of Life while Simultaneously
Preparing for the Blow of Death!

CHILDREN OF THE MOST HIGH:
PRISTINE YOUTH AND FAMILY SOLUTIONS, LLC.
SONS AND DAUGHTERS OF THE MOST HIGH PUBLISHERS &

OH, GRACIOUS MOST HIGH HEAVENLY FATHER, HOLY IS YOUR
NAME, YOUR WILL BE DONE NOW AND FOREVER!

After Malachi had completed his in-depth research, he held a family meeting with his parents and sister Jackie to display his findings to his family. Malachi outlined the following similarities:

- ♥ The Mosque of Allah teaches that Allah (the Most High) is alone and has no partners. The Church of the Lord and Savior Jesus Christ teaches that the Lord our God is one Lord, and the first and great commandment is: "Thou shalt love the Lord thy God with all thy heart, and with all thy soul, and with all thy mind."

- ♥ The Church of the Lord and Savior Jesus Christ teaches that Jesus is the Messiah, Son of God and Savior to the world. The Mosque of Allah teaches that Jesus (Issa) is Savior (Koran Chapter 2:136, Messiah (Koran Chapter 3:45, 4:157, 4:171, 4:172), Spirt and Soul of Allah (Koran Chapters 2:87, 2:253, 5:110, 4:171, 21:91), and Word (Kalima) of Allah (Koran Chapters 3:45, 4:157). Koran 4:159 states: "And verily, from the family of the scripture (from Adam to Muhammad) there is not anyone who should not believe by way of him (Jesus) before he [or she] dies, and the day of resurrection he (Jesus) will be a witness over them."

236

SPIRITUAL TRILLIONAIRE:
**Cherishing the Breath of Life while Simultaneously
Preparing for the Blow of Death!**

CHILDREN OF THE MOST HIGH:
PRISTINE YOUTH AND FAMILY SOLUTIONS, LLC.
SONS AND DAUGHTERS OF THE MOST HIGH PUBLISHERS ®

OH, GRACIOUS MOST HIGH HEAVENLY FATHER, HOLY IS YOUR
NAME, YOUR WILL BE DONE NOW AND FOREVER!

Unbeknown to Mrs. Fatimah Muhammad and her husband Mr. John Christian, their son Malachi's in-depth study into the Mosque of Allah's teachings and the Church of the Lord Jesus Christ teachings revealed that they had more similarities than differences in their teachings than they ever could have imagined. To Malachi and his sister Jackie's surprise, their parents decided not to get a divorce and to alternate going to the Mosque of Allah and the Church of the Lord Jesus Christ every other Sunday.

Mrs. Muhammad and Mr. Christian also became devout students of each other's teachings and converted over **999** married couples with different faith-based beliefs to focus on their similarities rather than the 3% or less of the differences that they disagree about. All of them unanimously agree that the Most High Heavenly Father is Love and is the Creator of the Boundless Universes by whatever name each person chooses to call on the Creator by.

The aforementioned information, if practiced daily by members of humanity, may lead to creating a world that is ruled by love and not ruled by negative emotions, greed, lust and love of money.

SPIRITUAL TRILLIONAIRE:
Cherishing the Breath of Life while Simultaneously
Preparing for the Blow of Death!

CHILDREN OF THE MOST HIGH:
PRISTINE YOUTH AND FAMILY SOLUTIONS, LLC.
SONS AND DAUGHTERS OF THE MOST HIGH PUBLISHERS ®

OH, GRACIOUS MOST HIGH HEAVENLY FATHER, HOLY IS YOUR
NAME, YOUR WILL BE DONE NOW AND FOREVER!

How does a person be or become an avid practitioner of "Self-Care" with no extra time in the day and multiple competing responsibilities?

In 2018, **Mr. Marcel Schwantes who is the founder and chief human officer of Leadership from the Core Inc.** wrote an article about Mr. Warren Buffet, he stated: "**Billionaire Warren Buffett**, the chairman and CEO of Berkshire Hathaway, is in his late eighties and still capturing the world's attention as the second richest person on the planet (as of this writing). So, how has he done it? Actually, it's not so much about *what he has done* as it is *what he hasn't done*. "With all the demands on him every day, **Buffett learned a long time ago that the greatest commodity of all is time**. He simply mastered the art and practice of setting boundaries for himself."

So, aspiring Spiritual Trillionaires must master the art of utilizing time wisely while simultaneously not allowing any person place, thing, life issues or life situations dominate the utilization of your time in a way keeps you from doing your Most High Heavenly Father preordained purpose for your life work!

SPIRITUAL TRILLIONAIRE:
Cherishing the Breath of Life while Simultaneously
Preparing for the Blow of Death!

CHILDREN OF THE MOST HIGH:
PRISTINE YOUTH AND FAMILY SOLUTIONS, LLC.
SONS AND DAUGHTERS OF THE MOST HIGH PUBLISHERS ®

OH, GRACIOUS MOST HIGH HEAVENLY FATHER, HOLY IS YOUR NAME, YOUR WILL BE DONE NOW AND FOREVER!

~OH, MOST HIGH HEAVENLY FATHER, PLEASE INSPIRE OUR MINDS TO ONLY BE COMMITTED TO LOVING YOU, OBEYING YOU, AND FOLLOWING YOUR GUIDANCE. WE SEEK YOUR ETERNAL PROTECTION FROM ALL WICKEDNESS AND FROM ALL DEPRAVED THINGS THAT MAY DISTRACT OUR MINDS FROM YOU. WE SEEK ETERNAL REFUGE IN YOU LIKE YOUR ANOINTED SON, THE MESSIAH YASHU'A (JESUS) DID AND DOES! NOW AND FOREVER. AMEN~

239

SPIRITUAL TRILLIONAIRE:
Cherishing the Breath of Life while Simultaneously
Preparing for the Blow of Death!

CHILDREN OF THE MOST HIGH:
PRISTINE YOUTH AND FAMILY SOLUTIONS, LLC.
SONS AND DAUGHTERS OF THE MOST HIGH PUBLISHERS ®

OH, GRACIOUS MOST HIGH HEAVENLY FATHER, HOLY IS YOUR
NAME, YOUR WILL BE DONE NOW AND FOREVER!

Chapter 8: How does the 9 Essential Elements in a Human Being and the 9 Essential Habits of Healing the physical body align with the Children of the Most High Pristine Youth and Family Solutions, LLC. 9X9 True Vine "Yashu'a" (Jesus) B.A.-K.A.-R.E. Sequential Order of Learning Habits of Success?

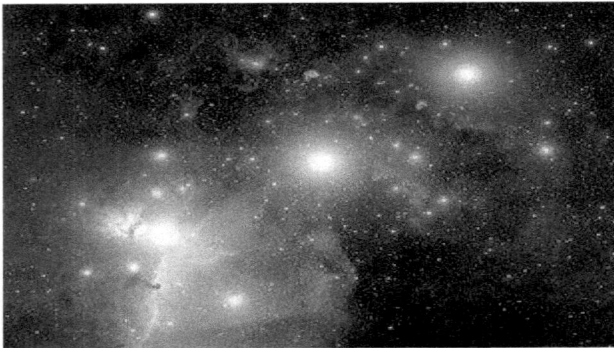

~OH, MOST HIGH HEAVENLY FATHER, PLEASE
CONTINUOUSLY DRAW US NEARER TO YOU MORE EACH
MOMENT THAT YOU ALLOW US TO LIVE AND EXIST,
NOW AND FOREVER. AMEN~

SPIRITUAL TRILLIONAIRE:
Cherishing the Breath of Life while Simultaneously
Preparing for the Blow of Death!

CHILDREN OF THE MOST HIGH:
PRISTINE YOUTH AND FAMILY SOLUTIONS, LLC.
SONS AND DAUGHTERS OF THE MOST HIGH PUBLISHERS ®

OH, GRACIOUS MOST HIGH HEAVENLY FATHER, HOLY IS YOUR
NAME, YOUR WILL BE DONE NOW AND FOREVER!

The 9 Essential Elements in a Human Being influences and empowers a person's overall well-being as it relates to acquiring, maintaining and sustaining positive spiritual health and positive spiritual wealth on the path to becoming a Spiritual Trillionaire. Those 9 Essential Elements are:

1. Spirit (KJV bible book of Genesis chapter 2 verse 7).
2. Mind (KJV bible book of Mathew chapter 22 verses 37-38).
3. Body (KJV bible book of Genesis chapter 2 verse 7).
4. Soul (KJV bible book of Genesis chapter 2 verse 7).
5. Plasma in you or Plasmatic You (KJV bible book of Leviticus chapter 17 verses 13-14, Life is in the blood).
6. Etheric (ether) you, is a person's genetic spiritual link to their Ancestors, the Ancient Ones and the Old Ones. (KJV bible book of Psalms chapter 82 verses 6-7).
7. Physical Heart (KJV bible book of Proverbs chapter 3 verses 5-6).
8. Spiritual Heart (KJV bible book of Revelation chapter 3 verse 20).
9. Spark of Life – Lifeforce of all living things (KJV bible book of John chapter 1 verses 1-5).

SPIRITUAL TRILLIONAIRE:
**Cherishing the Breath of Life while Simultaneously
Preparing for the Blow of Death!**

CHILDREN OF THE MOST HIGH:
PRISTINE YOUTH AND FAMILY SOLUTIONS, LLC.
SONS AND DAUGHTERS OF THE MOST HIGH PUBLISHERS ®

OH, GRACIOUS MOST HIGH HEAVENLY FATHER, HOLY IS YOUR
NAME, YOUR WILL BE DONE NOW AND FOREVER!

The 9 True Vine Yashu'a (Jesus) Essential Habits of Healing the physical body are:

1. Daily intake of healthy food. In the KJV bible book of Exodus chapter 23 verse 25; it states: "And ye shall serve the LORD your God, and he shall bless thy bread, and thy water; and I will take sickness away from the midst of thee."

2. Daily intake of plenty healthy water. In the KJV bible book of John chapter 4 verse 14; it states: "But whosoever drinketh of the water that I shall give him shall never thirst; but the water that I shall give him shall be in him a well of water springing up into everlasting life."

3. Daily Physical Health Self-Care – doing medical physician approved physical exercising (if possible). In the KJV bible book of 3rd John chapter 1 verse 2; states: "Beloved, I wish above all things that thou mayest prosper and be in health, even as thy soul prospereth."

SPIRITUAL TRILLIONAIRE:
**Cherishing the Breath of Life while Simultaneously
Preparing for the Blow of Death!**

CHILDREN OF THE MOST HIGH:
PRISTINE YOUTH AND FAMILY SOLUTIONS, LLC.
SONS AND DAUGHTERS OF THE MOST HIGH PUBLISHERS ®

OH, GRACIOUS MOST HIGH HEAVENLY FATHER, HOLY IS YOUR
NAME, YOUR WILL BE DONE NOW AND FOREVER!

4. Daily true-prayer supplication. In the KJV bible book of Philippians chapter 4 verse 6; it states: "Be careful for nothing; but in everything by prayer and supplication with thanksgiving let your requests be made known unto God."

5. Daily meditation, healthy breathing and healthy and sober relaxation. In the KJV bible book of Psalms chapter 1 verse 2; it states: "But his delight [is] in the law of the LORD; and in his law doth he meditates day and night."

6. Daily high-quality sufficient amounts of sleep. In the KJV bible book of Psalms chapter 127 verse 2; it states: "[It is] vain for you to rise up early, to sit up late, to eat the bread of sorrows: [for] so he giveth his beloved sleep."

SPIRITUAL TRILLIONAIRE:
Cherishing the Breath of Life while Simultaneously
Preparing for the Blow of Death!

CHILDREN OF THE MOST HIGH:
PRISTINE YOUTH AND FAMILY SOLUTIONS, LLC.
SONS AND DAUGHTERS OF THE MOST HIGH PUBLISHERS ®

OH, GRACIOUS MOST HIGH HEAVENLY FATHER, HOLY IS YOUR
NAME, YOUR WILL BE DONE NOW AND FOREVER!

7. Daily loving and obeying the Messiah Yashu'a (Jesus). In the KJV bible book of John chapter 14 verse 15; Yashu'a (Jesus) said: "If ye love me, keep my commandments."

8. Daily having and practicing True-Faith in the Most High Heavenly Father. In the KJV bible book of Mark chapter 11 verse 22; it states: "And Yashu'a (Jesus) answering saith unto them, "Have faith in God.""

9. Daily having and expressing divine love for the Most High Heavenly Father, loving and obeying the Most High Heavenly Father with all of your heart, with all your spirit, with all of your soul, and with all of your mind. In the KJV bible book of Matthew chapter 22 verse 37; Yashu'a (Jesus) said unto him: "Thou shalt love the Lord thy God with all thy heart, and with all thy soul, and with all thy mind."

SPIRITUAL TRILLIONAIRE:
Cherishing the Breath of Life while Simultaneously
Preparing for the Blow of Death!

CHILDREN OF THE MOST HIGH:
PRISTINE YOUTH AND FAMILY SOLUTIONS, LLC.
SONS AND DAUGHTERS OF THE MOST HIGH PUBLISHERS ®

OH, GRACIOUS MOST HIGH HEAVENLY FATHER, HOLY IS YOUR
NAME, YOUR WILL BE DONE NOW AND FOREVER!

Physical gardening and deep breathing exercises assist in a person's overall positive well-being. According to (Sogaa, Gastonb, and Yamaura, (2017), Review Gardening Article, physical gardening provides many health benefits. Some of those benefits include reductions in body mass index, depression, anxiety, increases in life satisfaction, quality of life, and sense of community.

"According to Goren (2018), he has identified ten strategies for building emotional intelligence, preventing burnout, identified Family practice management strategies, and discussed the benefits of deep breathing. Deep breathing is sometimes referred to as diaphragmatic breathing, abdominal breathing, and belly breathing, which medical science has proven is far healthier than chest breathing. Deep abdominal breathing allows the lungs to experience full oxygen exchange of the incoming oxygen for outgoing carbon dioxide which can slow the heartbeat and lower or stabilize blood pressure." Viveros and Schramm (2018), also support why stress management strategies work. Additional stress management strategies include almost all of the 9 True Vine "Yashu'a" (Jesus) Essential Habits of Healing the physical body.

SPIRITUAL TRILLIONAIRE:
Cherishing the Breath of Life while Simultaneously
Preparing for the Blow of Death!

CHILDREN OF THE MOST HIGH:
PRISTINE YOUTH AND FAMILY SOLUTIONS, LLC.
SONS AND DAUGHTERS OF THE MOST HIGH PUBLISHERS ®

OH, GRACIOUS MOST HIGH HEAVENLY FATHER, HOLY IS YOUR
NAME, YOUR WILL BE DONE NOW AND FOREVER!

So, in summary, if the 9 True Vine "Yashu'a" (Jesus) Essential
Habits of Healing the physical body are learned and practiced
every day in balance with the 9 Essential Elements in a Human
Being, it may help a person to overcome the 9 Deadly Venoms
of the Desires of the great dragon: that old serpent, called the
Devil, and Satan, which deceiveth the whole world. Doing so
may also help a person to acquire positive spiritual health and
positive spiritual wealth on the path to becoming a Spiritual
Trillionaire.

So, as it relates to a person beginning the process of acquiring,
maintaining and sustaining positive spiritual health and positive
spiritual wealth; a person must be devout to the Most High
Heavenly Father mentally, physically, emotionally and
spiritually. A person must also be willingly to be on the narrow
path of those who stand straight (**exhibit high moral character
and high moral integrity**) in the process of diligently,
intentionally and patiently working each moment to learn,
memorize and practice and apply the **Children of the Most
High Pristine Youth and Family Solutions, LLC. 9X9 True
Vine "Yashu'a" (Jesus) B.A.-K.A.-R.E. Sequential Order of
Learning Habits of Success.**

246

SPIRITUAL TRILLIONAIRE:
Cherishing the Breath of Life while Simultaneously
Preparing for the Blow of Death!

CHILDREN OF THE MOST HIGH:
PRISTINE YOUTH AND FAMILY SOLUTIONS, LLC.
SONS AND DAUGHTERS OF THE MOST HIGH PUBLISHERS ®

OH, GRACIOUS MOST HIGH HEAVENLY FATHER, HOLY IS YOUR NAME, YOUR WILL BE DONE NOW AND FOREVER!

If youth and adults apply the aforementioned on a daily basis as a lifestyle, they may reap the benefits personally, professionally and globally.

In chapter 7, you mentioned how becoming a Spiritual Trillionaire may benefit youth and adults personally, professionally and globally; how does that correlate with the Children of the Most High Pristine Youth and Family Solutions, LLC. 9X9 True Vine "Yashu'a" (Jesus) B.A.-K.A.-R.E. Sequential Order of Learning Habits of Success?

SPIRITUAL TRILLIONAIRE:
**Cherishing the Breath of Life while Simultaneously
Preparing for the Blow of Death!**

CHILDREN OF THE MOST HIGH:
PRISTINE YOUTH AND FAMILY SOLUTIONS, LLC.
SONS AND DAUGHTERS OF THE MOST HIGH PUBLISHERS ®

OH, GRACIOUS MOST HIGH HEAVENLY FATHER, HOLY IS YOUR
NAME, YOUR WILL BE DONE NOW AND FOREVER!

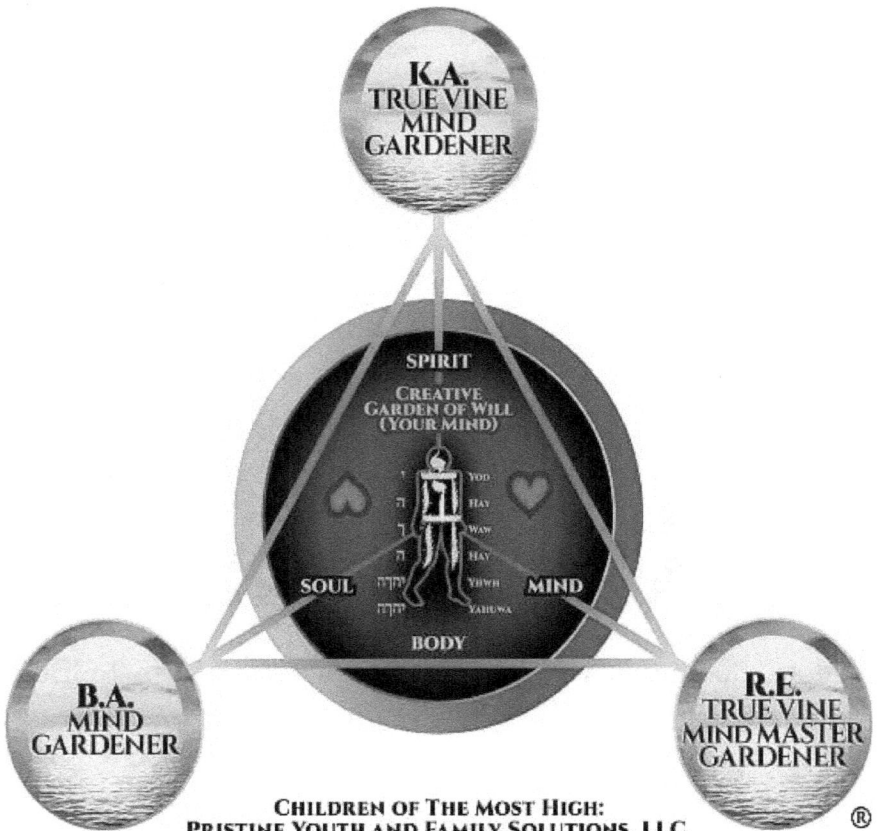

CHILDREN OF THE MOST HIGH:
PRISTINE YOUTH AND FAMILY SOLUTIONS, LLC.
9X9 TRUE VINE "YASHU'A" (JESUS) B.A.-K.A.-R.E.
SEQUENTIAL ORDER OF LEARNING®

248

SPIRITUAL TRILLIONAIRE:
Cherishing the Breath of Life while Simultaneously
Preparing for the Blow of Death!

CHILDREN OF THE MOST HIGH:
PRISTINE YOUTH AND FAMILY SOLUTIONS, LLC.
SONS AND DAUGHTERS OF THE MOST HIGH PUBLISHERS ®

OH, GRACIOUS MOST HIGH HEAVENLY FATHER, HOLY IS YOUR
NAME, YOUR WILL BE DONE NOW AND FOREVER!

Each child of the Most High has to willingly decide, out of love
for the Most High and love of the Messiah Yashu'a (Jesus);
whether or not they will utilize their **Creative Garden of Will
(Your Mind) to do their part in assisting in the process of
creating what the Children of the Most High: Pristine
Youth and Family Solutions, LLC. refer to as a global True
Vine "Yashu'a" (Jesus) <u>Farm-And-See</u> (which is
phonetically pronounced as: <u>Pharm-a-cy</u>) Garden of Love,
Positive Spiritual Health and Positive Spiritual Wealth. As
oppose to the present global Devil's Web <u>Far-From-Mercy</u>
(Pharm-a-cy) Garden of Poison Seeds.**

SPIRITUAL TRILLIONAIRE:
**Cherishing the Breath of Life while Simultaneously
Preparing for the Blow of Death!**

CHILDREN OF THE MOST HIGH:
PRISTINE YOUTH AND FAMILY SOLUTIONS, LLC.
SONS AND DAUGHTERS OF THE MOST HIGH PUBLISHERS

OH, GRACIOUS MOST HIGH HEAVENLY FATHER, HOLY IS YOUR
NAME, YOUR WILL BE DONE NOW AND FOREVER!

THE DEVIL'S WEB

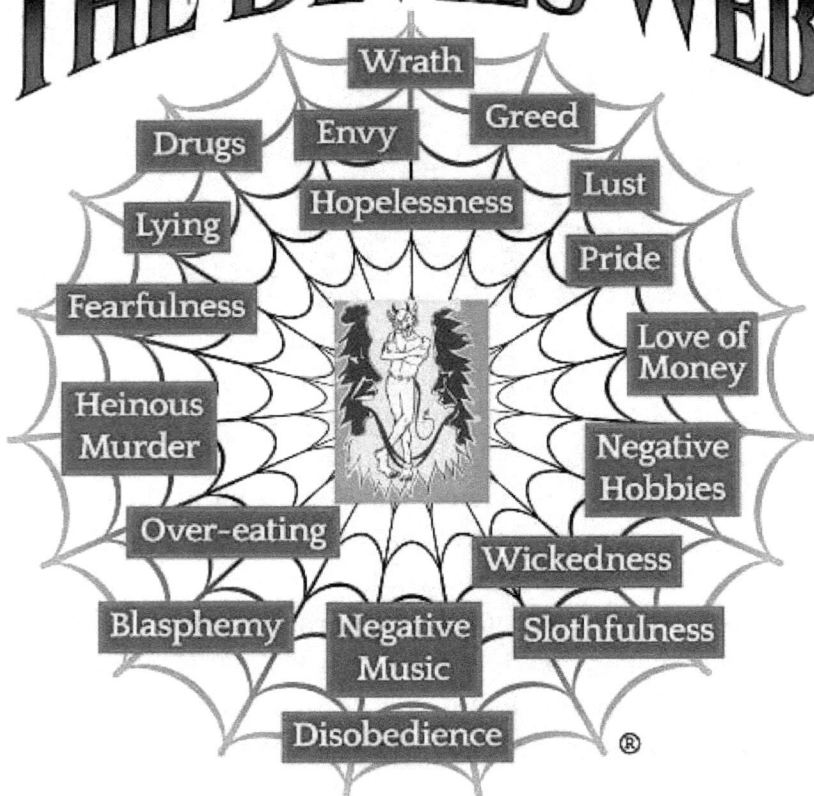

250

SPIRITUAL TRILLIONAIRE:
Cherishing the Breath of Life while Simultaneously
Preparing for the Blow of Death!

OH, GRACIOUS MOST HIGH HEAVENLY FATHER, HOLY IS YOUR
NAME, YOUR WILL BE DONE NOW AND FOREVER!

However, the children of the Most High who eat of the True
Vine "Yashu'a" (Jesus) Fruits of the Spirit, when you "See"
them, you see a reflection of the portion of the Most High that
is in them working through their "**Spiritual Majesty**" gifts
from the Most High to do the will of the Most High so that "Thy
Will Be Done on Earth as it is in Heaven!" And those who
see them, have a reminder and an opportunity to Glorify the
Most High! **The True Vine "Yashu'a (Jesus) Farm-And-See
Garden** grows True Vine "Yashu'a" (Jesus) Fruits of the Spirit
that feeds people mentally, spiritually, emotionally and
physically. **The True Vine "Yashu'a (Jesus) Farm-And-See
(which is phonetically pronounced as: Pharm-a-cy) Garden
foundation is** rooted in the "Will" of the Most High Heavenly
Father. The Messiah "Yashu'a (Jesus) proceeded from the Most
High Heavenly Father as the "**True Vine**". In the KJV bible
book of John chapter 15 verses 1-12;18-25; Yashu'a (Jesus)
said: "I am the true vine, and my Father is the husbandman.
Every branch in me that beareth not fruit he "taketh away:
and every branch that beareth fruit, he purgeth it, that it
may bring forth more fruit. Now ye are clean through the
word which I have spoken unto you. Abide in me, and I in
you.

SPIRITUAL TRILLIONAIRE:
Cherishing the Breath of Life while Simultaneously
Preparing for the Blow of Death!

CHILDREN OF THE MOST HIGH:
PRISTINE YOUTH AND FAMILY SOLUTIONS, LLC.
SONS AND DAUGHTERS OF THE MOST HIGH PUBLISHERS ®

OH, GRACIOUS MOST HIGH HEAVENLY FATHER, HOLY IS YOUR
NAME, YOUR WILL BE DONE NOW AND FOREVER!

As the branch cannot bear fruit of itself, except it abide in the vine; no more can ye, except ye abide in me. <u>I am the vine, ye are the branches: He that abideth in me, and I in him, the same bringeth forth much fruit: for without me ye can do nothing</u>. If a man [person] abide not in me, he is cast forth as a branch, and is withered; and men [human beings] gather them, and cast them into the fire, and they are burned. If ye abide in me, and my words abide in you, ye shall ask what ye will, and it shall be done unto you. Herein is my Father glorified, that ye bear much fruit; so, shall ye be my disciples. As the Father hath loved me, so have I loved you: continue ye in my love. If ye keep my commandments, ye shall abide in my love; even as I have kept my Father's commandments, and abide in his love. These things have I spoken unto you, that my joy might remain in you, and that your joy might be full. This is my commandment, that ye love one another, as I have loved you. <u>If the world hates you, ye know that it hated me before it hated you. If ye were of the world, the world would love his own: but because ye are not of the world, but I have chosen you out of the world, therefore the world hateth you</u>. Remember the word that I said unto you, the servant is not greater than his lord."

252

SPIRITUAL TRILLIONAIRE:
Cherishing the Breath of Life while Simultaneously
Preparing for the Blow of Death!

CHILDREN OF THE MOST HIGH:
PRISTINE YOUTH AND FAMILY SOLUTIONS, LLC.
SONS AND DAUGHTERS OF THE MOST HIGH PUBLISHERS ®

OH, GRACIOUS MOST HIGH HEAVENLY FATHER, HOLY IS YOUR
NAME, YOUR WILL BE DONE NOW AND FOREVER!

"If they have persecuted me, they will also persecute you; if they have kept my saying, they will keep yours also. But all these things will they do unto you for my name's sake, because they know not him that sent me. If I had not come and spoken unto them, they had not had sin: but now they have no cloke for their sin. He [a person] that hateth me hateth my Father also. If I had not done among them the works which none other man did, they had not had sin: but now have they both seen and hated both me and my Father. But this cometh to pass, that the word might be fulfilled that is written in their law, they hated me without a cause."

As it relates to a person being on the path to becoming a Spiritual Trillionaire, is there a correlation between what the bible refers to as sorcery, witchcraft, familiar spirits and the Mystery name of the Harlot who gave birth to the Global Devil's Web Far-From-Mercy (Pharm-a-cy) Garden of Poison Seeds? The 9 Deadly Venoms of the Desires of the great dragon, that old serpent called the devil and satan are in the devil's web, and are being grown continuously in the Global Devil's Web Far-From-Mercy (Pharm-a-cy) Garden of Poison Seeds.

253

SPIRITUAL TRILLIONAIRE:
Cherishing the Breath of Life while Simultaneously
Preparing for the Blow of Death!

CHILDREN OF THE MOST HIGH:
PRISTINE YOUTH AND FAMILY SOLUTIONS, LLC.
SONS AND DAUGHTERS OF THE MOST HIGH PUBLISHERS ℗

OH, GRACIOUS MOST HIGH HEAVENLY FATHER, HOLY IS YOUR
NAME, YOUR WILL BE DONE NOW AND FOREVER!

As oppose to being a child of the Most High who utilizes their
Creative Garden of Will (Your Mind) to do their part in
assisting in the process of creating a **Global True Vine
"Yashu'a" (Jesus) <u>Farm-And-See</u>** (which is phonetically
pronounced as: **<u>Pharm-a-cy</u>) Garden of Love, Positive
Spiritual Health and Positive Spiritual Wealth**. The **Global
Devil's Web <u>Far-From-Mercy</u> (Pharm-a-cy) Garden of
Poison Seeds** is the habitation of devils, the hold of every foul
spirit, and a cage of every unclean and hateful bird, slaves
(inclusive of human trafficking), and souls of people inclusive
of all nations of people were deceived by **sorceries** which is a
Mystery to those who do not know. In the KJV bible book of
Revelation chapter 17 verse 5; it states: "And upon her forehead
was a name written, **MYSTERY**, BABYLON THE GREAT,
THE MOTHER OF **HARLOTS** AND ABOMINATIONS OF
THE EARTH." The KJV bible Greek Strong's Concordance
word for "**MYSTERY**" is#3466 and is the word μυστήριον
mystērion which means **a hidden or secret thing, not obvious
to the understanding**. The KJV bible Greek Strong's
Concordance word for "**HARLOTS**" is#4204 and is the word
πόρνη **porne** which means **a prostitute, a harlot, an idolater,
one who yields themselves to defilement for the sake of gain**.

254

SPIRITUAL TRILLIONAIRE:
Cherishing the Breath of Life while Simultaneously
Preparing for the Blow of Death!

CHILDREN OF THE MOST HIGH:
PRISTINE YOUTH AND FAMILY SOLUTIONS, LLC.
SONS AND DAUGHTERS OF THE MOST HIGH PUBLISHERS ®

OH, GRACIOUS MOST HIGH HEAVENLY FATHER, HOLY IS YOUR
NAME, YOUR WILL BE DONE NOW AND FOREVER!

Porne is the **etymological root word** for "**Pornography**" which the Online American Heritage Dictionary (2019) defines to as: "Sexually explicit writing, images, video, or other material whose primary purpose is to cause sexual arousal. Lurid or sensational material. Often used in combination: violence pornography. [French pornographie, from pornographe, pornographer, from Late Greek pornographos, writing about prostitutes: **pornē**, prostitute; see per-5 in the Appendix of Indo-European roots + graphein, to write; see -GRAPHY."

SPIRITUAL TRILLIONAIRE:
Cherishing the Breath of Life while Simultaneously
Preparing for the Blow of Death!

CHILDREN OF THE MOST HIGH:
PRISTINE YOUTH AND FAMILY SOLUTIONS, LLC.
SONS AND DAUGHTERS OF THE MOST HIGH PUBLISHERS ®

OH, GRACIOUS MOST HIGH HEAVENLY FATHER, HOLY IS YOUR
NAME, YOUR WILL BE DONE NOW AND FOREVER!

So, the **MYSTERY** name of the **Harlot** in the KJV bible book
of Revelation chapter 17 that gave birth to the Global Devil's
Web **Far-From-Mercy** (**Pharm-a-cy**) Garden of Poison Seeds
is "**Porne**" or **Pornography**. "**Porne**" is rooted in "**Lusts**",
which is the 3rd of the 9 Deadly Venoms of Desires of the great
dragon, that old serpent called the devil and satan. Which is
what the Messiah Yashu'a (Jesus) warned us about in the KJV
bible book of John chapter 8:44; where he said to the Jews of
his day and time: "Ye are of your father the devil, and the
lusts of your father ye will do. He was a murderer from the
beginning, and abode not in the truth, because there is no
truth in him. When he speaketh a lie, he speaketh of his
own: for he is a liar, and the father of it." Also, the words,
he, **him** and **his** refers to **one** individual (phonetically is: **in-
the-visual** or "**I want to be seen or in-the-visual** (**individual**)
feeling of **P**ower") which denotes the "**I**" **principle** which
grows in Devil's Web **Far-From-Mercy** (**Pharm-a-cy**)
Garden of Poison Seeds, and it is rooted in "**Pride**", which is
the 1st of the 9 Deadly Venoms of Desires of the great dragon,
that old serpent called the devil and satan.

SPIRITUAL TRILLIONAIRE:
Cherishing the Breath of Life while Simultaneously
Preparing for the Blow of Death!

CHILDREN OF THE MOST HIGH:
PRISTINE YOUTH AND FAMILY SOLUTIONS, LLC.
SONS AND DAUGHTERS OF THE MOST HIGH PUBLISHERS ®

OH, GRACIOUS MOST HIGH HEAVENLY FATHER, HOLY IS YOUR NAME, YOUR WILL BE DONE NOW AND FOREVER!

When a person is in position of power in society, it does not change a person, it publicly reveals who the person who sits in the seat of power really is. Universal Love is against Individuality, which is why the word "Universe" consists of the two syllables of "Uni" (One) Verse (Against) or "ALL" or "The ALL" is against "Individuality"

"**Pride**", and the **Me**, **Myself** and **I Trinity** are the children of the "**EGO**, the KJV bible Greek Strong's Concordance#**1473** word: ἐγώ **egō** which means: **I, me, my**; a primary pronoun of the first person **I**" and are the greatest barriers to experiencing the Most High Heavenly Father through obedience to the "Will" and "Commandments" of Most High.

257

SPIRITUAL TRILLIONAIRE:
Cherishing the Breath of Life while Simultaneously
Preparing for the Blow of Death!

CHILDREN OF THE MOST HIGH:
PRISTINE YOUTH AND FAMILY SOLUTIONS, LLC.
SONS AND DAUGHTERS OF THE MOST HIGH PUBLISHERS ®

OH, GRACIOUS MOST HIGH HEAVENLY FATHER, HOLY IS YOUR
NAME, YOUR WILL BE DONE NOW AND FOREVER!

Remember: it was the "**EGO**" of the great dragon, that old serpent called the devil and satan that filled his chest with "**Pride**", and he got **very hot with great wrath (when a person gets very angry, their body temperature rises and their personality can change from positive to negative**) before him and his angels (messengers) got into a war with the Arch Angelic-Being Miykaa'el (Michael) and his Malaaikat (Angels/Messengers) in the KJV bible book of Revelation chapter 12 verses 7-12.

That's why the KJV bible book of Proverbs chapter 16 verse 18; states: "**Pride goeth before destruction, and a haughty** spirit before a fall." The KJV bible Hebrew Strong's Concordance#1363 for the word phrase "**and a haughty**" is גֹּבַהּ **gobahh and means arrogance, boastful, pouting out of anger, and full of pride.**"

The KJV bible book of Revelation chapter 12 verses 7-12; states: "And there was war in heaven: Michael and his angels fought against the dragon; and the dragon fought and his angels, and prevailed not; neither was their place found any more in heaven. And the great dragon was cast out, that old serpent,

SPIRITUAL TRILLIONAIRE:
**Cherishing the Breath of Life while Simultaneously
Preparing for the Blow of Death!**

CHILDREN OF THE MOST HIGH:
PRISTINE YOUTH AND FAMILY SOLUTIONS, LLC.
SONS AND DAUGHTERS OF THE MOST HIGH PUBLISHERS

OH, GRACIOUS MOST HIGH HEAVENLY FATHER, HOLY IS YOUR
NAME, YOUR WILL BE DONE NOW AND FOREVER!

called the Devil, and Satan, which deceiveth the whole world: he was cast out into the earth, and his angels were cast out with him. And I heard a loud voice saying in heaven, Now is come salvation, and strength, and the kingdom of our God, and the power of his Christ: for the accuser of our brethren is cast down, which accused them before our God day and night. And they overcame him by the blood of the Lamb, and by the word of their testimony; and they loved not their lives unto the death. Therefore rejoice, ye heavens, and ye that dwell in them. **Woe to the inhabitants of the earth and of the sea! for the devil is come down unto you, having great wrath, because he knoweth that he hath but a short time**."

So, as it relates to a person who aspires to become a Spiritual Trillionaire, **P**ride (**P**), **P**orne or Pornography (**P**) and the "I" principle that grows the "**I want to be seen or in-the-visual (individual)** feeling of **P**ower (**P**) are all from the **9 Deadly Venoms** of the great dragon which is revealed in the **3 PPPs'** being turned upside down as the numbers **666**. In the KJV bible book of Revelation chapter 13 verse 18; it states: "**Here is wisdom**. Let him that hath understanding count the number of the beast: **for it is the number of a man** (the KJV bible Greek Strong's Concordance#444 for the word "man" is ἄνθρωπος

259

SPIRITUAL TRILLIONAIRE:
**Cherishing the Breath of Life while Simultaneously
Preparing for the Blow of Death!**

CHILDREN OF THE MOST HIGH:
PRISTINE YOUTH AND FAMILY SOLUTIONS, LLC.
SONS AND DAUGHTERS OF THE MOST HIGH PUBLISHERS ®

OH, GRACIOUS MOST HIGH HEAVENLY FATHER, HOLY IS YOUR
NAME, YOUR WILL BE DONE NOW AND FOREVER!

Anthrōpos and means a person or human being, whether male or female); and his (or her or their) number is Six hundred threescore and six (**666**)."

It is not possible to achieve positive spiritual health and positive spiritual wealth without surrendering the "**I**" principle and converting the "**EGO**" into the eternal obedient service to the "**Will**" of the Most High Heavenly Father. By surrendering the "**I**" principle, over time with a lot of personal hard work on yourself, a person may become free from all of the 9 Deadly Venoms of the Desires of the great dragon, that old serpent called the devil and satan.

In the KJV bible book of Revelation chapter 18 verses 1, 2, 13 and 23 states: "And after these things I saw another angel come down from heaven, having great power; and the earth was lightened with his glory. And he cried mightily with a strong voice, saying, Babylon the great is fallen, is fallen, and **is become the habitation of devils, and the hold of every foul spirit, and a cage of every unclean and hateful bird**."

SPIRITUAL TRILLIONAIRE:
Cherishing the Breath of Life while Simultaneously
Preparing for the Blow of Death!

CHILDREN OF THE MOST HIGH:
PRISTINE YOUTH AND FAMILY SOLUTIONS, LLC.
SONS AND DAUGHTERS OF THE MOST HIGH PUBLISHERS ®

OH, GRACIOUS MOST HIGH HEAVENLY FATHER, HOLY IS YOUR
NAME, YOUR WILL BE DONE NOW AND FOREVER!

And cinnamon, and odours, and ointments, and frankincense, and wine, and oil, and fine flour, and wheat, and beasts, and sheep, and horses, and chariots, and **slaves, and souls of men**. And the light of a candle shall shine no more at all in thee; and the voice of the bridegroom and of the bride shall be heard no more at all in thee: for thy merchants were the great men of the earth; for by thy **sorceries** were all nations deceived."

In the KJV bible book of Revelation chapter 18 verse 23; the word for "**sorceries**" is the KJV bible Greek Strong's Concordance#5331word: **φαρμακεία pharmakeia** which is the original Greek root word of where the word **"Pharmacy and Pharmaceuticals" originates from.** In the KJV bible book of Galatians chapter 5 verses 19-21; states: "Now the works of the flesh are manifest, which are these; Adultery, fornication, uncleanness, lasciviousness, Idolatry, **witchcraft**, hatred, variance, emulations, wrath, strife, seditions, heresies, Envyings, murders, drunkenness, reveling, and such like: of the which I tell you before, as I have also told you in time past, that they which do such things shall not inherit the kingdom of God."

SPIRITUAL TRILLIONAIRE:
Cherishing the Breath of Life while Simultaneously
Preparing for the Blow of Death!

CHILDREN OF THE MOST HIGH:
PRISTINE YOUTH AND FAMILY SOLUTIONS, LLC.
SONS AND DAUGHTERS OF THE MOST HIGH PUBLISHERS ®

OH, GRACIOUS MOST HIGH HEAVENLY FATHER, HOLY IS YOUR
NAME, YOUR WILL BE DONE NOW AND FOREVER!

In the KJV bible book of Galatians chapter 5 verse 20; the word for "**witchcraft**" is the KJV bible Greek Strong's Concordance#5331word: **φαρμακεία pharmakeia** which is the original Greek root word of where the word "**Pharmacy and Pharmaceuticals**" originates from. **The Pharmaceutical companies** make opioids and pain medication that many people have become **addicted** to which introduced the world to opioids, and the opioids "**addiction**" crisis in America. **However, in fairness, many people have taken opioids as prescribed by their medical physicians and did not become addicted to opioids.**

SPIRITUAL TRILLIONAIRE:
Cherishing the Breath of Life while Simultaneously
Preparing for the Blow of Death!

CHILDREN OF THE MOST HIGH:
PRISTINE YOUTH AND FAMILY SOLUTIONS, LLC.
SONS AND DAUGHTERS OF THE MOST HIGH PUBLISHERS ®

OH, GRACIOUS MOST HIGH HEAVENLY FATHER, HOLY IS YOUR
NAME, YOUR WILL BE DONE NOW AND FOREVER!

Opioids "**addiction**" adds to preexisting **addictions** such as tobacco, alcohol, illegal and legal substance abuse **addictions** which continues to grow the number of people who become **addicted** to pharmaceutical drugs and become **addicts** amongst members of humanity. **Leviathan**, as a sex force, utilizes **Porne to grow** "**Lusts**", the 3rd of the 9 Deadly Venoms of Desires of the great dragon, that old serpent called the devil and satan in the **global Devil's Web** <u>**Far-From-Mercy**</u> **(Pharm-a-cy) Garden of Poison Seeds**.

DANGER

POISON

In the KJV bible book of Leviticus chapter 19 verse 31; states: "Regard <u>**not them that have familiar spirits**</u>, neither seek after <u>**wizards**</u> "to be defiled by them: I [am] the LORD your God."

SPIRITUAL TRILLIONAIRE:
**Cherishing the Breath of Life while Simultaneously
Preparing for the Blow of Death!**

CHILDREN OF THE MOST HIGH:
PRISTINE YOUTH AND FAMILY SOLUTIONS, LLC.
SONS AND DAUGHTERS OF THE MOST HIGH PUBLISHERS

OH, GRACIOUS MOST HIGH HEAVENLY FATHER, HOLY IS YOUR
NAME, YOUR WILL BE DONE NOW AND FOREVER!

In the KJV bible book of Leviticus chapter 20 verse 6; states:
"And the soul that turneth after **such as have familiar spirits**,
and after **wizards**, to go a whoring after them, I will even set
my face against that soul, and will cut him off from among his
people." "In the KJV bible book of Leviticus chapter 19 verse
31, and Leviticus chapter 20 verse 6; the word for "**wizards**" is
the KJV bible Hebrew Strong's Concordance#3045 word:
"**Yiddehonee**" יִדְּעֹנִי **yidd@`oniy which means soothsayer,
necromancer, a knowing one; specifically, a conjurer; (by
implication) a ghost; wizard.**"

יִדְּעֹנִי. m. pl. יִדְּעֹנִים.—(1) properly knowing, wise,
hence *a prophet, a wizard*, always used in a bad
sense of false prophets. Lev. 19:31; 20:6; Deut.
18:11; 1 Sa. 28:3, 9 (comp. عالِم prop. knowing, a
magician, like the Germ. weiſer Mann, kluge Frau, used
of wizards uttering words to the deluded people.)
(2) *a spirit of divination, a spirit of python*
with which these soothsayers were believed to be in
communication. Lev. 20:27; comp. אוֹב.

SPIRITUAL TRILLIONAIRE:
Cherishing the Breath of Life while Simultaneously
Preparing for the Blow of Death!

OH, GRACIOUS MOST HIGH HEAVENLY FATHER, HOLY IS YOUR
NAME, YOUR WILL BE DONE NOW AND FOREVER!

In the previous KJV bible book of Leviticus chapter 19 verse 31, and Leviticus chapter 20 verse 6; the word for phrases "**not them that have familiar spirits** and **such as have familiar spirits**" is the KJV bible Hebrew Strong's Concordance#178 word: אוֹב 'owb which means **ghost**, **spirit of a dead one**. So, in summary, the aforementioned information explains the correlation between what the bible refers to as sorcery, witchcraft, familiar spirits and the Mystery name of the Harlot who gave birth to the Global Devil's Web **Far-From-Mercy** (Pharmacy) Garden of Poison Seeds as it relates to a person being on the path to becoming a Spiritual Trillionaire.

It also clarifies **why God (Elohiym) is** against the children of the Most High utilizing or experimenting with **Ouija boards or spirit boards, porne, soothsayers, necromancers, sorceries, witchcraft, familiar spirits and overcoming the "I" principle, as it relates to preventing a person from being able to acquire, maintain and sustain positive spiritual health and positive spiritual wealth**. So, it is crucial that all aspiring Spiritual Trillionaires set True Vine (Yashu'a, Jesus) P.A.S.S.I.O.N.A.T.E. P.A.T.H.F.I.N.D.E.R.S. of the Most High **Predetermined S.M.A.R.T. (Single-Minded, Achievable,**

SPIRITUAL TRILLIONAIRE:
Cherishing the Breath of Life while Simultaneously
Preparing for the Blow of Death!

CHILDREN OF THE MOST HIGH:
PRISTINE YOUTH AND FAMILY SOLUTIONS, LLC.
SONS AND DAUGHTERS OF THE MOST HIGH PUBLISHERS ®

OH, GRACIOUS MOST HIGH HEAVENLY FATHER, HOLY IS YOUR
NAME, YOUR WILL BE DONE NOW AND FOREVER!

Reasonable, Timed) Goals for themselves to intentionally, acquire, maintain, and sustain positive spiritual health and positive spiritual wealth. Becoming a Spiritual Trillionaire requires a person to commit themselves with a sincere and compassionate heart to the service of the Most High Heavenly Father ONLY! Service is the vehicle by which an aspiring Spiritual Trillionaire, child of the Most High Heavenly Father travels in life.

Shirley Chisholm said: "Service is the rent we pay for the privilege of living on the earth."

Rev. Dr. Martin Luther King Jr. said:

Everybody Can Be Great Because Everybody Can Serve

SPIRITUAL TRILLIONAIRE:
Cherishing the Breath of Life while Simultaneously
Preparing for the Blow of Death!

CHILDREN OF THE MOST HIGH:
PRISTINE YOUTH AND FAMILY SOLUTIONS, LLC.
SONS AND DAUGHTERS OF THE MOST HIGH PUBLISHERS ®

OH, GRACIOUS MOST HIGH HEAVENLY FATHER, HOLY IS YOUR
NAME, YOUR WILL BE DONE NOW AND FOREVER!

Love is the zeal and speed of the vehicle by which an aspiring
Spiritual Trillionaire, child of the Most High Heavenly Father
travels in life, and wisdom is the way that an aspiring Spiritual
Trillionaire, child of the Most High Heavenly Father travels in
life.

SPIRITUAL TRILLIONAIRE:
Cherishing the Breath of Life while Simultaneously
Preparing for the Blow of Death!

CHILDREN OF THE MOST HIGH:
PRISTINE YOUTH AND FAMILY SOLUTIONS, LLC.
SONS AND DAUGHTERS OF THE MOST HIGH PUBLISHERS ®

OH, GRACIOUS MOST HIGH HEAVENLY FATHER, HOLY IS YOUR
NAME, YOUR WILL BE DONE NOW AND FOREVER!

What are the Children of the Most High Pristine Youth and
Family Solutions, LLC. 9X9 True Vine "Yashu'a" (Jesus)
B.A.-K.A.-R.E. Sequential Order of Learning Habits of
Success that can help a person to become a Spiritual
Trillionaire?

The **1st of the 9X9** True Vine "Yashu'a" (Jesus) B.A.-K.A.-
R.E. Sequential Order of Learning Habits of Success which
introduce the mind to thoughts that give birth to new ideas;
are **the 9 True Vine Yashu'a (Jesus) Mind Gardening
Memorization Keys to Success** that may help a person to
becoming a Spiritual Trillionaire. They are:

1. **G**lorify the Most High Heavenly Father through the
   Messiah Yashu'a (Jesus).

2. **A**pply the Most High's Scriptural Knowledge in all that
   you do.

SPIRITUAL TRILLIONAIRE:
**Cherishing the Breath of Life while Simultaneously
Preparing for the Blow of Death!**

CHILDREN OF THE MOST HIGH:
PRISTINE YOUTH AND FAMILY SOLUTIONS, LLC.
SONS AND DAUGHTERS OF THE MOST HIGH PUBLISHERS ®

OH, GRACIOUS MOST HIGH HEAVENLY FATHER, HOLY IS YOUR
NAME, YOUR WILL BE DONE NOW AND FOREVER!

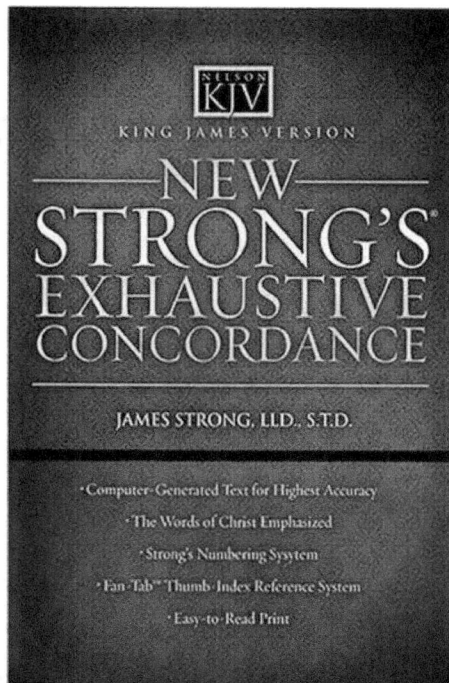

3. **R**evere the Most High and have moral reverence for the Most High.

4. **D**ecrease so that the Messiah Yashu'a (Jesus) can increase within you.

269

SPIRITUAL TRILLIONAIRE:
Cherishing the Breath of Life while Simultaneously
Preparing for the Blow of Death!

CHILDREN OF THE MOST HIGH:
PRISTINE YOUTH AND FAMILY SOLUTIONS, LLC.
SONS AND DAUGHTERS OF THE MOST HIGH PUBLISHERS ®

OH, GRACIOUS MOST HIGH HEAVENLY FATHER, HOLY IS YOUR
NAME, YOUR WILL BE DONE NOW AND FOREVER!

5. Except a person be born again, he or she cannot see the kingdom of the Most High.

6. Nourish yourself and others with the Most High's Scriptural Knowledge.

7. Inform yourself and others about the Most High's Scriptural Knowledge.

8. Narrow is the way that leads unto eternal life through the Messiah Yashu'a (Jesus).

9. Grace and truth came by way of the Messiah Yashu'a (Jesus).

Explain how the 9 True Vine Yashu'a (Jesus) Mind Gardening Memorization Keys to Success concept of Gardening relates to Mind Gardening and its relationship to the Most High, the True Vine (the Messiah Yashu'a, Jesus), the branches, obeying the laws of the Most High, mind, heart, and grace?

SPIRITUAL TRILLIONAIRE:
Cherishing the Breath of Life while Simultaneously
Preparing for the Blow of Death!

CHILDREN OF THE MOST HIGH:
PRISTINE YOUTH AND FAMILY SOLUTIONS, LLC.
SONS AND DAUGHTERS OF THE MOST HIGH PUBLISHERS ®

OH, GRACIOUS MOST HIGH HEAVENLY FATHER, HOLY IS YOUR
NAME, YOUR WILL BE DONE NOW AND FOREVER!

The **Most High Heavenly Father is the Creator** of the **Mind**
and on a **macro level from the people on earth viewpoint, the
Boundless Universes combined may be one of the Most
High's Garden's?**

The Messiah Yashu'a (Jesus) is **the True Vine** as stated in the
KJV bible book of John chapter 15 verse 1; he said: "I am the
true vine, and my Father is the husbandman." Aspiring
Spiritual Trillionaires who accept the Messiah Yashu'a (Jesus)
into their **hearts** as their savior, will be **the branches** as
Yashu'a (Jesus) said in the KJV bible book of John chapter 15
verse 4; he said: (I am the vine, ye are the branches: He that
abideth in me, and I in him, the same bringeth forth much
fruit: for without me ye can do nothing)."

Growth occurs over time by learning and obeying the laws of
the Most High which initiates all thoughts through the
activating of the "**Will**" of the Most High Heavenly Father in
the minds of aspiring Spiritual Trillionaires. Once this occurs,
Yashu'a (Jesus) makes them into **Mind Gardeners** who
become practitioners of **Mind Gardening!** In the KJV bible
book of Hebrews 8 verse 10; it states: "For this is the covenant

271

SPIRITUAL TRILLIONAIRE:
Cherishing the Breath of Life while Simultaneously
Preparing for the Blow of Death!

CHILDREN OF THE MOST HIGH:
PRISTINE YOUTH AND FAMILY SOLUTIONS, LLC.
SONS AND DAUGHTERS OF THE MOST HIGH PUBLISHERS ®

OH, GRACIOUS MOST HIGH HEAVENLY FATHER, HOLY IS YOUR
NAME, YOUR WILL BE DONE NOW AND FOREVER!

that I will make with the house of Israel after those days, saith
the Lord; I will put my laws into their mind, and write them in
their hearts: and I will be to them a God, and they shall be to
me a people."

In the KJV bible book of Revelation chapter 22 verse 14; it
states: "Blessed are they that do his commandments, that they
may have right to the tree of life, and may enter in through the
gates into the city." As it relates to **Mind Gardening, what
does the heart have to do with the mind**? As a necessary
essential Spiritual Trillionaire growth requirement, a person
must have a clean or pure heart that is forgiven of all sins
through repentance which is why the Messiah Yashu'a (Jesus)
stands at the door of the **hearts** of people offering **grace**, **truth**
(KJV bible book of John chapter 1 verse 17) and **eternal life**.
The Messiah Yashu'a (Jesus) said in the KJV bible book of
Revelation chapter 3 verse 20; he said: "Behold, I stand at the
door, and knock: if any man [person] hear my voice, and
open the door [of the **heart**], I will come in to him, and will
sup with him [or her], and he [or she] with me."

SPIRITUAL TRILLIONAIRE:
Cherishing the Breath of Life while Simultaneously
Preparing for the Blow of Death!

CHILDREN OF THE MOST HIGH:
PRISTINE YOUTH AND FAMILY SOLUTIONS, LLC.
SONS AND DAUGHTERS OF THE MOST HIGH PUBLISHERS ®

OH, GRACIOUS MOST HIGH HEAVENLY FATHER, HOLY IS YOUR
NAME, YOUR WILL BE DONE NOW AND FOREVER!

"The word "**Grace**" is the KJV bible Greek Strong's
Concordance #5485 word: χάρις **charis** (**khar`-ece**), which
means graciousness (as gratifying), of manner or act (abstract
or concrete; literal, figurative or spiritual; especially the divine
influence upon the heart, and its reflection in the life; including
gratitude): acceptable, benefit, favor, gift, grace(- ious), joy,
liberality, pleasure, thank(-s, -worthy)." This is why the
Messiah Yashu'a (Jesus) said in the KJV bible book of Matthew
chapter 6 verse 21; he said: "For where your treasure is, there
will your heart be also." **Therefore; allowing the Most High
to divide the disagreeable from agreeable in our hearts is
essential to acquiring, maintaining and sustaining positive
spiritual health and positive spiritual wealth on the path of
becoming a Spiritual Trillionaire!**

WHAT DO YOU VALUE THE MOST?

SPIRITUAL TRILLIONAIRE:
Cherishing the Breath of Life while Simultaneously
Preparing for the Blow of Death!

CHILDREN OF THE MOST HIGH:
PRISTINE YOUTH AND FAMILY SOLUTIONS, LLC.
SONS AND DAUGHTERS OF THE MOST HIGH PUBLISHERS ®

OH, GRACIOUS MOST HIGH HEAVENLY FATHER, HOLY IS YOUR
NAME, YOUR WILL BE DONE NOW AND FOREVER!

Rev. Dr. Martin Luther King Jr. said: "No one really know why they are alive until they know what they'd die for."

Rev. Dr. Martin Luther King Jr. said: "the arc of the moral universe is long, but it bends toward justice."

SPIRITUAL TRILLIONAIRE:
Cherishing the Breath of Life while Simultaneously
Preparing for the Blow of Death!

CHILDREN OF THE MOST HIGH:
PRISTINE YOUTH AND FAMILY SOLUTIONS, LLC.
SONS AND DAUGHTERS OF THE MOST HIGH PUBLISHERS ®

OH, GRACIOUS MOST HIGH HEAVENLY FATHER, HOLY IS YOUR
NAME, YOUR WILL BE DONE NOW AND FOREVER!

Explain the 9 True Vine Yashu'a (Jesus) Mind Gardening Memorization Keys to Success of <u>Gardening</u> as it relates to the Mind Gardening from the Original language of the Bible verses where they come from?

The 9 True Vine (Yashu'a, Jesus) Memorization Keys to Success acronyms of <u>Gardening</u> as it relates to the True Vine Yashu'a (Jesus) Mind Gardening from the original language that the Bible verses were revealed in is listed below:

1. <u>G</u>lorify – In the KJV bible book of Matthew chapter 5 verse 16; Yashu'a (Jesus) said: "Let your light so shine before men, that they may see your good works, and glorify your Father which is in heaven." In this verse, the word for "**glorify**", is the KJV bible Greek Strong's Concordance#1392 word: δοξάζω **doxazo** (**dox-ad`-zo**), which means to render (or esteem) glorious (in a wide application): (make) glorify(-ious), full of (have) glory, honor, magnify.

SPIRITUAL TRILLIONAIRE:
Cherishing the Breath of Life while Simultaneously
Preparing for the Blow of Death!

CHILDREN OF THE MOST HIGH:
PRISTINE YOUTH AND FAMILY SOLUTIONS, LLC.
SONS AND DAUGHTERS OF THE MOST HIGH PUBLISHERS ®

OH, GRACIOUS MOST HIGH HEAVENLY FATHER, HOLY IS YOUR
NAME, YOUR WILL BE DONE NOW AND FOREVER!

2. Apply - In the KJV bible book of Psalms chapter 90 verse 12; it states: "So teach us to number our days, **that we may apply our hearts unto wisdom."** In this verse, the KJV bible Hebrew Strong's Concordance#935 word: בּוֹא **bow'** (bō), which is the word for "**apply**" which means to apply, attain, get, follow.

3. <u>R</u>evere or <u>R</u>everence – In the KJV bible book of Proverbs chapter 1 verse 7; it states: "**The <u>fear</u> of the LORD is the beginning of knowledge: but fools** אֱוִיל **'eviyl,** the word for "**fools**" is KJV bible Hebrew Strong's Concordance#191 word "<u>ev·ēl</u>" meaning to be perverse, be foolish, foolish, of one who despises wisdom, of one who mocks when guilty, of one who is quarrelsome, of one who is licentious silly: fool(-ish). **despise wisdom and instruction."** In this verse, the word for "**fear**" is the KJV bible Hebrew Strong's Concordance#3374 word: יִרְאָה **yir'ah** (yir·ä'), which means to "**fear**", to respect, reverence, piety revered respect, having moral reverence.

CHILDREN OF THE MOST HIGH:
PRISTINE YOUTH AND FAMILY SOLUTIONS, LLC.
SONS AND DAUGHTERS OF THE MOST HIGH PUBLISHERS ®

OH, GRACIOUS MOST HIGH HEAVENLY FATHER, HOLY IS YOUR NAME, YOUR WILL BE DONE NOW AND FOREVER!

4. <u>D</u>ecrease – In the KJV bible book of John chapter 3 verse 30; it states: "He must increase, but I **must decrease**." In this verse, the word for "**decrease**" is the KJV bible Greek Strong's Concordance#1642 word: ἐλαττόω **elattoo (el-at-to`-o)**, which means to lessen, make lower to make less or inferior: in dignity, to be made less or inferior: in dignity; to decrease in authority or popularity.

5. <u>E</u>xcept – In the KJV bible book of John chapter 3 verse 3; Yashu'a (Jesus) said unto him: "Verily, verily, I say unto thee, **except** a man be born again, he cannot see the kingdom of God." In this verse, the word for "**except**" is the KJV bible Greek Strong's Concordance #3362 word: ἐὰν μή **ean mē (eh-an`-may)**, which means if not, unless, before, but, except.

SPIRITUAL TRILLIONAIRE:
**Cherishing the Breath of Life while Simultaneously
Preparing for the Blow of Death!**

CHILDREN OF THE MOST HIGH:
PRISTINE YOUTH AND FAMILY SOLUTIONS, LLC.
SONS AND DAUGHTERS OF THE MOST HIGH PUBLISHERS ®

OH, GRACIOUS MOST HIGH HEAVENLY FATHER, HOLY IS YOUR
NAME, YOUR WILL BE DONE NOW AND FOREVER!

6. <u>N</u>ourish – In the KJV bible book of Genesis chapter 50 verse 21; it states: "Now therefore fear ye not: **I will nourish you**, and your little ones. And he comforted them, and spake kindly unto them." In this verse, the word for "**nourish**" is the KJV bible Hebrew Strong's Concordance#3557 word: כּוּל **kuwl** (kool), which means to maintain, sustain, provide sustenance.

7. <u>I</u>nform – In the KJV bible book of Deuteronomy chapter 17 verse 10; it states: "And thou shalt do according to the sentence, which they of that place which the LORD shall choose shall shew thee; and thou shalt observe to do **according to all that they inform** thee." In this verse, the word for "**inform**" is the KJV bible Hebrew Strong's Concordance#3384 word: יָרָה **yarah** (yaw-raw`), which means to teach, direct, teach through, instruct, inform.

SPIRITUAL TRILLIONAIRE:
Cherishing the Breath of Life while Simultaneously
Preparing for the Blow of Death!

CHILDREN OF THE MOST HIGH:
PRISTINE YOUTH AND FAMILY SOLUTIONS, LLC.
SONS AND DAUGHTERS OF THE MOST HIGH PUBLISHERS ®

OH, GRACIOUS MOST HIGH HEAVENLY FATHER, HOLY IS YOUR
NAME, YOUR WILL BE DONE NOW AND FOREVER!

8. Narrow – In the KJV bible book of Matthew chapter 7 verse 14; Yashu'a (Jesus) said: "Because strait is the gate, and narrow is the way, which leadeth unto life, and few there be that find it." In this verse, the word for "narrow" is the KJV bible Greek King James Strong Concordance#2346 word: θλίβω thlibō (thlee`-bo), which means thin, tight, small width, slim, slender, limited in extent, amount, or scope; restricted, narrow.

9. Grace – In the KJV bible book of Matthew chapter 1 verse 7; it stated: "For the law was given by Moses, but grace and truth came by Jesus Christ." In this verse, the word for "grace" is the KJV bible Greek King James Strong Concordance #5485 word: χάρις charis (khä'-rēs) means graciousness (as gratifying), of manner or act (abstract or concrete; literal, figurative or spiritual; especially the divine influence upon the heart, and its reflection in the life; including gratitude); acceptable, benefit, favor, gift, grace(- ious), joy, liberality, pleasure, thank(-s, -worthy).

SPIRITUAL TRILLIONAIRE:
Cherishing the Breath of Life while Simultaneously
Preparing for the Blow of Death!

CHILDREN OF THE MOST HIGH:
PRISTINE YOUTH AND FAMILY SOLUTIONS, LLC.
SONS AND DAUGHTERS OF THE MOST HIGH PUBLISHERS ®

OH, GRACIOUS MOST HIGH HEAVENLY FATHER, HOLY IS YOUR
NAME, YOUR WILL BE DONE NOW AND FOREVER!

The **9 True Vine Yashu'a (Jesus) Memorization Keys to Success**, if learned and practiced every day, it may help a person to overcome the 9 Deadly Venoms of the Desires of the great dragon: that old serpent, called the Devil, and Satan, which deceiveth the whole world. They may also help a person to acquire positive spiritual health and positive spiritual wealth on the path to becoming a Spiritual Trillionaire.

SPIRITUAL TRILLIONAIRE:
Cherishing the Breath of Life while Simultaneously
Preparing for the Blow of Death!

CHILDREN OF THE MOST HIGH:
PRISTINE YOUTH AND FAMILY SOLUTIONS, LLC.
SONS AND DAUGHTERS OF THE MOST HIGH PUBLISHERS ®

OH, GRACIOUS MOST HIGH HEAVENLY FATHER, HOLY IS YOUR
NAME, YOUR WILL BE DONE NOW AND FOREVER!

The **2nd of the 9X9** True Vine "Yashu'a" (Jesus) B.A.-K.A.-R.E. Sequential Order of Learning Habits of Success are **the 9 True Vine Yashu'a (Jesus) Elements of Healthy Living** that may help a person's overall well-being of as it relates to acquiring, maintaining and sustaining positive spiritual health and positive spiritual on the path to becoming a Spiritual Trillionaire, which are:

1. **<u>A Resilient - Sound Mind</u>** – In the KJV bible book of 2nd Timothy chapter 1 verse 7; it states: "For God hath not given us the spirit of fear; but of power, and of love, and of a sound mind." In the KJV bible book of Hebrews chapter 8 verse 10; it states: "For this is the covenant that I will make with the house of Israel after those days, saith the Lord; I will put my laws into their mind, and write them in their hearts: and I will be to them a God, and they shall be to me a people."

SPIRITUAL TRILLIONAIRE:
**Cherishing the Breath of Life while Simultaneously
Preparing for the Blow of Death!**

CHILDREN OF THE MOST HIGH:
PRISTINE YOUTH AND FAMILY SOLUTIONS, LLC.
SONS AND DAUGHTERS OF THE MOST HIGH PUBLISHERS ®

OH, GRACIOUS MOST HIGH HEAVENLY FATHER, HOLY IS YOUR
NAME, YOUR WILL BE DONE NOW AND FOREVER!

2. **A Clean Soul** – In the KJV bible book of Mark chapter 7 verses 20-23; the Messiah Yashu'a (Jesus) said: "That which cometh out of the man, that defileth the man [or person]. For from within, out of the heart of men, proceed evil thoughts, adulteries, fornications, murders, thefts, covetousness, wickedness, deceit, lasciviousness, an evil eye, blasphemy, pride, foolishness: All these evil things come from within, and defile the man [or person]."

3. **A Holy Spirit** – In the KJV bible book of Luke chapter 11 verse 13; the Messiah Yashu'a (Jesus) said: "If ye then, being evil, know how to give good gifts unto your children: how much more shall your heavenly Father give the Holy Spirit to them that ask him?" In the KJV bible book of Isaiah chapter 11 verse 2; it states: "And the spirit of the LORD shall rest upon him, the spirit of wisdom and understanding, the spirit of counsel and might, the spirit of knowledge and of the fear of the LORD."

SPIRITUAL TRILLIONAIRE:
Cherishing the Breath of Life while Simultaneously
Preparing for the Blow of Death!

CHILDREN OF THE MOST HIGH:
PRISTINE YOUTH AND FAMILY SOLUTIONS, LLC.
SONS AND DAUGHTERS OF THE MOST HIGH PUBLISHERS ®

OH, GRACIOUS MOST HIGH HEAVENLY FATHER, HOLY IS YOUR NAME, YOUR WILL BE DONE NOW AND FOREVER!

4. **A Clear Conscious** – In the KJV bible book of 1ˢᵗ John chapter 1 verse 9; it states: "If we confess our sins, he is faithful and just to forgive us our sins, and to cleanse us from all unrighteousness."

5. **A Clean Heart** – In the KJV bible book of Psalms chapter 51 verse 10; it states: "Create in me a clean heart, O God; and renew a right spirit within me." In the KJV bible book of Deuteronomy chapter 6 verses 4-7; it states: "Hear, O Israel: The LORD our God is one LORD: And thou shalt love the LORD thy God with all thine heart, and with all thy soul, and with all thy might. And these words, which I command thee this day, shall be in thine heart: And thou shalt teach them diligently unto thy children, and shalt talk of them when thou sittest in thine house, and when thou walkest by the way, and when thou liest down, and when thou risest up."

SPIRITUAL TRILLIONAIRE:
**Cherishing the Breath of Life while Simultaneously
Preparing for the Blow of Death!**

CHILDREN OF THE MOST HIGH:
PRISTINE YOUTH AND FAMILY SOLUTIONS, LLC.
SONS AND DAUGHTERS OF THE MOST HIGH PUBLISHERS &

OH, GRACIOUS MOST HIGH HEAVENLY FATHER, HOLY IS YOUR
NAME, YOUR WILL BE DONE NOW AND FOREVER!

6. <u>**A Caring Person**</u> – In the KJV bible book of John chapter 13 verses 34-35 Yashu'a (Jesus) said: "A new commandment I give unto you, that ye love one another; as I have loved you, that ye also love one another. By this shall all men [women and children] know that ye are my disciples, if ye have love one to another."

7. <u>**An Honest Personality**</u> – In the KJV bible book of James chapter 4 verse 8; it states: "Draw nigh to God, and he will draw nigh to you. Cleanse your hands, ye sinners; and purify your hearts, ye double minded."

8. <u>**A Being who is Loving**</u> – In the KJV bible book of 1st John chapter 4 verse 8; it states: "He that loveth not knoweth not God; for God is love." In the KJV bible book of John chapter 13 verses 34-35; the Messiah Yashu'a (Jesus) said: "A new commandment I give unto you, that ye love one another; as I have loved you, that ye also love one another. By this shall all men [women and children] know that ye are my disciples, if ye have love one to another."

284

SPIRITUAL TRILLIONAIRE:
Cherishing the Breath of Life while Simultaneously
Preparing for the Blow of Death!

CHILDREN OF THE MOST HIGH:
PRISTINE YOUTH AND FAMILY SOLUTIONS, LLC.
SONS AND DAUGHTERS OF THE MOST HIGH PUBLISHERS ®

OH, GRACIOUS MOST HIGH HEAVENLY FATHER, HOLY IS YOUR
NAME, YOUR WILL BE DONE NOW AND FOREVER!

9. **A Clean Healthy Body** in a Sound Environment that receives daily high dosages of quality sleep. In the KJV bible book of John chapter 15 verse 3; the Messiah Yashu'a (Jesus) said: "Now ye are clean through the word which I have spoken unto you." In the KJV bible book of Matthew chapter 6 verse 22; the Messiah Yashu'a (Jesus) said: "The light of the body is the eye: if therefore thine eye be single; thy whole body shall be full of light."

The 9 True Vine "Yashu'a" (Jesus) Elements of Healthy Living, if learned and practiced every day, it may help a person to overcome the 9 Deadly Venoms of the Desires of the great dragon: that old serpent, called the Devil, and Satan, which deceiveth the whole world. They may also help a person to acquire positive spiritual health and positive spiritual wealth on the path to becoming a Spiritual Trillionaire.

The **3rd** of the 9X9 True Vine "Yashu'a" (Jesus) B.A.-K.A.-R.E. Sequential Order of Learning Habits of Success are **the 9 True Vine Yashu'a (Jesus) Attributes as habits of success** that may help a person's overall well-being as it relates to

285

SPIRITUAL TRILLIONAIRE:
**Cherishing the Breath of Life while Simultaneously
Preparing for the Blow of Death!**

CHILDREN OF THE MOST HIGH:
PRISTINE YOUTH AND FAMILY SOLUTIONS, LLC.
SONS AND DAUGHTERS OF THE MOST HIGH PUBLISHERS ®

OH, GRACIOUS MOST HIGH HEAVENLY FATHER, HOLY IS YOUR
NAME, YOUR WILL BE DONE NOW AND FOREVER!

acquiring, maintaining and sustaining positive spiritual health and positive spiritual wealth on the path to becoming a Spiritual Trillionaire, which are:

1. **Willing-Sacrifice** – In the KJV bible book of Luke chapter 22 verse 44; the Messiah Yashu'a (Jesus) said: "Father, if thou be willing, remove this cup from me: nevertheless, not my will, but thine, be done." In the KJV bible book of John chapter 15 verse 13; the Messiah Yashu'a (Jesus) said: "Greater love hath no man **[person]** than this, that a man **[person]** lay down his life for his friends." Instead of taking innocent people lives and suicide; **aspiring Spiritual Trillionaires must become willing to sacrifice our lives to the service of the Most High Heavenly Father NOW and FOREVER!** This response conquers the deadly venom of desire of **Heinous Murder.**

Rev. Dr. Martin Luther King Jr. said:
"Use me, God. Show me how to take who I am, who I want to be, and what I can do, and use it for a purpose greater than myself."

SPIRITUAL TRILLIONAIRE:
Cherishing the Breath of Life while Simultaneously
Preparing for the Blow of Death!

CHILDREN OF THE MOST HIGH:
PRISTINE YOUTH AND FAMILY SOLUTIONS, LLC.
SONS AND DAUGHTERS OF THE MOST HIGH PUBLISHERS ®

OH, GRACIOUS MOST HIGH HEAVENLY FATHER, HOLY IS YOUR
NAME, YOUR WILL BE DONE NOW AND FOREVER!

In the KJV bible book of Genesis, chapter 14 verse 18; it states: "And Melchizedek (Malkiy-Tsedeq, מַלְכִּי־צֶדֶק) king of Salem brought forth bread and wine: and he was the priest of the Most High (ELYOWN עֶלְיוֹן EL אֵל) God." In the KJV bible book of Psalms chapter 82 verse 6; states: "I have said, Ye are gods; and all of you are children of the Most High (is the KJV bible Hebrew Strong's Concordance#5945 which is the title: ELYOWN עֶלְיוֹן (the God) EL אֵל)." In the KJV bible book of Numbers chapter 23 verse 19; states: "God (EL אֵל) is not a man, that he should lie; neither the son of man, that he should repent: hath he said, and shall he not do it? or hath he spoken, and shall he not make it good?" However, for clarification it is critical that all children of the Most High know that in the KJV bible book of Genesis Chapter 1 verse 1; the original Aramic (Hebrew) word for "God" is "Elohiym" not the Most High (ELYOWN עֶלְיוֹן EL אֵל), the Sustainer, the Nourisher, the Provider of all Life, and the Omnipotent and the Omnipresent Creator of the boundless universes. So, the children of the Most High: Pristine Youth and Family Solutions, LLC. hopes that all children of the Most High acquire an overstanding of the differences between "God" ("אֱלֹהִים 'Elohiym") in the KJV bible book of Genesis chapter 1 verse 1, "the LORD, יְהֹוָה Yёhovah, (Yahuwa, Yahweh, Jehovah, Yahayyu)" who repented to the Most High (ELYOWN עֶלְיוֹן EL אֵל) in the KJV bible book of Genesis chapter 6 verse 6; who is referred to as: "the LORD; and the יְהֹוָה Yёhovah "God" "אֱלֹהִים 'Elohiym" who gets jealous in the KJV bible book of Exodus chapter 20 verse 5; ARE NOT TO BE CONFUSED AS BEING the Most High (ELYOWN עֶלְיוֹן EL אֵל), the Sustainer, the Nourisher, the Provider of all Life, and the Omnipotent and the Omnipresent Creator of the boundless universes who they all worship and do the 'Will" of!

SPIRITUAL TRILLIONAIRE:
**Cherishing the Breath of Life while Simultaneously
Preparing for the Blow of Death!**

CHILDREN OF THE MOST HIGH:
PRISTINE YOUTH AND FAMILY SOLUTIONS, LLC.
SONS AND DAUGHTERS OF THE MOST HIGH PUBLISHERS ®

OH, GRACIOUS MOST HIGH HEAVENLY FATHER, HOLY IS YOUR
NAME, YOUR WILL BE DONE NOW AND FOREVER!

2. **Kindness** – In the KJV bible book of Hebrews chapter 13 verse 2; it states: "Be not forgetful to entertain strangers: for thereby some have entertained angels unawares." In the KJV bible book of Matthew chapter 25 verse 35; the Messiah Yashu'a (Jesus) said: "For I was an hungred, and ye gave me meat: I was thirsty, and ye gave me drink: I was a stranger, and ye took me in." Aspiring Spiritual Trillionaires must have kindness rooted in their hearts and minds and be courageous practitioners and the best examples of inspirational kindness in action towards all members of humanity and towards all of nature in eternal obedience to the Most High Heavenly Father. This response conquers the deadly venom of desire of **Hopeless-Fear-Disobedience**.

3. **Faithful-Giver** – In the KJV bible book of Revelation chapter 3 verse 14; the Messiah Yashu'a (Jesus) said: "And unto the angel of the church of the Laodiceans write; These things saith the Amen, the faithful and true witness, the beginning of the creation of God;"

SPIRITUAL TRILLIONAIRE:
Cherishing the Breath of Life while Simultaneously
Preparing for the Blow of Death!

CHILDREN OF THE MOST HIGH:
PRISTINE YOUTH AND FAMILY SOLUTIONS, LLC.
SONS AND DAUGHTERS OF THE MOST HIGH PUBLISHERS ®

OH, GRACIOUS MOST HIGH HEAVENLY FATHER, HOLY IS YOUR
NAME, YOUR WILL BE DONE NOW AND FOREVER!

In the KJV bible book of Luke chapter 6 verse 38; the Messiah Yashu'a (Jesus) said: "Give, and it shall be given unto you; good measure, pressed down, and shaken together, and running over, shall men give into your bosom. For with the same measure that ye mete withal it shall be measured to you again." Aspiring Spiritual Trillionaires must have faithful-giving rooted in their hearts and minds and be true-faith practitioners and the best examples of giving back in action towards all members of humanity and towards all of nature in eternal obedience to the Most High Heavenly Father. This response conquers the deadly venom of desire of **Greed**.

SPIRITUAL TRILLIONAIRE:
**Cherishing the Breath of Life while Simultaneously
Preparing for the Blow of Death!**

CHILDREN OF THE MOST HIGH:
PRISTINE YOUTH AND FAMILY SOLUTIONS, LLC.
SONS AND DAUGHTERS OF THE MOST HIGH PUBLISHERS &

OH, GRACIOUS MOST HIGH HEAVENLY FATHER, HOLY IS YOUR
NAME, YOUR WILL BE DONE NOW AND FOREVER!

4. **Loving** – In the KJV bible book of John chapter 13 verses 34-35; the Messiah Yashu'a (Jesus) said: "A new commandment I give unto you, that ye love one another; as I have loved you, that ye also love one another. By this shall all [men] [women and children] know that ye are my disciples, if ye have love one to another." In the KJV bible book of Proverbs chapter 10 verse 12; it states: "Hatred stirreth up strifes: but love covereth all sins."

Dr. George Washington Carver said: "Human need is really a great spiritual vacuum which God seeks to fill...With one hand in the hand of a fellow man in need and the other hand of Christ, He could get across the vacuum."

SPIRITUAL TRILLIONAIRE:
**Cherishing the Breath of Life while Simultaneously
Preparing for the Blow of Death!**

CHILDREN OF THE MOST HIGH:
PRISTINE YOUTH AND FAMILY SOLUTIONS, LLC.
SONS AND DAUGHTERS OF THE MOST HIGH PUBLISHERS ®

OH, GRACIOUS MOST HIGH HEAVENLY FATHER, HOLY IS YOUR
NAME, YOUR WILL BE DONE NOW AND FOREVER!

Aspiring Spiritual Trillionaires must have lovingness rooted in their hearts and minds and be loving practitioners and the best examples of lovingness in action towards all members of humanity and towards all of nature in eternal obedience to the Most High Heavenly Father. This response conquers the deadly venom of desire of **Wickedness**.

5. **Self-Disciplined** – In the KJV bible book of Galatians chapter 5 verse 23; it states: "Meekness, temperance: against such there is no law. Aspiring Spiritual Trillionaires must have Meekness rooted in their hearts and minds and be practitioners of meekness and the best examples of meekness in action towards all members of humanity and towards all of nature in eternal obedience to the Most High Heavenly Father. This response conquers the deadly venom of desire of **Lust**.

6. **Humble** – In the KJV bible book of James chapter 4: verse 10; it states: "Humble yourselves in the sight of the Lord, and he shall lift you up." In the KJV bible book of Matthew chapter 23 verse 12; the Messiah Yashu'a (Jesus) said: "And whosoever shall exalt himself shall

SPIRITUAL TRILLIONAIRE:
Cherishing the Breath of Life while Simultaneously
Preparing for the Blow of Death!

CHILDREN OF THE MOST HIGH:
PRISTINE YOUTH AND FAMILY SOLUTIONS, LLC.
SONS AND DAUGHTERS OF THE MOST HIGH PUBLISHERS ®

OH, GRACIOUS MOST HIGH HEAVENLY FATHER, HOLY IS YOUR
NAME, YOUR WILL BE DONE NOW AND FOREVER!

be abased; and he that shall humble himself shall be
exalted."

In the KJV bible book of 2nd Chronicles chapter 7 verse
14; it states: "If my people, which are called by my
name, shall humble themselves, and pray, and seek my
face, and turn from their wicked ways; then will I hear
from heaven, and will forgive their sin, and will heal
their land. One of the definitions of humility is
humbleness. In the KJV bible book of Proverbs chapter
29 verse 23; it states: "A man's pride shall bring him
low: but honor shall uphold the humble in spirit."
Aspiring Spiritual Trillionaires must have humbleness
rooted in their hearts and minds and be practitioners of
humbleness and the best examples of humbleness in
action towards all members of humanity and towards all
of nature in eternal obedience to the Most High
Heavenly Father. This response conquers the deadly
venom of desire of **Pride**.

SPIRITUAL TRILLIONAIRE:
Cherishing the Breath of Life while Simultaneously
Preparing for the Blow of Death!

CHILDREN OF THE MOST HIGH:
PRISTINE YOUTH AND FAMILY SOLUTIONS, LLC.
SONS AND DAUGHTERS OF THE MOST HIGH PUBLISHERS ®

OH, GRACIOUS MOST HIGH HEAVENLY FATHER, HOLY IS YOUR
NAME, YOUR WILL BE DONE NOW AND FOREVER!

7. **Honest** – In the KJV bible book of Luke chapter 8 verse 15; the Messiah Yashu'a (Jesus) said: "But that on the good ground are they, which in an honest and good heart, having heard the word, keep it, and bring forth fruit with patience." Aspiring Spiritual Trillionaires must have honesty rooted in their hearts and minds and be practitioners of honesty and the best examples of being honest in action towards all members of humanity and towards all of nature in eternal obedience to the Most High Heavenly Father. This response conquers the deadly venom of desire of **Lying**.

8. **Patient** – In the KJV bible book of Hebrews chapter 6 verse 15; it states: "And so, after he had patiently endured, he obtained the promise." Aspiring Spiritual Trillionaires must have patience rooted in their hearts and minds and be practitioners of patience and the best examples of being patience in action towards all members of humanity and towards all of nature in eternal obedience to the Most High Heavenly Father. This response conquers the deadly venom of desire of **Wrath**.

SPIRITUAL TRILLIONAIRE:
**Cherishing the Breath of Life while Simultaneously
Preparing for the Blow of Death!**

CHILDREN OF THE MOST HIGH:
PRISTINE YOUTH AND FAMILY SOLUTIONS, LLC.
SONS AND DAUGHTERS OF THE MOST HIGH PUBLISHERS ®

OH, GRACIOUS MOST HIGH HEAVENLY FATHER, HOLY IS YOUR
NAME, YOUR WILL BE DONE NOW AND FOREVER!

9. **Hard Working** – In the KJV bible book of John chapter 9 verse 4; the Messiah Yashu'a (Jesus) said: "I must work the works of him that sent me, while it is day: the night cometh, when no man can."

Aspiring Spiritual Trillionaires must have the habit of working hard rooted in their hearts and minds and be practitioners of working hard and the best examples of being hard working in action on behalf of all members of humanity and towards all of nature in eternal obedience to the Most High Heavenly Father. This response conquers the deadly venom of desire of **Slothful**.

The 9 True Vine "Yashu'a" Jesus Attributes as habits of success, if learned and practiced every day, it may help a person to overcome the 9 Deadly Venoms of the Desires of the great dragon: that old serpent, called the Devil, and Satan, which deceiveth the whole world. They may also help a person to acquire positive spiritual health and positive spiritual wealth on the path to becoming a Spiritual Trillionaire.

SPIRITUAL TRILLIONAIRE:
Cherishing the Breath of Life while Simultaneously
Preparing for the Blow of Death!

CHILDREN OF THE MOST HIGH:
PRISTINE YOUTH AND FAMILY SOLUTIONS, LLC.
SONS AND DAUGHTERS OF THE MOST HIGH PUBLISHERS ®

OH, GRACIOUS MOST HIGH HEAVENLY FATHER, HOLY IS YOUR
NAME, YOUR WILL BE DONE NOW AND FOREVER!

The **4th of the 9X9** True Vine "Yashu'a" (Jesus) B.A.-K.A.-R.E. Sequential Order of Learning Habits of Success are **the 9 True Vine Yashu'a (Jesus) Mental Transformation Principles** that may help a person's overall well-being of as it relates to acquiring, maintaining and sustaining positive spiritual health and positive spiritual on the path to becoming a Spiritual Trillionaire, which are:

1. **Love the Most High Heavenly Father with all of your heart, with all your spirit and soul, and with all your mind and entire being**. In the KJV bible book of Matthew chapter 22 verses 37-38; Yashu'a (Jesus) said: unto him, "Thou shalt love the Lord thy God with all thy heart, and with all thy soul, and with all thy mind. This is the first and great commandment." There is no knowledge higher than love. The Most High Heavenly Father is Love, and the Most High Heavenly Father loves us! Love replenishes everything without limitations. Truth and Love move, but are not ever moved! Aspiring Spiritual Trillionaires must always remember: you can't build your happiness on other peoples' sorrows without sowing your own seeds of sorrow that will only bring forth your own unhappiness!

SPIRITUAL TRILLIONAIRE:
**Cherishing the Breath of Life while Simultaneously
Preparing for the Blow of Death!**

CHILDREN OF THE MOST HIGH:
PRISTINE YOUTH AND FAMILY SOLUTIONS, LLC.
SONS AND DAUGHTERS OF THE MOST HIGH PUBLISHERS ®

OH, GRACIOUS MOST HIGH HEAVENLY FATHER, HOLY IS YOUR
NAME, YOUR WILL BE DONE NOW AND FOREVER!

2. **Be sincere about being obedient to the Most High while working to overcome the temptations of this world**. In the KJV bible book of Revelation chapter 3 verse 10; the Messiah Yashu'a (Jesus) said: "Because thou hast kept the word of my patience, I also will keep thee from the hour of temptation, which shall come upon all the world, to try them that dwell upon the earth."

3. **Be non-judgmental of others while striving for perfection through peace, patience and truth**. In the KJV bible book of Matthew chapter 7 verse 1; the Messiah Yashu'a (Jesus) said: "Judge not, that ye be not judged." In the KJV bible book of Matthew chapter 5 verse 48; the Messiah Yashu'a (Jesus) said: "Be ye therefore perfect, even as your Father which is in heaven is perfect." The KJV bible Greek Strong's Concordance word for "**perfect**" is τέλειος **teleios** and means complete (in various applications of labor, growth, mental and moral character, etc.); being balanced mentally, spiritually and emotionally; completeness: of full age, perfect.

296

SPIRITUAL TRILLIONAIRE:
Cherishing the Breath of Life while Simultaneously
Preparing for the Blow of Death!

CHILDREN OF THE MOST HIGH:
PRISTINE YOUTH AND FAMILY SOLUTIONS, LLC.
SONS AND DAUGHTERS OF THE MOST HIGH PUBLISHERS ®

OH, GRACIOUS MOST HIGH HEAVENLY FATHER, HOLY IS YOUR
NAME, YOUR WILL BE DONE NOW AND FOREVER!

However, it does not mean the English perception of not ever making another mistake or physically being without defect or blemish. The True Vine "Yashu'a (Jesus) is the Perfect and Best Example of a Spiritual Trillionaire! However, Yashu'a (Jesus) said to all aspiring Spiritual Trillionaires: "Be ye therefore <u>perfect</u>, even as your Father which is in heaven is <u>perfect</u>." Now that we know how the KJV bible Greek Strong's Concordance defines "**perfect**" as τέλειος teleios, and that the Messiah Yashu'a (Jesus) told us to be perfect, why do many Ministers preach that it is impossible (**I'm-possible**) to become perfect while in human form?

In the KJV bible book of 2nd Corinthians chapter 11 verses 13-15; it states: "For such are false apostles, deceitful workers, transforming themselves into the apostles of Christ. **And no marvel; for Satan himself is transformed into an angel of light. Therefore, it is no great thing if his ministers also be transformed as the ministers of righteousness**; whose end shall be according to their works." In the KJV bible book of Mathew chapter 7 verse 15; the Messiah Yashu'a (Jesus) said:

"Beware of false prophets, which come to you in sheep's clothing, but inwardly they are ravening wolves." So, aspiring Spiritual Trillionaires; Be Aware; don't fall into the Devil's Web of being deceived by the children of the devil

SPIRITUAL TRILLIONAIRE:
Cherishing the Breath of Life while Simultaneously
Preparing for the Blow of Death!

CHILDREN OF THE MOST HIGH:
PRISTINE YOUTH AND FAMILY SOLUTIONS, LLC.
SONS AND DAUGHTERS OF THE MOST HIGH PUBLISHERS ®

OH, GRACIOUS MOST HIGH HEAVENLY FATHER, HOLY IS YOUR NAME, YOUR WILL BE DONE NOW AND FOREVER!

and their **wolves in sheep clothing or ministers of satan** who preach and teach that you can't be **perfect** as Yashu'a (Jesus) told us to do.

298

SPIRITUAL TRILLIONAIRE:
Cherishing the Breath of Life while Simultaneously
Preparing for the Blow of Death!

CHILDREN OF THE MOST HIGH:
PRISTINE YOUTH AND FAMILY SOLUTIONS, LLC.
SONS AND DAUGHTERS OF THE MOST HIGH PUBLISHERS ®

OH, GRACIOUS MOST HIGH HEAVENLY FATHER, HOLY IS YOUR
NAME, YOUR WILL BE DONE NOW AND FOREVER!

According to the Online American Heritage Dictionary (2019), the word "**Minister**" is from "Middle English **ministre**, from Old French, from Latin minister, meaning **servant**; to attend to the wants and needs of others: Volunteers ministered to the homeless after the flood." The first part of the word "**Minis**ter" is "**Minis**" which phonetically sounds exactly like the word "**Menace**", which are what the **Ministers of Satan** are; **trouble-makers**, not to be confused with the children of the Most High who Ad**minister** the Most High's doctrine to members of humanity. "According to the Online American Heritage Dictionary (2019), the word "**Menace**" from "Middle English manace, from Old French, from Late Latin minācia, sing. of Latin mināciae, threats, menaces, from mināx, mināc-, threatening, from minārī, to threaten, from minae, threats; a possible danger; a threat: a careless driver who was a menace to public safety. The quality of being threatening: a hint of menace in his voice. To constitute a threat to; endanger: A troublesome or annoying person: or considered her little brother to be a menace, tr.v. men·aced, men·ac·ing, men·ac·es."

Also, as it relates the Messiah Yashu'a (Jesus) saying: "Be ye therefore perfect, even as your Father which is in heaven is perfect." Remember, the Messiah Yashu'a (Jesus) spoke the **Aramic/Hebrew language** and the **Galilaean/Syriac language** which are very close in dialect.

SPIRITUAL TRILLIONAIRE:
Cherishing the Breath of Life while Simultaneously
Preparing for the Blow of Death!

CHILDREN OF THE MOST HIGH:
PRISTINE YOUTH AND FAMILY SOLUTIONS, LLC.
SONS AND DAUGHTERS OF THE MOST HIGH PUBLISHERS ®

OH, GRACIOUS MOST HIGH HEAVENLY FATHER, HOLY IS YOUR
NAME, YOUR WILL BE DONE NOW AND FOREVER!

At the day of Pentecost, in the KJV bible book of Acts chapter 2, **the devout men were all filled with the Holy Ghost**, and began to speak with other **tongues γλῶσσα glōssa (languages)**, **as the Spirit gave them utterance being able to understand one another in Yashu'a (Jesus) Galilaean language that he spoke**, which is why to the onlookers of this miraculous event asked: "are not all these which speak **Galilaeans**?" **Yashu'a (Jesus) did not speak the English and Greek languages**, therefore, it would be best to investigate the **Aramic/Hebrew** word for "**Perfect**" in Yashu'a (Jesus) own language or languages to overstand the meaning of the word from his perspective. What does the word "**perfect**" mean in **Aramic/Hebrew**? In the KJV bible book of Genesis chapter 6 verse 9; it states with Hebrew inserts:

6:9 אֵלֶּה תּוֹלְדֹת נֹחַ נֹחַ אִישׁ צַדִּיק תָּמִים הָיָה בְּדֹרֹתָיו אֶת־הָאֱלֹהִים הִתְהַלֶּךְ־
נֹחַ:

"These are the generations of Noah: Noah was a just man **and perfect** in his generations, and Noah walked with God."

SPIRITUAL TRILLIONAIRE:
Cherishing the Breath of Life while Simultaneously
Preparing for the Blow of Death!

CHILDREN OF THE MOST HIGH:
PRISTINE YOUTH AND FAMILY SOLUTIONS, LLC.
SONS AND DAUGHTERS OF THE MOST HIGH PUBLISHERS ®

OH, GRACIOUS MOST HIGH HEAVENLY FATHER, HOLY IS YOUR
NAME, YOUR WILL BE DONE NOW AND FOREVER!

In the KJV bible Hebrew Strong's Concordance#8549, the word for the phrase "**and perfect**" is תָּמִים tamiym which means **moral integrity**, entire (literally, figuratively or morally); also (as noun) integrity, truth: —without blemish, complete, full, perfect, sincerely (-ity), sound, without spot, undefiled, upright(-ly), whole." So, it is essential that all aspiring Spiritual Trillionaire character reflects **moral integrity**. The Online American Heritage Dictionary defines **moral** and **integrity** as teaching or exhibiting goodness or correctness of character and behavior: Steadfast adherence to a strict moral or ethical code: a leader of great integrity. The quality or condition of being whole or undivided; completeness."

4. <u>**Have selfless True-Faith in the Most High Heavenly Father**</u>. In the KJV bible book of Hebrews chapter 10 verse 21; it states: "**Let us draw near with a true heart in full assurance of faith, having our hearts sprinkled from an evil conscience, and our bodies washed with pure water.**"

SPIRITUAL TRILLIONAIRE:
Cherishing the Breath of Life while Simultaneously
Preparing for the Blow of Death!

CHILDREN OF THE MOST HIGH:
PRISTINE YOUTH AND FAMILY SOLUTIONS, LLC.
SONS AND DAUGHTERS OF THE MOST HIGH PUBLISHERS ®

OH, GRACIOUS MOST HIGH HEAVENLY FATHER, HOLY IS YOUR
NAME, YOUR WILL BE DONE NOW AND FOREVER!

5. **Actively, generously, and selflessly further the progress of the well-being of others**. In the KJV bible book of Proverbs chapter 14 verse 31; it states: "**He [or She] that oppresseth the poor reproacheth his Maker: but he [or she] that honoureth him hath mercy on the poor.**" In the KJV bible book of Proverbs chapter 29 verse 7; it states: "**The righteous considereth the cause of the poor: [but] the wicked regardeth not to know [it].**" In the KJV bible book of Isaiah chapter 25 verse 4; it states: Isaiah 25:4: "**For thou hast been a strength to the poor, a strength to the needy in his distress, a refuge from the storm, a shadow from the heat, when the blast of the terrible ones [is] as a storm [against] the wall.**"

6. **Utilize will and faith to overcome material desires of the mind and heart**. In the KJV bible book of 1st John chapter 4 verse 4; it states: "Ye are of God, little children, and have overcome them: because greater is he that is in you, than he that is in the world." In the KJV bible book of 1st John chapter 5 verses 4-5; it states: "Whatsoever is born of God overcometh the world: and

SPIRITUAL TRILLIONAIRE:
Cherishing the Breath of Life while Simultaneously
Preparing for the Blow of Death!

CHILDREN OF THE MOST HIGH:
PRISTINE YOUTH AND FAMILY SOLUTIONS, LLC.
SONS AND DAUGHTERS OF THE MOST HIGH PUBLISHERS ®

OH, GRACIOUS MOST HIGH HEAVENLY FATHER, HOLY IS YOUR
NAME, YOUR WILL BE DONE NOW AND FOREVER!

this is the victory that overcometh the world, even our faith. Who is he that overcometh the world, but he that believeth that Jesus is the Son of God?" In the KJV bible book of Revelation chapter 3 verse 12; Yashu'a (Jesus) said: "Him [or Her] that overcometh will I make a pillar in the temple of my God, and he [or she] shall go no more out: and I will write upon him [or her] the name of my God, and the name of the city of my God, which is new Jerusalem, which cometh down out of heaven from my God: and I will write upon him [or her] my new name." In the KJV bible book of Revelation chapter 3 verse 21; Yashu'a (Jesus) said: "To him [or her] that overcometh will I grant to sit with me in my throne, even as I also overcame, and am set down with my Father in his throne."

7. **Allow Divine Love from the Most High and for the Most High through the Messiah Yashu'a (Jesus) to not be conquered by carnal love**. In the KJV bible book of John chapter 3 verse 16; Yashu'a (Jesus) said: "For God so loved the world, that he gave his only begotten Son, that whosoever believeth in him should not perish, but have everlasting life."

SPIRITUAL TRILLIONAIRE:
Cherishing the Breath of Life while Simultaneously
Preparing for the Blow of Death!

CHILDREN OF THE MOST HIGH:
PRISTINE YOUTH AND FAMILY SOLUTIONS, LLC.
SONS AND DAUGHTERS OF THE MOST HIGH PUBLISHERS ®

OH, GRACIOUS MOST HIGH HEAVENLY FATHER, HOLY IS YOUR
NAME, YOUR WILL BE DONE NOW AND FOREVER!

8. **Conquer grief, hope, fears and all human emotions
that arise from human loves and desires through the
Messiah Yashu'a (Jesus)**. In the KJV bible book of 1st
John chapter 4 verse 18; it states: "**There is no fear in
love; but perfect love casteth out fear: because fear
hath torment. He [or She] that feareth is not made
perfect in love.**"

9. **Exercise patience in all that you are allowed the
ability to do**. In the KJV bible book of Hebrews chapter
10 verse 36; it states: "**For ye have need of patience,
that, after ye have done the will of God, ye might
receive the promise.**" In the KJV bible book of
Hebrews chapter 6 verse 12; it states: "**That ye be not
slothful, but followers of them who through faith and
patience inherit the promises.**" In the KJV bible book
of Revelation chapter 14 verse 12; it states: "**Here is the
patience of the saints: here are they that keep the
commandments of God [the Most High Heavenly
Father], and the faith of Jesus [Yashu'a].**"

SPIRITUAL TRILLIONAIRE:
Cherishing the Breath of Life while Simultaneously
Preparing for the Blow of Death!

CHILDREN OF THE MOST HIGH:
PRISTINE YOUTH AND FAMILY SOLUTIONS, LLC.
SONS AND DAUGHTERS OF THE MOST HIGH PUBLISHERS ®

OH, GRACIOUS MOST HIGH HEAVENLY FATHER, HOLY IS YOUR
NAME, YOUR WILL BE DONE NOW AND FOREVER!

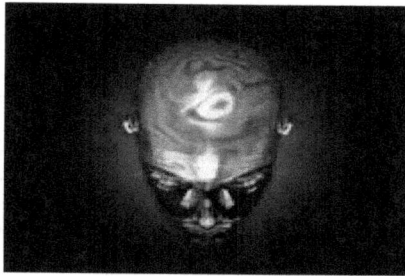

The 9 True Vine "Yashu'a" Jesus Mental Transformation Principles, if learned and practiced every day, it may help a person to overcome the 9 Deadly Venoms of the Desires of the great dragon: that old serpent, called the Devil, and Satan, which deceiveth the whole world. They may also help a person to acquire positive spiritual health and positive spiritual wealth on the path to becoming a Spiritual Trillionaire.

305

SPIRITUAL TRILLIONAIRE:
Cherishing the Breath of Life while Simultaneously
Preparing for the Blow of Death!

CHILDREN OF THE MOST HIGH:
PRISTINE YOUTH AND FAMILY SOLUTIONS, LLC.
SONS AND DAUGHTERS OF THE MOST HIGH PUBLISHERS ®

OH, GRACIOUS MOST HIGH HEAVENLY FATHER, HOLY IS YOUR
NAME, YOUR WILL BE DONE NOW AND FOREVER!

The **5th of the 9X9** True Vine "Yashu'a" (Jesus) B.A.-K.A.-R.E. Sequential Order of Learning Habits of Success are **the 9 True Vine Yashu'a (Jesus) Spiritual Gifts** that may help a person's overall well-being of as it relates to acquiring, maintaining and sustaining positive spiritual health and positive spiritual on the path to becoming a Spiritual Trillionaire, which are:

1. **The Spirit of the Word of Wisdom** (In the KJV bible book of 1st Corinthians chapter 12 verse 8).

2. **The Spirit of the Word of Knowledge** (In the KJV bible book of 1st Corinthians chapter 12 verse 8).

3. **The Spirit of Faith** (In the KJV bible book of 1st Corinthians chapter 12 verse 9).

4. **The Spirit of Healing** (In the KJV bible book of 1st Corinthians chapter 12 verse 9).

5. **The Spirit of Working Miracles** (In the KJV bible book of 1st Corinthians chapter 12 verse 10).

6. **The Spirit of Prophecy** (In the KJV bible book of 1st Corinthians chapter 12 verse 10).

7. **The Spirit of Discerning of Spirits** (In the KJV bible book of 1st Corinthians chapter 12 verse 10).

SPIRITUAL TRILLIONAIRE:
**Cherishing the Breath of Life while Simultaneously
Preparing for the Blow of Death!**

CHILDREN OF THE MOST HIGH:
PRISTINE YOUTH AND FAMILY SOLUTIONS, LLC.
SONS AND DAUGHTERS OF THE MOST HIGH PUBLISHERS ®

OH, GRACIOUS MOST HIGH HEAVENLY FATHER, HOLY IS YOUR
NAME, YOUR WILL BE DONE NOW AND FOREVER!

8. **The Spirit of Diverse kinds of Tongues** (In the KJV bible book of 1st Corinthians chapter 12 verse 10).
9. **The Spirit of Interpretation of Tongues** (In the KJV bible book of 1st Corinthians chapter 12 verse 10).

If a person is blessed to receive one or more of **the 9 True Vine "Yashu'a" (Jesus) Spiritual Gifts**, if learned and practiced every day, it may help a person to overcome the 9 Deadly Venoms of the Desires of the great dragon: that old serpent, called the Devil, and Satan, which deceiveth the whole world. They may also help a person to acquire positive spiritual health and positive spiritual wealth on the path to becoming a Spiritual Trillionaire.

The **6th of the 9X9** True Vine "Yashu'a" (Jesus) B.A.-K.A.-R.E. Sequential Order of Learning Habits of Success are **the 9 True Vine Yashu'a (Jesus) Titles of Divinity** that may help a person's overall well-being of as it relates to acquiring, maintaining and sustaining positive spiritual health and positive spiritual on the path to becoming a Spiritual Trillionaire, which are:

SPIRITUAL TRILLIONAIRE:
Cherishing the Breath of Life while Simultaneously
Preparing for the Blow of Death!

CHILDREN OF THE MOST HIGH:
PRISTINE YOUTH AND FAMILY SOLUTIONS, LLC.
SONS AND DAUGHTERS OF THE MOST HIGH PUBLISHERS ®

OH, GRACIOUS MOST HIGH HEAVENLY FATHER, HOLY IS YOUR
NAME, YOUR WILL BE DONE NOW AND FOREVER!

1. **The True Vine** – The Messiah Yashu'a (Jesus) said in the KJV bible book of John chapter 15 verse 1: "I am the true vine, and my Father is the husbandman."

2. **The only begotten Son** – In the KJV bible book of John chapter 1 verse 18; states: "**No man hath seen God at any time; the only begotten Son, which is in the bosom of the Father, he hath declared him.**"

3. **Light of the world** – The Messiah Yashu'a (Jesus) said in the KJV bible book of John chapter 8 verse 12: "I am the light of the world: he that followeth me shall not walk in darkness, but shall have the light of life."

4. **The Lamb of God** – In the KJV bible book of John chapter 1 verse 29; it states: "The next day John seeth Jesus coming unto him, and saith, **Behold the Lamb of God**, which taketh away the sin of the world."

SPIRITUAL TRILLIONAIRE:
Cherishing the Breath of Life while Simultaneously
Preparing for the Blow of Death!

CHILDREN OF THE MOST HIGH:
PRISTINE YOUTH AND FAMILY SOLUTIONS, LLC.
SONS AND DAUGHTERS OF THE MOST HIGH PUBLISHERS ®

OH, GRACIOUS MOST HIGH HEAVENLY FATHER, HOLY IS YOUR
NAME, YOUR WILL BE DONE NOW AND FOREVER!

5. **The Resurrection and the Life** – The Messiah
Yashu'a (Jesus) said in the KJV bible book of John
chapter 11 verse 25: "I am the resurrection, and the
life: he that believeth in me, though he were dead,
yet shall he live."

6. **The Word of God Made Flesh** – In the KJV bible
book of John chapter 1 verse 14; it states: "**And the
Word was made flesh**, and dwelt among us, (and we
beheld his glory, the glory as of the only begotten of
the Father,) full of grace and truth."

7. **The Savior of the World** – In the KJV bible book of
1st John chapter 4 verse 14; it states: "And we have
seen and do testify that the Father sent **the Son to be
the Savior of the world**."

8. **The Son of the Most High God** – In the KJV bible
book of Mark chapter 5 verse 7: "And cried with a
loud voice, and said, what have I to do with thee,
Jesus, thou Son of the Most High God? I adjure thee
by God, that thou torment me not."

SPIRITUAL TRILLIONAIRE:
**Cherishing the Breath of Life while Simultaneously
Preparing for the Blow of Death!**

CHILDREN OF THE MOST HIGH:
PRISTINE YOUTH AND FAMILY SOLUTIONS, LLC.
SONS AND DAUGHTERS OF THE MOST HIGH PUBLISHERS ®

OH, GRACIOUS MOST HIGH HEAVENLY FATHER, HOLY IS YOUR
NAME, YOUR WILL BE DONE NOW AND FOREVER!

9. <u>**The Messiah, which is called Christ**</u> – In the KJV bible book of John chapter 1 verse 41; it states: "He first findeth his own brother Simon, and saith unto him, <u>**we have found the Messias, which is, being interpreted, the Christ**</u>."

If a person utilizes **the 9 True Vine "Yashu'a" (Jesus) Titles of Divinity Spiritual Gifts as inspiration**, it may help a person to overcome the 9 Deadly Venoms of the Desires of the great dragon: that old serpent, called the Devil, and Satan, which deceiveth the whole world. They may also help a person to acquire positive spiritual health and positive spiritual wealth on the path to becoming a Spiritual Trillionaire.

The **7th of the 9X9** True Vine "Yashu'a" (Jesus) B.A.-K.A.-R.E. Sequential Order of Learning Habits of Success are **the 9 True Vine Yashu'a (Jesus) Fruits of the Spirit of Positive Character-Building Essentials** that may help a person's overall well-being of as it relates to acquiring, maintaining and sustaining positive spiritual health and positive spiritual on the path to becoming a Spiritual Trillionaire, which are:

SPIRITUAL TRILLIONAIRE:
**Cherishing the Breath of Life while Simultaneously
Preparing for the Blow of Death!**

CHILDREN OF THE MOST HIGH:
PRISTINE YOUTH AND FAMILY SOLUTIONS, LLC.
SONS AND DAUGHTERS OF THE MOST HIGH PUBLISHERS ®

OH, GRACIOUS MOST HIGH HEAVENLY FATHER, HOLY IS YOUR
NAME, YOUR WILL BE DONE NOW AND FOREVER!

1: **Love** – ἀγάπη **Agápē, ag-ah'-pay**; from KJV Bible Strong's Greek # G25; which means: love, i.e. affection or benevolence; specially (plural) a love-feast: — (feast of) charity(-ably), dear, love. Affection, good will, love, benevolence, brotherly love, love feasts. In KJV bible book of Galatians chapter 5 verse 22; it states: "But the fruit of the Spirit is **love**, joy, peace, longsuffering, gentleness, goodness, faith."

The True Vine Yashu'a (Jesus) Fruit of the Spirit of Positive Character-Building Essential of "Love" in action through true-faith in the Most High Heavenly Father to overcome and resist the 5th of the 9 Deadly Venoms of the Desires of the great dragon, that old serpent called the devil and satan which deceiveth the whole world known as "**Lust**" by expressing divine love for the most High Heavenly Father, loving the Messiah Yashu'a to overcoming the longing for something that is forbidden (**Love – ἀγάπη Agápē**) according to the commandments of the Most High.

SPIRITUAL TRILLIONAIRE:
Cherishing the Breath of Life while Simultaneously
Preparing for the Blow of Death!

CHILDREN OF THE MOST HIGH:
PRISTINE YOUTH AND FAMILY SOLUTIONS, LLC.
SONS AND DAUGHTERS OF THE MOST HIGH PUBLISHERS ®

OH, GRACIOUS MOST HIGH HEAVENLY FATHER, HOLY IS YOUR
NAME, YOUR WILL BE DONE NOW AND FOREVER!

2: **Joy** – χαρά Chará, Khar-ah'; from KJV Bible Strong's Greek #**G5463**; which means: cheerfulness, i.e. calm delight:— gladness, × greatly, (X be exceeding) joy(-ful, -fully, -fulness, -ous). Joy, gladness, the joy received from you, the cause or occasion of joy, of persons who are one's joy. In KJV bible book of Galatians chapter 5 verse 22; it states: "But the fruit of the Spirit is love, **joy**, peace, longsuffering, gentleness, goodness, faith."

According to "**The will to Kill**": **Making sense of senseless murder** (2018), over 90% of all **Heinous Murder**s were committed by people who were not joyful, but were very angry or enraged. The **True Vine Yashu'a (Jesus) Fruit of the Spirit of Positive Character-Building Essential of "Joy"** in action through true-faith in the Most High Heavenly Father to overcome and resist the **8th of the 9 Deadly Venoms of the Desires of the great dragon, that old serpent called the devil and satan which deceiveth the whole world** known as "**Heinous Murder**" by learning and practicing being happy inside, **cheerful, calm** and **delightful (Joy – χαρά Chará, Khar-ah')** every day.

312

SPIRITUAL TRILLIONAIRE:
Cherishing the Breath of Life while Simultaneously
Preparing for the Blow of Death!

CHILDREN OF THE MOST HIGH:
PRISTINE YOUTH AND FAMILY SOLUTIONS, LLC.
SONS AND DAUGHTERS OF THE MOST HIGH PUBLISHERS ®

OH, GRACIOUS MOST HIGH HEAVENLY FATHER, HOLY IS YOUR
NAME, YOUR WILL BE DONE NOW AND FOREVER!

3: **Peace** – εἰρήνη Eirēnē, i-ray'-nay; from KJV Bible Strong's Greek **#1515** probably from a primary verb εἴρω eírō (to join); which means: peace (literally or figuratively); by implication, prosperity: one, peace, quietness, rest, + set at one again. A state of national tranquility, exemption from the rage and havoc of war, peace between individuals, i.e. harmony, concord, security, safety, prosperity, felicity, (because peace and harmony make and keep things safe and prosperous); of the Messiah's peace, the way that leads to peace (salvation), the blessed state of **devout and upright** men after death. In KJV bible book of Galatians chapter 5 verse 22; it states: "But the fruit of the Spirit is love, joy, **peace**, longsuffering, gentleness, goodness, faith." The **True Vine Yashu'a (Jesus) Fruit of the Spirit of Positive Character-Building Essential of "Peace"** through true-faith in the Most High Heavenly Father to overcome and resist the **7th of the 9 Deadly Venoms of the Desires of the great dragon, that old serpent called the devil and satan which deceiveth the whole world** known as "**Lying**" by learning and practicing being **peaceful, devout and upright (Peace** – εἰρήνη Eirēnē).

313

SPIRITUAL TRILLIONAIRE:
**Cherishing the Breath of Life while Simultaneously
Preparing for the Blow of Death!**

CHILDREN OF THE MOST HIGH:
PRISTINE YOUTH AND FAMILY SOLUTIONS, LLC.
SONS AND DAUGHTERS OF THE MOST HIGH PUBLISHERS ®

OH, GRACIOUS MOST HIGH HEAVENLY FATHER, HOLY IS YOUR
NAME, YOUR WILL BE DONE NOW AND FOREVER!

4: <u>**Longsuffering**</u> – μακροθυμία **makrothymía**, mak-roth-oo-mee'-ah; from the same as <u>G3116</u>; longanimity, i.e. which means: (objectively) forbearance or (subjectively) fortitude, patience, endurance, constancy, steadfastness, perseverance, longsuffering, slowness in avenging wrongs. In KJV bible book of Galatians chapter 5 verse 22; it states: "But the fruit of the Spirit is love, joy, peace, **longsuffering**, gentleness, goodness, faith." The **True Vine Yashu'a (Jesus) Fruit of the Spirit of Positive Character-Building Essential of** "**longsuffering**" in action through true-faith in the Most High Heavenly Father to overcome and resist the **2nd of the 9 Deadly Venoms of the Desires of the great dragon, that old serpent called the devil and satan which deceiveth the whole world** known as "**Wrath**" by learning and practicing **longsuffering** μακροθυμία **makrothymía** which overcomes **Wrath**. Wrath is a negative unhealthy energy in action through <u>e</u>-motion or energy in <u>m</u>otion ($E=mc$). When a person gives into wrath, for those moments, they are literally out of their positive mind and are controlled by emotions. Energy in motion equals emotions ($E=mc$) which can become dangerous when they are in motion. These are the identical emotions that are the roots for hate, war, lust, greed, envy, pride and fear.

314

SPIRITUAL TRILLIONAIRE:
Cherishing the Breath of Life while Simultaneously
Preparing for the Blow of Death!

CHILDREN OF THE MOST HIGH:
PRISTINE YOUTH AND FAMILY SOLUTIONS, LLC.
SONS AND DAUGHTERS OF THE MOST HIGH PUBLISHERS ®

OH, GRACIOUS MOST HIGH HEAVENLY FATHER, HOLY IS YOUR
NAME, YOUR WILL BE DONE NOW AND FOREVER!

5: "**Gentleness – Chrēstotēs** χρηστότης KJV Bible Strong's Concordance#5544 which means: khray-stot'-ace; from G5543; **usefulness**, i.e. morally, excellence (in character or demeanor):—gentleness, good(-ness), kindness. Overcomes being **Slothful**. In KJV bible book of Galatians chapter 5 verse 22; it states: "But the fruit of the Spirit is love, joy, peace, longsuffering, **gentleness**, goodness, faith." So, a person who has **accepted the Lord Jesus Christ (Yashu'a Ha Mashiakh – Jesus the Messiah or Yehoshu'a – Yahayyu is Salvation or Yahayyu Saves) as their Savior, is in the Body of Christ** and can access **the True Vine Yashu'a (Jesus) Fruits of the Spirit Positive Character-Building Essentials** of "Gentleness – Chrēstotēs (χρηστότης)" in action through true-faith in the Most High Heavenly Father to overcome and resist the **1 of 9 Deadly Venoms of the Desires of the great dragon, that old serpent called the devil and satan which deceiveth the whole world** known as "**Slothfulness**" by being kind to all life and positively useful every day.

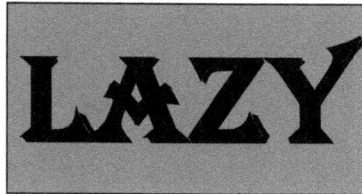

SPIRITUAL TRILLIONAIRE:
Cherishing the Breath of Life while Simultaneously
Preparing for the Blow of Death!

CHILDREN OF THE MOST HIGH:
PRISTINE YOUTH AND FAMILY SOLUTIONS, LLC.
SONS AND DAUGHTERS OF THE MOST HIGH PUBLISHERS ®

OH, GRACIOUS MOST HIGH HEAVENLY FATHER, HOLY IS YOUR
NAME, YOUR WILL BE DONE NOW AND FOREVER!

6: <u>Goodness</u> - ἀγαθωσύνη **Agathōsýnē, ag-ath-o-soo'-nay**; from KJV Bible Strong's Greek #G18; which means: goodness, uprightness of heart and life, kindness, i.e. virtue or beneficence. In KJV bible book of Galatians chapter 5 verse 22; it states: "But the fruit of the Spirit is love, joy, peace, longsuffering, gentleness, **goodness**, faith." The **True Vine Yashu'a (Jesus) Fruit of the Spirit of Positive Character-Building Essential** of "Goodness" in action through true-faith in the Most High Heavenly Father to overcome and resist the **9th of the 9 Deadly Venoms of the Desires of the great dragon, that old serpent called the devil and satan which deceiveth the whole world** known as "Wickedness" by learning and practicing goodness, uprightness of heart and life, kindness, and the virtue of beneficence (**Goodness - ἀγαθωσύνη Agathōsýnē**) every day.

GOOD

316

SPIRITUAL TRILLIONAIRE:
Cherishing the Breath of Life while Simultaneously
Preparing for the Blow of Death!

CHILDREN OF THE MOST HIGH:
PRISTINE YOUTH AND FAMILY SOLUTIONS, LLC.
SONS AND DAUGHTERS OF THE MOST HIGH PUBLISHERS ®

OH, GRACIOUS MOST HIGH HEAVENLY FATHER, HOLY IS YOUR
NAME, YOUR WILL BE DONE NOW AND FOREVER!

7: **Faith** - πίστις **Pístis, pis'-tis**; from KJV Bible Strong's Greek #**G3982**; which means: persuasion, i.e. credence; moral conviction (of religious truth, or the truthfulness of God or a religious teacher), especially reliance upon Christ for salvation; abstractly, constancy in such profession; by extension, the system of religious (Gospel) truth itself: —assurance, belief, believe, faith, fidelity. In KJV bible book of Galatians chapter 5 verse 22; it states: "But the fruit of the Spirit is love, joy, peace, longsuffering, gentleness, goodness, **faith**." The **True Vine Yashu'a (Jesus) Fruit of the Spirit of Positive Character-Building Essential** of "**Faith**" in action through true-faith in the Most High Heavenly Father to overcome and resist the **6th of the 9 Deadly Venoms of the Desires of the great dragon, that old serpent called the devil and satan which deceiveth the whole world** known as "**Hopeless-Fear-Disobedience**" by learning and practicing **true-faith (Faith - πίστις Pístis**) in the Most High heavenly Father through the Messiah Yashu'a (Jesus). "**Hopeless Fear Disobedience**" are rooted in a lack of faith in the Most High Heavenly Father. Real fear is the lack of true-faith in the Most High Heavenly Father.

SPIRITUAL TRILLIONAIRE:
Cherishing the Breath of Life while Simultaneously
Preparing for the Blow of Death!

CHILDREN OF THE MOST HIGH:
PRISTINE YOUTH AND FAMILY SOLUTIONS, LLC.
SONS AND DAUGHTERS OF THE MOST HIGH PUBLISHERS ®

OH, GRACIOUS MOST HIGH HEAVENLY FATHER, HOLY IS YOUR
NAME, YOUR WILL BE DONE NOW AND FOREVER!

8: <u>Meekness</u> - πραότης praiótēs, prah-ot'-ace; from <u>G4235</u>; which means: gentleness, mildness by implication, humility. In KJV bible book of Galatians chapter 5 verse 23; it states: "**Meekness**, temperance: against such there is no law." The **True Vine Yashu'a (Jesus) Fruit of the Spirit of Positive Character-Building Essential** of "Meekness" in action through true-faith in the Most High Heavenly Father to overcome and resist the **3rd of the 9 Deadly Venoms of the Desires of the great dragon, that old serpent called the devil and satan which deceiveth the whole world** known as "**Pride**" by learning and practicing **Meekness - πραότης praiótēs true-faith (Faith - πίστις Pístis)** which overcomes pride.

9: <u>Temperance</u> ἐγκράτεια Enkráteia, eng-krat'-i-ah; from KJV Bible Strong's Greek **#G1468**; which means: self-control (especially continence): temperance. Self-control (the virtue of one who masters his or her desires and passions, esp. his sensual appetites). In KJV bible book of Galatians chapter 5 verse 23; it states: "Meekness, **temperance**: against such there is no law." The **True Vine Yashu'a (Jesus) Fruit of the Spirit of Positive Character-Building Essential** of "Temperance" through in action true-faith in the Most High Heavenly Father to overcome and resist the **4th of the 9 Deadly Venoms of the Desires of the great dragon, that old serpent called the devil and satan which deceiveth the whole world** known as "**Greed**" by learning and practicing self-control which is the virtue of one who masters his or her desires and passions every day.

SPIRITUAL TRILLIONAIRE:
Cherishing the Breath of Life while Simultaneously
Preparing for the Blow of Death!

CHILDREN OF THE MOST HIGH:
PRISTINE YOUTH AND FAMILY SOLUTIONS, LLC.
SONS AND DAUGHTERS OF THE MOST HIGH PUBLISHERS ®

OH, GRACIOUS MOST HIGH HEAVENLY FATHER, HOLY IS YOUR
NAME, YOUR WILL BE DONE NOW AND FOREVER!

The 9 True Vine "Yashu'a" (Jesus) Fruits of the Spirit of
Positive Character-Building Essentials, if learned and
practiced every day, it may help a person to overcome the 9
Deadly Venoms of the Desires of the great dragon: that old
serpent, called the Devil, and Satan, which deceiveth the whole
world. They may also help a person to acquire positive spiritual
health and positive spiritual wealth on the path to becoming a
Spiritual Trillionaire.

The **8ᵗʰ of the 9X9** True Vine "Yashu'a" (Jesus) B.A.-K.A.-
R.E. Sequential Order of Learning Habits of Success are **the 9
True Vine Yashu'a (Jesus) Work Ethics** that may help a
person's overall well-being of as it relates to acquiring,
maintaining and sustaining positive spiritual health and positive
spiritual on the path to becoming a Spiritual Trillionaire, which
are:

1. <u>**Responsible**</u> – In the KJV bible book of Romans
   chapter 14 verse 12; it states: "So then every one of us
   shall give account of himself [or herself] to God."

SPIRITUAL TRILLIONAIRE:
**Cherishing the Breath of Life while Simultaneously
Preparing for the Blow of Death!**

CHILDREN OF THE MOST HIGH:
PRISTINE YOUTH AND FAMILY SOLUTIONS, LLC.
SONS AND DAUGHTERS OF THE MOST HIGH PUBLISHERS ®

OH, GRACIOUS MOST HIGH HEAVENLY FATHER, HOLY IS YOUR
NAME, YOUR WILL BE DONE NOW AND FOREVER!

2. **Active Listener** – In the KJV bible book of James chapter 1 verse 19; it states: "Wherefore, my beloved brethren [or sisters], let every man [woman and child] be swift to hear, slow to speak, slow to wrath."

3. **Trustworthy** – In the KJV bible book of Proverbs chapter 3 verses 5-6; it states: "Trust in the LORD with all thine heart; and lean not unto thine own understanding. In all thy ways acknowledge him, and he shall direct thy **paths**." In the KJV bible book of Matthew chapter 10 verse 13; it states: The Messiah Yashu'a (Jesus) said: "And if the house be worthy, let your peace come upon it: but if it be not worthy, let your peace return to you." In the KJV bible book of Matthew chapter 10 verses 37-38; the Messiah Yashu'a (Jesus) said: "He [or She] that loveth father or mother more than me is not worthy of me: and he [or She] that loveth son or daughter more than me is not worthy of me. And he [or she] that taketh not his cross, and followeth after me, is not worthy of me."

SPIRITUAL TRILLIONAIRE:
**Cherishing the Breath of Life while Simultaneously
Preparing for the Blow of Death!**

CHILDREN OF THE MOST HIGH:
PRISTINE YOUTH AND FAMILY SOLUTIONS, LLC.
SONS AND DAUGHTERS OF THE MOST HIGH PUBLISHERS ®

OH, GRACIOUS MOST HIGH HEAVENLY FATHER, HOLY IS YOUR
NAME, YOUR WILL BE DONE NOW AND FOREVER!

4. <u>**Respectful**</u> – In the KJV bible book of Psalms chapter 119 verse 6; it states: "Then shall I not be ashamed, when I have respect unto all thy commandments." In the KJV bible book of Psalms chapter 119 verse 15; it states: "I will meditate in thy precepts, and have respect unto thy ways." In the KJV bible book of Psalms chapter 119 verse 117; it states: "Hold thou me up, and I shall be safe: and I will have respect unto thy statutes continually."

5. <u>**Dependable**</u> – In the KJV bible book of 2nd Samuel chapter 22 verse 3; it states: "The God of my rock; in him will I trust [and depend upon]: he is my shield, and the horn of my salvation, my high tower, and my refuge, my savior; thou savest me from violence." In the KJV bible book of Revelation chapter 21 verse 23; it states: "And the city had no need of the sun, neither of the moon, to shine in it: for the glory of God did lighten it, and the Lamb is the light thereof."

SPIRITUAL TRILLIONAIRE:
Cherishing the Breath of Life while Simultaneously
Preparing for the Blow of Death!

CHILDREN OF THE MOST HIGH:
PRISTINE YOUTH AND FAMILY SOLUTIONS, LLC.
SONS AND DAUGHTERS OF THE MOST HIGH PUBLISHERS ®

OH, GRACIOUS MOST HIGH HEAVENLY FATHER, HOLY IS YOUR
NAME, YOUR WILL BE DONE NOW AND FOREVER!

6. **Positive Attitude** – In the KJV bible book of Psalms chapter 45 verse 7; it states: "Thou lovest righteousness, and hatest wickedness: therefore God, thy God, hath anointed thee with the oil of gladness above thy fellows."

7. **Positive Behavior** – In the KJV bible book of Philippians chapter 4 verse 8; it states: "Finally, brethren, whatsoever things are true, whatsoever things [are] honest, whatsoever things [are] just, whatsoever things [are] pure, whatsoever things [are] lovely, whatsoever things [are] of good report; if [there be] any virtue, and if [there be] any praise, think on these things."

8. **Impactful** – In the KJV bible book of Proverbs chapter 13 verse 20; it states: "He that walketh with wise [men] shall be wise: but a companion of fools shall be destroyed."

SPIRITUAL TRILLIONAIRE:
Cherishing the Breath of Life while Simultaneously
Preparing for the Blow of Death!

CHILDREN OF THE MOST HIGH:
PRISTINE YOUTH AND FAMILY SOLUTIONS, LLC.
SONS AND DAUGHTERS OF THE MOST HIGH PUBLISHERS ®

OH, GRACIOUS MOST HIGH HEAVENLY FATHER, HOLY IS YOUR
NAME, YOUR WILL BE DONE NOW AND FOREVER!

9. **Team Player** – In the KJV bible book of Ecclesiastes chapter 4 verses 9-10; it states: "Two [are] better than one; because they have a good reward for their labor. For if they fall, the one will lift up his fellow: but woe to him [or her] [that is] alone when he [or she] falleth; for [he hath] [or she hath] not another to help him [or her] up."

The 9 True Vine "Yashu'a" (Jesus) Work Ethics, if learned and practiced every day, it may help a person to overcome the 9 Deadly Venoms of the Desires of the great dragon: that old serpent, called the Devil, and Satan, which deceiveth the whole world. They may also help a person to acquire positive spiritual health and positive spiritual wealth on the path to becoming a Spiritual Trillionaire.

323

SPIRITUAL TRILLIONAIRE:
Cherishing the Breath of Life while Simultaneously
Preparing for the Blow of Death!

CHILDREN OF THE MOST HIGH:
PRISTINE YOUTH AND FAMILY SOLUTIONS, LLC.
SONS AND DAUGHTERS OF THE MOST HIGH PUBLISHERS ®

OH, GRACIOUS MOST HIGH HEAVENLY FATHER, HOLY IS YOUR
NAME, YOUR WILL BE DONE NOW AND FOREVER!

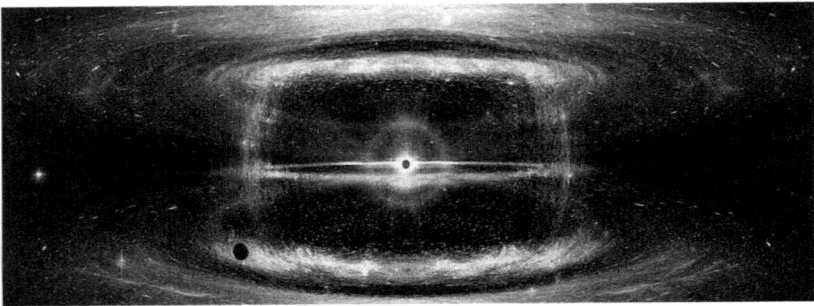

The **9th of the 9X9** True Vine "Yashu'a" (Jesus) B.A.-K.A.-R.E. Sequential Order of Learning Habits of Success are **the 9 True Vine Yashu'a (Jesus) Values** that may help a person's overall well-being of as it relates to acquiring, maintaining and sustaining positive spiritual health and positive spiritual on the path to becoming a Spiritual Trillionaire, which are:

1. **God is love**. In the KJV bible book of 1st John chapter 4 verse 8; it states: "He [or She] that loveth not knoweth not God; for God is love." In the KJV bible book of 1st John chapter 4 verse 16; it states: "And we have known and believed the love that God hath to us. God is love; and he [or she] that dwelleth in love dwelleth in God, and God in him [or her]."

324

SPIRITUAL TRILLIONAIRE:
Cherishing the Breath of Life while Simultaneously
Preparing for the Blow of Death!

CHILDREN OF THE MOST HIGH:
PRISTINE YOUTH AND FAMILY SOLUTIONS, LLC.
SONS AND DAUGHTERS OF THE MOST HIGH PUBLISHERS ®

OH, GRACIOUS MOST HIGH HEAVENLY FATHER, HOLY IS YOUR
NAME, YOUR WILL BE DONE NOW AND FOREVER!

2. **Love thy Neighbor**. In the KJV bible book of Matthew chapter 22 verse 39; the Messiah Yashu'a (Jesus) said: "Thou shalt love thy neighbor as thyself."

3. **Love One Another**. In the KJV bible book of John chapter 13 verses 34-36; the Messiah Yashu'a (Jesus) said: "A new commandment I give unto you, that ye love one another; as I have loved you, that ye also love one another. By this shall all men [women and children] know that ye are my disciples, if ye have love one to another."

4. **Love Your Enemies**. In the KJV bible book of Matthew chapter 5 verse 44; the Messiah Yashu'a (Jesus) said: "But I say unto you, love your enemies, bless them that curse you, do good to them that hate you, and pray for them which despitefully use you, and persecute you."

5. **Be ye therefore perfect**, even as your Father which is in heaven is perfect. In the KJV bible book of Matthew chapter 5 verse 48; the Messiah Yashu'a (Jesus) said:

SPIRITUAL TRILLIONAIRE:
**Cherishing the Breath of Life while Simultaneously
Preparing for the Blow of Death!**

CHILDREN OF THE MOST HIGH:
PRISTINE YOUTH AND FAMILY SOLUTIONS, LLC.
SONS AND DAUGHTERS OF THE MOST HIGH PUBLISHERS ®

OH, GRACIOUS MOST HIGH HEAVENLY FATHER, HOLY IS YOUR
NAME, YOUR WILL BE DONE NOW AND FOREVER!

"Be ye therefore perfect, even as your Father which
is in heaven is perfect."

6. **Glorify your Father which is in heaven**. In the KJV
bible book of Matthew chapter 5 verse 16; the Messiah
Yashu'a (Jesus) said: "Let your light so shine before
men, that they may see your good works, and glorify
your Father which is in heaven."

7. **Bless them that curse you**. In the KJV bible book of
Matthew chapter 5 verse 44; the Messiah Yashu'a
(Jesus) said: "But I say unto you, love your enemies,
bless them that curse you, do good to them that hate
you, and pray for them which despitefully use you,
and persecute you."

8. **Do good to them that hate you**. In the KJV bible book
of Matthew chapter 5 verse 44; the Messiah Yashu'a
(Jesus) said: "But I say unto you, love your enemies,
bless them that curse you, do good to them that hate
you, and pray for them which despitefully use you,
and persecute you."

SPIRITUAL TRILLIONAIRE:
Cherishing the Breath of Life while Simultaneously
Preparing for the Blow of Death!

CHILDREN OF THE MOST HIGH:
PRISTINE YOUTH AND FAMILY SOLUTIONS, LLC.
SONS AND DAUGHTERS OF THE MOST HIGH PUBLISHERS ®

OH, GRACIOUS MOST HIGH HEAVENLY FATHER, HOLY IS YOUR
NAME, YOUR WILL BE DONE NOW AND FOREVER!

9. **Pray for them which despitefully use you, and persecute you**. In the KJV bible book of Matthew chapter 5 verse 44; the Messiah Yashu'a (Jesus) said: "But I say unto you, love your enemies, bless them that curse you, do good to them that hate you, and pray for them which despitefully use you, and persecute you."

The 9 True Vine "Yashu'a" Jesus Values, if learned and practiced every day, it may help a person to overcome the 9 Deadly Venoms of the Desires of the great dragon: that old serpent, called the Devil, and Satan, which deceiveth the whole world. They may also help a person to acquire positive spiritual health and positive spiritual wealth on the path to becoming a Spiritual Trillionaire.

~OH, MOST HIGH HEAVENLY FATHER, WE SEEK YOUR
HELP BY WAY OF PATIENCE AND PRAYER AS LONG AS
WE LIVE AND EXIST, NOW AND FOREVER. AMEN~

SPIRITUAL TRILLIONAIRE:
Cherishing the Breath of Life while Simultaneously
Preparing for the Blow of Death!

CHILDREN OF THE MOST HIGH:
PRISTINE YOUTH AND FAMILY SOLUTIONS, LLC.
SONS AND DAUGHTERS OF THE MOST HIGH PUBLISHERS ®

OH, GRACIOUS MOST HIGH HEAVENLY FATHER, HOLY IS YOUR
NAME, YOUR WILL BE DONE NOW AND FOREVER!

Chapter 9: What are the Children of the Most High: Pristine Youth and Family Solutions, LLC. Purpose and Responsibilities? Proclamation? And What is Life and the Blow of Death?

~OH, MOST HIGH HEAVENLY FATHER, ALL PRAISES
AND GLORY BE TO YOU IN THE MORNING, AFTERNOON
AND EVENING, NOW AND FOREVER. AMEN~

SPIRITUAL TRILLIONAIRE:
Cherishing the Breath of Life while Simultaneously
Preparing for the Blow of Death!

CHILDREN OF THE MOST HIGH:
PRISTINE YOUTH AND FAMILY SOLUTIONS, LLC.
SONS AND DAUGHTERS OF THE MOST HIGH PUBLISHERS ®

OH, GRACIOUS MOST HIGH HEAVENLY FATHER, HOLY IS YOUR
NAME, YOUR WILL BE DONE NOW AND FOREVER!

The Children of the Most High; Pristine Youth and Family Solutions, LLC. Purpose is:

1). To do the will of the Most High Heavenly Father.

2). To dispel the diversity of confusion by helping people to mentally break free from the mental imprisonment of the blinding light of misinformation.

3). To encourage people to love themselves and members of humanity in a healthy, positive, caring, non- egotistical way.

4). To help people to practice being caring and loving to one another in an effort to be obedient to what the Messiah Yashu'a (Jesus) commanded us to do when he said in the KJV book of John chapter 13 verses 34-35; the Messiah Yashu'a (Jesus) said: "A new commandment I give unto you, that ye love one another; as I have loved you, that ye also love one another. By this shall all men [women and children] know that ye are my disciples, if ye have love one to another)."

5). To help youth and adults to improve the overall quality of their lives.

SPIRITUAL TRILLIONAIRE:
Cherishing the Breath of Life while Simultaneously
Preparing for the Blow of Death!

CHILDREN OF THE MOST HIGH:
PRISTINE YOUTH AND FAMILY SOLUTIONS, LLC.
SONS AND DAUGHTERS OF THE MOST HIGH PUBLISHERS ®

OH, GRACIOUS MOST HIGH HEAVENLY FATHER, HOLY IS YOUR
NAME, YOUR WILL BE DONE NOW AND FOREVER!

7). To remind members of humanity to love the Most High Heavenly Father with all of their heart, and with all of their spirit and soul, with all of their mind, and entire being.

8). Defend the poor, the motherless, fatherless, the underserved underrepresented, afflicted members of humanity; and do what is morally right for them.

9). Deliver the poor and needy out of the hands of the wicked.

SPIRITUAL TRILLIONAIRE:
Cherishing the Breath of Life while Simultaneously
Preparing for the Blow of Death!

CHILDREN OF THE MOST HIGH:
PRISTINE YOUTH AND FAMILY SOLUTIONS, LLC.
SONS AND DAUGHTERS OF THE MOST HIGH PUBLISHERS ®

OH, GRACIOUS MOST HIGH HEAVENLY FATHER, HOLY IS YOUR
NAME, YOUR WILL BE DONE NOW AND FOREVER!

What are the Children of the Most High Pristine Youth and Family Solutions LLC. responsibilities? The Children of the Most High; Pristine Youth and Family Solutions LLC. have the following **W**arn, **I**nform, **T**each (**W.I.T.**) responsibilities:

1). We have the responsibility to **W**arn members of humanity who are children of the Most High to be on their guard against the children of the devil (who look like any person that you may see at any time), and to remind members of humanity what the Messiah Yashu'a (Jesus) said to the children of the devil in the KJV bible book of John chapter 8 verse 44: "Ye are of your father the devil, and the lusts of your father ye will do. He was a murderer from the beginning, and abode not in the truth, because there is no truth in him. When he speaketh a lie, he speaketh of his own: for he is a liar, and the father of it."

2). We have the responsibility to **I**nform those children of the Most High who we are sent to, to tell them to repent to the Most High Heavenly Father through the Messiah Yashu'a (Jesus) who said in the KJV bible book of John chapter 14 verse 6: "I am the way, the truth, and the life: no man [woman or child] cometh unto the Father, but by me."

SPIRITUAL TRILLIONAIRE:
**Cherishing the Breath of Life while Simultaneously
Preparing for the Blow of Death!**

CHILDREN OF THE MOST HIGH:
PRISTINE YOUTH AND FAMILY SOLUTIONS, LLC.
SONS AND DAUGHTERS OF THE MOST HIGH PUBLISHERS &

OH, GRACIOUS MOST HIGH HEAVENLY FATHER, HOLY IS YOUR
NAME, YOUR WILL BE DONE NOW AND FOREVER!

3). We have the responsibility to **T**each True Vine (Jesus) education and positive life skills to youth and adults who are children of the Most High through **the Children of the Most High Pristine Youth and Family Solutions, LLC. 9X9 True Vine "Yashu'a" (Jesus) B.A.-K.A.-R.E. Sequential Order of Learning Habits of Success**. This occurs in an effort to assist youth and adults who are children of the Most High in the process of achieving what they define as positive success, their positive life aspirations and all of their positive predetermined life goals. We seek to inspire and empower all children of the Most High to pristinely make the world a safe and healthy place for all members of humanity. In hopes to create a world that is ruled by **Love** and the **"Will"** of the Most High, void of negative emotions, greed, lusts and love of money. We also have the responsibility to **T**each the doctrine of the Most High Heavenly Father to the children of the Most High who we are sent to by explaining the scriptures from the original language it was revealed in so that youth and adults will learn how to best apply the Most High Heavenly Father's truth in all situations to achieve success. The Messiah Yashu'a (Jesus) said in the KJV bible book of John chapter 8 verse 32: "And ye shall know the truth, and the truth shall make you free."

SPIRITUAL TRILLIONAIRE:
Cherishing the Breath of Life while Simultaneously
Preparing for the Blow of Death!

CHILDREN OF THE MOST HIGH:
PRISTINE YOUTH AND FAMILY SOLUTIONS, LLC.
SONS AND DAUGHTERS OF THE MOST HIGH PUBLISHERS

OH, GRACIOUS MOST HIGH HEAVENLY FATHER, HOLY IS YOUR
NAME, YOUR WILL BE DONE NOW AND FOREVER!

SPIRITUAL TRILLIONAIRE:
Cherishing the Breath of Life while Simultaneously
Preparing for the Blow of Death!

CHILDREN OF THE MOST HIGH:
PRISTINE YOUTH AND FAMILY SOLUTIONS, LLC.
SONS AND DAUGHTERS OF THE MOST HIGH PUBLISHERS ®

OH, GRACIOUS MOST HIGH HEAVENLY FATHER, HOLY IS YOUR
NAME, YOUR WILL BE DONE NOW AND FOREVER!

What is the Children of the Most High: Pristine Youth and Family Solutions, LLC. Proclamation?

"We greet all in peace with a sincere heart. We are non-violent and agree with the Reverend Dr. Martin Luther King Jr. when he said: "At the center of non-violence stands the principle of love." We stay sober, we don't drink alcohol, we don't become intoxicated, we eat healthy, we exercise, and we don't smoke anything for the body is a temple where the spirit of the Most High dwells; so, our bodies and minds must be in a state of cleanliness! We respect nature, we respect the laws of nature, and the Most High Heavenly Father who is the source of it all. We don't hate any race, creed, religion, or sexual orientation. We advocate that humanity practice being just to the depressed, in mind or circumstances, the poor, and underserved underrepresented members of humanity. We advocate that humanity practice defending the poor, motherless and fatherless from all injustices. We seek to help deliver the poor and needy out of the hands of the wicked by teaching them how to activate the latent potential in them through their inborn gifts, by learning and applying the Most High's doctrine in all that they do, through repentance, and through the acceptance of the Messiah Yashu'a (Jesus), and through the eternal obedience to the Most High Heavenly Father's "Will" and commandments. We seek to help empower members of humanity to take that which is evil and to turn it into good. We seek to work with all members of humanity to help make the world a safer, peaceful, healthy, and poverty free environment for all youth and all adults to live in; and we obey Yashu'a (Jesus) commandment to love one another."

SPIRITUAL TRILLIONAIRE:
Cherishing the Breath of Life while Simultaneously
Preparing for the Blow of Death!

CHILDREN OF THE MOST HIGH:
PRISTINE YOUTH AND FAMILY SOLUTIONS, LLC.
SONS AND DAUGHTERS OF THE MOST HIGH PUBLISHERS ®

OH, GRACIOUS MOST HIGH HEAVENLY FATHER, HOLY IS YOUR
NAME, YOUR WILL BE DONE NOW AND FOREVER!

What is the meaning of the Children of the Most High: Pristine Youth and Family Solutions, LLC. LOGO?

The Children of the Most High: Pristine Youth and Family Solutions LLC. LOGO **is a federal registered LOGO.**

CHILDREN OF THE MOST HIGH:
PRISTINE YOUTH AND FAMILY SOLUTIONS, LLC.
SONS AND DAUGHTERS OF THE MOST HIGH PUBLISHERS ®

The gold image that looks like a person is a **modern Aramic (Hebrew) symbol** that **originated** from **Ancient Africa**. In the Greek language it is referred to as a **Tetragrammaton** (the four letters word that represents the sacred name of the Almighty in Aramic (Hebrew) biblical text. In the Aramic (Hebrew) language, a person would read from right to left, not left to right like a person would read in the English language. If we read the following: **Tetragrammaton,** the four letters word that represents the sacred name of the Almighty in Aramic (Hebrew) biblical text in modern Aramic

SPIRITUAL TRILLIONAIRE:
Cherishing the Breath of Life while Simultaneously
Preparing for the Blow of Death!

CHILDREN OF THE MOST HIGH:
PRISTINE YOUTH AND FAMILY SOLUTIONS, LLC.
SONS AND DAUGHTERS OF THE MOST HIGH PUBLISHERS ®

OH, GRACIOUS MOST HIGH HEAVENLY FATHER, HOLY IS YOUR
NAME, YOUR WILL BE DONE NOW AND FOREVER!

(Hebrew), we get the letters: **Y-W-H-W** for the **Tetragrammaton**. If we read the **Tetragrammaton** letters: **Y-W-H-W** from right to left as we would in the Aramic (Hebrew) language, we would read the letters: **W-H-W-Y**. The modern day Aramic (Hebrew) symbol **Tetragrammaton** letters: **W-H-W-Y** originated from the Ancient African: **H-U-H-I** which literally means: **the creative force of will**. In modern Aramic (Hebrew), the "**I**" was changed into a "**Y**" and the "**U**" was changed into a **double** "**U**" called a "**W**". In Ancient Africa, **HU** is the masculine creative force of will which in science is called **centripetal**. **HI** is the feminine creative force of will which in science is called **centrifugal**. These principals exist in other cultures as **Shen** and **Sham** in Ancient Africa, **Yin** and **Yang** in Asian culture, **male** and **female** to many, or **positive** and **negative**.

However, positive and negative from a creative perspective **is not synonymous with good or bad**. For example, most drivable vehicles have a battery under their hood that if it is working properly, it will be able to start and drive.

SPIRITUAL TRILLIONAIRE:
Cherishing the Breath of Life while Simultaneously
Preparing for the Blow of Death!

CHILDREN OF THE MOST HIGH:
PRISTINE YOUTH AND FAMILY SOLUTIONS, LLC.
SONS AND DAUGHTERS OF THE MOST HIGH PUBLISHERS ®

OH, GRACIOUS MOST HIGH HEAVENLY FATHER, HOLY IS YOUR
NAME, YOUR WILL BE DONE NOW AND FOREVER!

The **vehicle battery has a positive post and a negative post on it. If either of the posts are not working together, the battery won't work**. So, the creative force of will is necessary for all life to occur. So, the Children of the Most High: Pristine

Youth and Family Solutions LLC. utilizes the ▇ symbol that has different meanings at different stages in a person's growth. **For example: At another stage in the Children of the Most High: Pristine Youth and Family Solutions LLC. growth, this symbol: represents the active True Vine Yashu'a (Jesus) Mind Master Gardner – children of the Most High (God) mind**.

As it relates to the symbol resembling a person, the person would be or may be in the process of becoming a child of the Most High who accepts the Messiah Yashu'a (Jesus) as their savior, and commits their life to doing the will of the Most High Heavenly Father, now and forever.

SPIRITUAL TRILLIONAIRE:
Cherishing the Breath of Life while Simultaneously
Preparing for the Blow of Death!

CHILDREN OF THE MOST HIGH:
PRISTINE YOUTH AND FAMILY SOLUTIONS, LLC.
SONS AND DAUGHTERS OF THE MOST HIGH PUBLISHERS ®

OH, GRACIOUS MOST HIGH HEAVENLY FATHER, HOLY IS YOUR
NAME, YOUR WILL BE DONE NOW AND FOREVER!

The Children of the Most High: Pristine Youth and Family

Solutions LLC. also utilizes the ▉ symbol to represent the portion of the Most High that exists in "**YOU**" and in every person according the KJV bible book of John chapter 1 verses 1-5 and 9.

(1). A person's physical body is composed of 70-75% **water.**

(2). The human body is composed of the 99 natural elements on the **earth.**

(3). Human breathing is represented in **wind** (oxygen).

(4). A person's inner **fire** is referred to as a solar plexus.

(5). The totality of a person's entire being is **the (5th) fifth element** as **a creative force of will personified** who utilizes the **9X9 True Vine "Yashu'a" (Jesus) B.A.-K.A.-R.E. Sequential Order of Learning Habits of Success** to help improve every aspect of their life.

338

SPIRITUAL TRILLIONAIRE:
Cherishing the Breath of Life while Simultaneously
Preparing for the Blow of Death!

CHILDREN OF THE MOST HIGH:
PRISTINE YOUTH AND FAMILY SOLUTIONS, LLC.
SONS AND DAUGHTERS OF THE MOST HIGH PUBLISHERS ®

OH, GRACIOUS MOST HIGH HEAVENLY FATHER, HOLY IS YOUR
NAME, YOUR WILL BE DONE NOW AND FOREVER!

What keeps a fire burning? Something flammable and oxygen keeps a fire burning. What element does a fire give off? A fire gives off carbon dioxide. What do we as human beings breathe in? We breathe in oxygen. What do we exhale? We exhale the element carbon dioxide. So, there must be something burning inside of each person. When we breathe in **wind** (oxygen) and when blood leaves the heart through the pulmonic valve, into the pulmonary artery and to the lungs, it is oxygenated, it becomes infused or charged like a combustion, **fire**, inside

our hearts through the "**True Light**" which lighteth every person that comes into the world. In the KJV bible book of John chapter 1 verses 1-5,9; it states: "In the beginning was the Word, and the Word was with God, and the Word was God. The same was in the beginning with God. All things were made by him; and without him was not anything made that was made. In him was life; and the life was the light of men. And the light shineth in darkness; and the darkness comprehended it not. [9] That was the true Light, which lighteth every man that cometh into the world."

SPIRITUAL TRILLIONAIRE:
**Cherishing the Breath of Life while Simultaneously
Preparing for the Blow of Death!**

CHILDREN OF THE MOST HIGH:
PRISTINE YOUTH AND FAMILY SOLUTIONS, LLC.
SONS AND DAUGHTERS OF THE MOST HIGH PUBLISHERS ®

OH, GRACIOUS MOST HIGH HEAVENLY FATHER, HOLY IS YOUR
NAME, YOUR WILL BE DONE NOW AND FOREVER!

Air   **Fire**

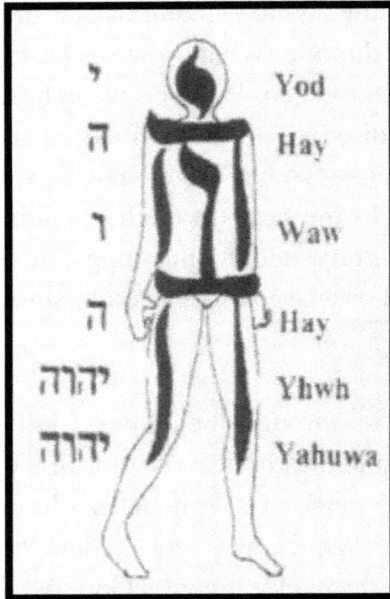

Water   **Earth**

The aforementioned symbol is referred to as the tetragrammaton. Tetragrammaton is a Greek word composed of **tetra**-meaning "**four**", and **gramma**-meaning "**letter**" and has been variously transliterated as Jhvh, Yhve, Jhwh, Yhwh, Yahayyu, Yahweh, Jehovah, and Yahuwa.

340

SPIRITUAL TRILLIONAIRE:
**Cherishing the Breath of Life while Simultaneously
Preparing for the Blow of Death!**

CHILDREN OF THE MOST HIGH:
PRISTINE YOUTH AND FAMILY SOLUTIONS, LLC.
SONS AND DAUGHTERS OF THE MOST HIGH PUBLISHERS ®

OH, GRACIOUS MOST HIGH HEAVENLY FATHER, HOLY IS YOUR
NAME, YOUR WILL BE DONE NOW AND FOREVER!

THE FOUR LETTERS ARE:

YOD IS THE HAND THAT CREATED ALL
HAI IS LIFE
WAW IS THE EYE THAT WATCHES OVER
HAI ALL LIFE

TRANSLATION OF יהוה
O HE WHO IS WHOM HE IS
THE HIDDEN MEANING OF יהוה

WITH HIS HAND HE CREATED ALL
LIFE AND WITH HIS EYE HE WATCHES
OVER ALL LIFE.

YOD also represented all manifested power of the hand. It is symbolized by the extended finger on the right hand.

HAI also represents the breath of life in men, women, and children, and the spirit and soul.

WAW also signifies the ear and is the wind.

SPIRITUAL TRILLIONAIRE:
Cherishing the Breath of Life while Simultaneously
Preparing for the Blow of Death!

CHILDREN OF THE MOST HIGH:
PRISTINE YOUTH AND FAMILY SOLUTIONS, LLC.
SONS AND DAUGHTERS OF THE MOST HIGH PUBLISHERS ®

OH, GRACIOUS MOST HIGH HEAVENLY FATHER, HOLY IS YOUR
NAME, YOUR WILL BE DONE NOW AND FOREVER!

YOD represents all manifested power of the hand. It is symbolized by the extended finger on the right hand. **HAI** represents the breath of life in men, women, and children, and the spirit and soul. **WAW** represents and signifies the ear and the wind. If we read the **Tetragrammaton** letters: **Y-W-H-W** from right to left as we would in the Aramic (Hebrew) language, we would read the letters: **W-H-W-Y**. The modern day Aramic (Hebrew) symbol **Tetragrammaton** letters: **W-H-W-Y** originated from the Ancient African: **H-U-H-I** which literally means: **the creative force of will**. In modern Aramic (Hebrew), the "**I**" was changed into a "**Y**" and the "**U**" was changed into a **double** "**U**" called a "**W**". In Ancient Africa, **HU** is the masculine creative force of will which in science is called **centripetal**. **HI** is the feminine creative force of will which in science is called **centrifugal**. So, the Ancient African **HUHI** (Creative Force of Will) became the Aramic (Hebrew) **YWHW** (LORD of the Bible) and **YWHW** is phonetically and literally, the reverse of **HUHI**. **YWHW** translates into the English bible equivalent of "**The LORD**" (Yahayyu – Living or Existing One, or Yahweh, Yahuwa,

SPIRITUAL TRILLIONAIRE:
Cherishing the Breath of Life while Simultaneously
Preparing for the Blow of Death!

CHILDREN OF THE MOST HIGH:
PRISTINE YOUTH AND FAMILY SOLUTIONS, LLC.
SONS AND DAUGHTERS OF THE MOST HIGH PUBLISHERS ®

OH, GRACIOUS MOST HIGH HEAVENLY FATHER, HOLY IS YOUR
NAME, YOUR WILL BE DONE NOW AND FOREVER!

Yehovah or Jehovah in the KJV bible Hebrew Strong's Concordance# 3068 יהוה. The KJV bible book of Isaiah chapter 19 verse 25, states: "Whom **the Lord** (Yahayyu or Yahweh, Yehovah or Jehovah – Living or Existing One 3068 יהוה) Whom the Lord of hosts shall bless, saying, **Blessed be Egypt my people**, and Assyria the work of my hands, and Israel mine inheritance." The KJV bible book of Isaiah chapter 19 verse 25 with Hebrew inserts:

אשר ברכו יהוה צבאות לאמר ברוך עמי מצרים ומעשה ידי אשור ונחלתי ישראל

Where does "**The Lord**" of the bible come from? According KJV bible book of Hosea chapter 12 verse 9; it states: "**And I that am the Lord** (Yahayyu or Yahweh, Yehovah or Jehovah – Living or Existing One) **from the land of Egypt (In this verse, Egypt is translated as: "מִצְרַיִם"** "Miṣ·Rā·Yim" KJV Bible Hebrew Strong's Concordance# 4714, and sometimes Egypt is translated as "Cush" in the KJV bible) **will yet make thee to dwell in tabernacles, as in the days of the solemn feast.**" In KJV bible book of Hosea chapter 13 verse 4; it states: "**Yet I am the Lord thy God from the land of Egypt, and thou shalt know no god but me: for there is no Saviour** (**Saviour** or **Savior** ישע is: "YaShu'a" – Savior is defined as one who saves, Yâsha', Yaw-Shah'; KJV bible Hebrew

SPIRITUAL TRILLIONAIRE:
Cherishing the Breath of Life while Simultaneously
Preparing for the Blow of Death!

CHILDREN OF THE MOST HIGH:
PRISTINE YOUTH AND FAMILY SOLUTIONS, LLC.
SONS AND DAUGHTERS OF THE MOST HIGH PUBLISHERS ®

OH, GRACIOUS MOST HIGH HEAVENLY FATHER, HOLY IS YOUR
NAME, YOUR WILL BE DONE NOW AND FOREVER!

Strong's Concordance Number: **3467) beside me**." The **inverted heart** represents **divine love from the Most High coming down from above that enters the hearts of the children of the Most High**. The **upright heart** represents the **divine love** that the children of the Most High have for the Most High that ascends upward to the Most High.

The **3 suns** have multiple meanings at various stages of growth. For this first degree of the True Vine (Yashu'a, Jesus) youth and adult learning, the **1ˢᵗ Sun** represents a person **Becoming Aware as a Mind Gardner**. The **2ⁿᵈ Sun** represents a person having the Elohiym (God's) A.W.A.R.E. **Knowledge** that they **Apply** in all that they do as a True Vine (Yashu'a, Jesus), **Mind Gardner.** The **3ʳᵈ Sun** represents a person having and applying the Elohiym (God's) A.W.A.R.E. knowledge over time and now are able to **Reflect** back on their **Experiences** of their utilization of the Elohiym (God's) A.W.A.R.E. knowledge. BA-KA-**RE** (**RE** is Pronounced as RAY). The **9X9 True Vine "Yashu'a" (Jesus) B.A.-K.A.-R.E. Sequential Order of Learning Habits of Success LOGO is a Children of the Most High: Pristine Youth and Family Solutions, LLC. Federal Registered LOGO.**

SPIRITUAL TRILLIONAIRE:
**Cherishing the Breath of Life while Simultaneously
Preparing for the Blow of Death!**

CHILDREN OF THE MOST HIGH:
PRISTINE YOUTH AND FAMILY SOLUTIONS, LLC.
SONS AND DAUGHTERS OF THE MOST HIGH PUBLISHERS ®

OH, GRACIOUS MOST HIGH HEAVENLY FATHER, HOLY IS YOUR
NAME, YOUR WILL BE DONE NOW AND FOREVER!

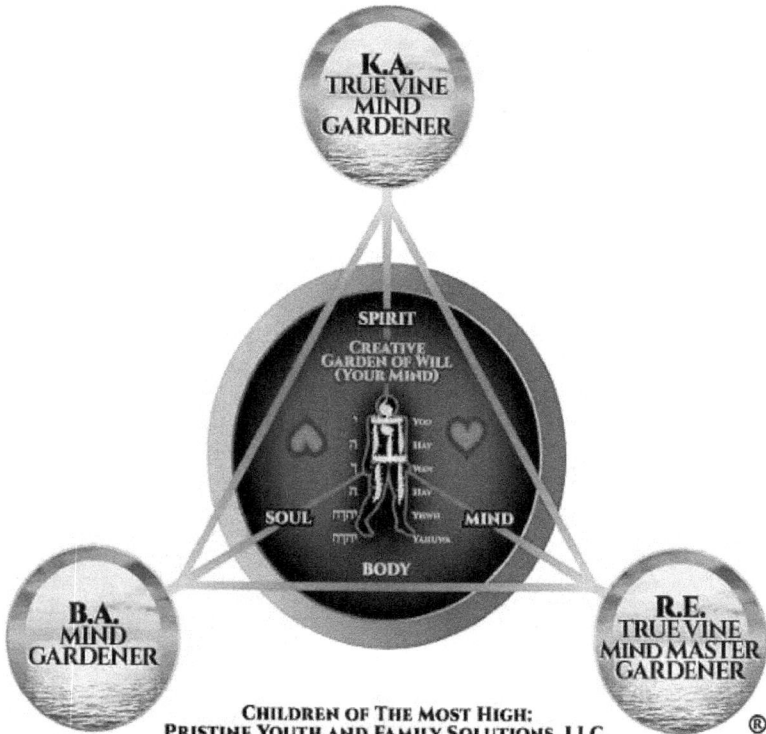

CHILDREN OF THE MOST HIGH:
PRISTINE YOUTH AND FAMILY SOLUTIONS, LLC.
9X9 TRUE VINE "YASHU'A" (JESUS) B.A.-K.A.-R.E.
SEQUENTIAL ORDER OF LEARNING®

345

SPIRITUAL TRILLIONAIRE:
**Cherishing the Breath of Life while Simultaneously
Preparing for the Blow of Death!**

CHILDREN OF THE MOST HIGH:
PRISTINE YOUTH AND FAMILY SOLUTIONS, LLC.
SONS AND DAUGHTERS OF THE MOST HIGH PUBLISHERS ®

OH, GRACIOUS MOST HIGH HEAVENLY FATHER, HOLY IS YOUR
NAME, YOUR WILL BE DONE NOW AND FOREVER!

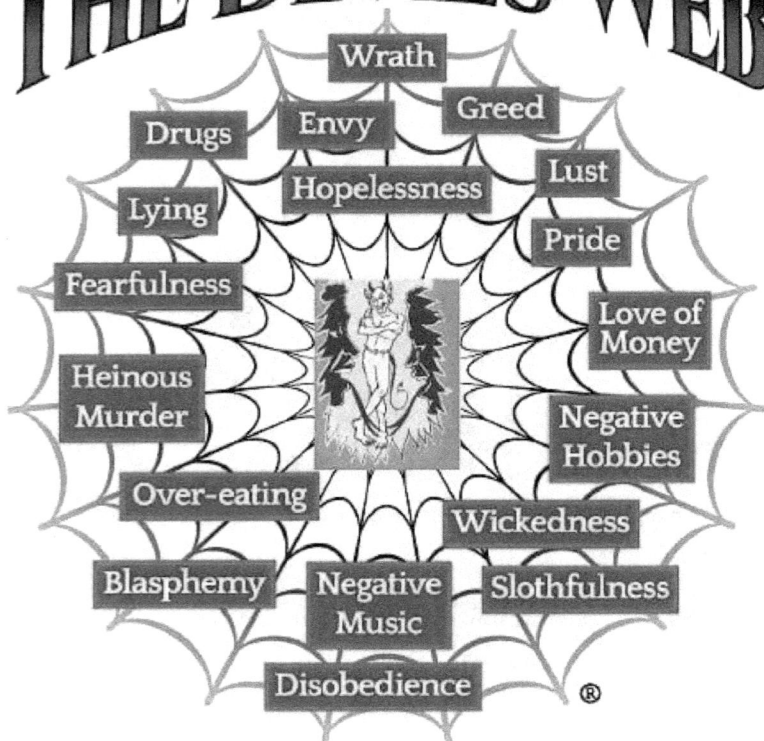

SPIRITUAL TRILLIONAIRE:
Cherishing the Breath of Life while Simultaneously
Preparing for the Blow of Death!

CHILDREN OF THE MOST HIGH:
PRISTINE YOUTH AND FAMILY SOLUTIONS, LLC.
SONS AND DAUGHTERS OF THE MOST HIGH PUBLISHERS ℗

OH, GRACIOUS MOST HIGH HEAVENLY FATHER, HOLY IS YOUR
NAME, YOUR WILL BE DONE NOW AND FOREVER!

The Children of the Most High Pristine Youth and Family
Solutions, LLC. 9X9 True Vine "Yashu'a" (Jesus) B.A.-K.A.-
R.E. Sequential Order of Learning Habits of Success also
teaches youth and adults how to be aware of the children of the
devil who advocate, teach and preach **the great dragon, that
old serpent, called the Devil, and Satan, which deceiveth the
whole world and his angels** (ἄγγελος Angelos, meaning
Messengers), messages of the 9 Deadly Venoms of the Desires
of the great dragon, that old serpent, called the Devil, and Satan,
which deceiveth the whole world. The 9 Deadly Venoms of the
Desires are: Slothful, Wrath, Pride, Greed, Lust, Hopeless Fear
Disobedience, Lying, Heinous Murder, and Wickedness.
Beware of the devil's web! Be in the world, but not of the
world! Stay in grace! Come you all, out of the world, do not
drink the intoxicating spirit of Satan. Come you all into the
world ruled by the master Yashu'a (Jesus), for he is of the
Heavenly Father, and the Heavenly Father is in him. Blessed
are they who learn true love. Rewarded are they who share true
love in their Heavenly Father's name. **The Children of the
Most High: Pristine Youth and Family Solutions, LLC.
Devil's Web Image is also a Federally Registered image.**

347

SPIRITUAL TRILLIONAIRE:
Cherishing the Breath of Life while Simultaneously
Preparing for the Blow of Death!

CHILDREN OF THE MOST HIGH:
PRISTINE YOUTH AND FAMILY SOLUTIONS, LLC.
SONS AND DAUGHTERS OF THE MOST HIGH PUBLISHERS ®

OH, GRACIOUS MOST HIGH HEAVENLY FATHER, HOLY IS YOUR
NAME, YOUR WILL BE DONE NOW AND FOREVER!

The darkness that surrounds the [symbol] symbol, represents that the Almighty dwells in thick darkness as stated in the KJV bible book of 1st Kings chapter 8 verse 12; it states: "Then spake Solomon, The Lord said that he would dwell in the thick darkness." On the Children of the Most High: Pristine Youth and Family Solution LLC. Logo, the words: "**Children of the Most High**:" are in the **1st darkest black** which is symbolic of the receiver of the message from the Most High who is the conveyer of the message that results in **God's (Elohiym) Al Wise Abundant Right Exact (A.W.A.R.E) reasoning**. The

message is life [symbol] HAI, the breath of life in men, women, and children, and the spirit and soul, and the conveyer is existence. **The first degree of darkness is also symbolic of the first stage in triple darkness** which is **before light, before energy**, and **before matter**. The words: "**Pristine Youth and Family Solutions, LLC,**" is the **2nd darkest black** as symbolic of **the second stage in triple darkness** which is **before time, before place**, and **before space**. The words: "**Sons and Daughters of the Most High Publishers**" is in **the 3rd darkest**

SPIRITUAL TRILLIONAIRE:
Cherishing the Breath of Life while Simultaneously
Preparing for the Blow of Death!

CHILDREN OF THE MOST HIGH:
PRISTINE YOUTH AND FAMILY SOLUTIONS, LLC.
SONS AND DAUGHTERS OF THE MOST HIGH PUBLISHERS ®

**OH, GRACIOUS MOST HIGH HEAVENLY FATHER, HOLY IS YOUR
NAME, YOUR WILL BE DONE NOW AND FOREVER!**

black as symbolic of the **third stage in triple darkness** which is **before body**, **before soul**, and **before spirit**. So, an aspiring Spiritual Trillionaire will have an opportunity to acquire a more in depth meaning of **the Children of the Most High Pristine Youth and Family Solutions, LLC. 9X9 True Vine "Yashu'a" (Jesus) B.A.-K.A.-R.E. Sequential Order of Learning Habits of Success** as they advance in their growth and development over time.

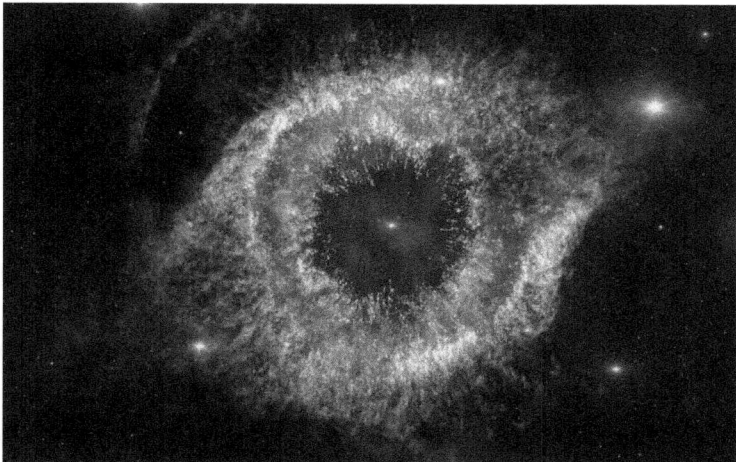

SPIRITUAL TRILLIONAIRE:
Cherishing the Breath of Life while Simultaneously
Preparing for the Blow of Death!

CHILDREN OF THE MOST HIGH:
PRISTINE YOUTH AND FAMILY SOLUTIONS, LLC.
SONS AND DAUGHTERS OF THE MOST HIGH PUBLISHERS ®

OH, GRACIOUS MOST HIGH HEAVENLY FATHER, HOLY IS YOUR
NAME, YOUR WILL BE DONE NOW AND FOREVER!

According to Children of the Most High: Pristine Youth and Family Solutions LLC., Define Pristine, Youth, Family, and Solutions?

Pristine is defined as: belonging to the earliest period or state: original: not spoiled, not corrupted, or not polluted (as by civilization): pure: fresh and clean as or as if new.

Youth is defined as: the period between childhood and adult age.

Family is defined as the Messiah Yashu'a (Jesus) said in the KJV bible book of Matthew chapter 12 verse 50; Yashu'a (Jesus) said: "For whosoever shall do the will of my Father which is in heaven, the same is my brother, and sister, and mother."

Solutions is defined as: a means of solving a problem or issues or successfully working through a difficult issue or situations. The story of life is designed to unfold the secret of us. It is very simple to make life circumstances or issues complex.

SPIRITUAL TRILLIONAIRE:
Cherishing the Breath of Life while Simultaneously
Preparing for the Blow of Death!

CHILDREN OF THE MOST HIGH:
PRISTINE YOUTH AND FAMILY SOLUTIONS, LLC.
SONS AND DAUGHTERS OF THE MOST HIGH PUBLISHERS

OH, GRACIOUS MOST HIGH HEAVENLY FATHER, HOLY IS YOUR
NAME, YOUR WILL BE DONE NOW AND FOREVER!

Who are the Sons and Daughters of the Most High Publishers? The Sons and Daughters of the Most High Publisher's is the name of the Publishers of the Children of the Most High: Pristine Youth and Family Solutions, LLC. publications of peace. For more information about scheduling workshops or presentations, please visit our website at: www.childrenofthemosthigh.com or you can call **478-538-1918** for all inquiries. All workshops or presentations can be conveniently designed to meet your specific, unique needs of the youth or adults targeted audiences that you work with **based on our scheduling availability**.

What are the True Vine (Yashu'a, Jesus) Mind Gardening Daily Individual or Family Household Habits of Success? The True Vine (Yashu'a, Jesus) Mind Gardening Daily Individual or Family Household Habits of Success are:

1. **Obey the Most High Heavenly Father's will and commandments now and forever!**

SPIRITUAL TRILLIONAIRE:
Cherishing the Breath of Life while Simultaneously
Preparing for the Blow of Death!

CHILDREN OF THE MOST HIGH:
PRISTINE YOUTH AND FAMILY SOLUTIONS, LLC.
SONS AND DAUGHTERS OF THE MOST HIGH PUBLISHERS ®

OH, GRACIOUS MOST HIGH HEAVENLY FATHER, HOLY IS YOUR
NAME, YOUR WILL BE DONE NOW AND FOREVER!

2. Love the Most High Heavenly Father with all of your heart, all of your spirit, all of your soul, all of your mind, and all of your entire being!

3. Decrease so that the Spirit of the Messiah Yashu'a (Jesus) can increase in you!

4. Do unto others as you would want others to do unto you!

5. Always think positive!

6. Always be positive!

7. Always have a positive attitude!

8. Open your heart before you open your mouth!

9. Remember, words should be soft, not hard!

10. It's nice to be important, but it is more important to be nice!

SPIRITUAL TRILLIONAIRE:
Cherishing the Breath of Life while Simultaneously
Preparing for the Blow of Death!

CHILDREN OF THE MOST HIGH:
PRISTINE YOUTH AND FAMILY SOLUTIONS, LLC.
SONS AND DAUGHTERS OF THE MOST HIGH PUBLISHERS ®

OH, GRACIOUS MOST HIGH HEAVENLY FATHER, HOLY IS YOUR
NAME, YOUR WILL BE DONE NOW AND FOREVER!

11. Mine your mind for the jewels of your soul!

12. Pray together daily!

13. Eat together in the same room a minimum of once a week!

14. Observe the Sabbath (Shu-Bat) weekly as a family!

15. Study and read the scriptures of the Most High as a family a minimum of once a week!

16. Watch a TV show or movie at home a minimum of once a week!

17. Workout together as a family or ensure that all family members are working out on a weekly basis if their medical physicians have approved of them doing so.

SPIRITUAL TRILLIONAIRE:
**Cherishing the Breath of Life while Simultaneously
Preparing for the Blow of Death!**

CHILDREN OF THE MOST HIGH:
PRISTINE YOUTH AND FAMILY SOLUTIONS, LLC.
SONS AND DAUGHTERS OF THE MOST HIGH PUBLISHERS ®

OH, GRACIOUS MOST HIGH HEAVENLY FATHER, HOLY IS YOUR
NAME, YOUR WILL BE DONE NOW AND FOREVER!

18. Have family meetings once a week to discuss everyone's overall well-being, current events or anything else that is on any family member's mind, without the TV or any other electronic devices being on as a potential conversation distraction. One person speaks at a time, no arguing, no vulgarity, and all family members must respect each other!

19. Do some agreed upon, healthy, fun, and safe family event a minimum of once a month or weekly or bi-weekly together as a family.

What is Life?

The Online American Heritage Dictionary defines the word "life" as: **the time for which something exists or functions**. The word "life" is mentioned for the first time in the KJV bible book of Genesis chapter 1 verse 20; and it states: "And God said, Let the waters bring forth abundantly the moving creature that hath **life**, and fowl that may fly above the earth in the open firmament of heaven." The KJV bible Hebrew Strong's Concordance#**2416** word for **life** is:

SPIRITUAL TRILLIONAIRE:
**Cherishing the Breath of Life while Simultaneously
Preparing for the Blow of Death!**

CHILDREN OF THE MOST HIGH:
PRISTINE YOUTH AND FAMILY SOLUTIONS, LLC.
SONS AND DAUGHTERS OF THE MOST HIGH PUBLISHERS ®

OH, GRACIOUS MOST HIGH HEAVENLY FATHER, HOLY IS YOUR
NAME, YOUR WILL BE DONE NOW AND FOREVER!

Khah-Ee חַי (**Khay** or **Chay**) and means **living**, **alive**.

The Ashuric/Syriac (Arabic) Word For "Life" Is Hayaat (حياة) In

Greek The Word Is Zoe (Ζωη); Meaning *"The Time You Spend*

alive or living; the time for which something exists or
functions.

What is the Blow of Death?

THE BLOW OF DEATH IS WHEN A PERSON OR LIVING LIFE
FORM THAT BREATHES TAKES HIS OR HER OR ITS LAST
BREATH!

355

SPIRITUAL TRILLIONAIRE:
Cherishing the Breath of Life while Simultaneously
Preparing for the Blow of Death!

CHILDREN OF THE MOST HIGH:
PRISTINE YOUTH AND FAMILY SOLUTIONS, LLC.
SONS AND DAUGHTERS OF THE MOST HIGH PUBLISHERS ®

OH, GRACIOUS MOST HIGH HEAVENLY FATHER, HOLY IS YOUR
NAME, YOUR WILL BE DONE NOW AND FOREVER!

In the KJV bible book of 1st John chapter 1 verse 9-10; it states: "If we confess our sins, he is faithful and just to forgive us our sins, and to cleanse us from all unrighteousness. If we say that we have not sinned, we make him (Yashu'a, Jesus) a liar, and his word is not in us."

Below is a Prayer of Repentance:

In the KJV bible book of Psalms chapter 51 verses 1-19; it states:

"51 Have mercy upon me, O God, according to thy lovingkindness: according unto the multitude of thy tender mercies blot out my transgressions. ² Wash me throughly from mine iniquity, and cleanse me from my sin. ³ For I acknowledge my transgressions: and my sin is ever before me. ⁴ Against thee, thee only, have I sinned, and done this evil in thy sight: that thou mightest be justified when thou speakest, and be clear when thou judgest. ⁵ Behold, I was shapen in iniquity; and in sin did my mother conceive me. ⁶ Behold, thou desirest truth in the inward parts: and in the hidden part thou shalt make me to know wisdom. ⁷ Purge me with hyssop, and I shall be clean: wash me, and I shall

SPIRITUAL TRILLIONAIRE:
Cherishing the Breath of Life while Simultaneously
Preparing for the Blow of Death!

CHILDREN OF THE MOST HIGH:
PRISTINE YOUTH AND FAMILY SOLUTIONS, LLC.
SONS AND DAUGHTERS OF THE MOST HIGH PUBLISHERS

OH, GRACIOUS MOST HIGH HEAVENLY FATHER, HOLY IS YOUR
NAME, YOUR WILL BE DONE NOW AND FOREVER!

be whiter than snow. [8] Make me to hear joy and gladness; that the bones which thou hast broken may rejoice. [9] Hide thy face from my sins, and blot out all mine iniquities. [10] Create in me a clean heart, O God; and renew a right spirit within me. [11] Cast me not away from thy presence; and take not thy holy spirit from me. [12] Restore unto me the joy of thy salvation; and uphold me with thy free spirit. [13] Then will I teach transgressors thy ways; and sinners shall be converted unto thee. [14] Deliver me from bloodguiltiness, O God, thou God of my salvation: and my tongue shall sing aloud of thy righteousness. [15] O Lord, open thou my lips; and my mouth shall shew forth thy praise. [16] For thou desirest not sacrifice; else would I give it: thou delightest not in burnt offering. [17] The sacrifices of God are a broken spirit: a broken and a contrite heart, O God, thou wilt not despise. [18] Do good in thy good pleasure unto Zion: build thou the walls of Jerusalem. [19] Then shalt thou be pleased with the sacrifices of righteousness, with burnt offering and whole burnt offering: then shall they offer bullocks upon thine altar."

SPIRITUAL TRILLIONAIRE:
Cherishing the Breath of Life while Simultaneously
Preparing for the Blow of Death!

CHILDREN OF THE MOST HIGH:
PRISTINE YOUTH AND FAMILY SOLUTIONS, LLC.
SONS AND DAUGHTERS OF THE MOST HIGH PUBLISHERS ®

OH, GRACIOUS MOST HIGH HEAVENLY FATHER, HOLY IS YOUR
NAME, YOUR WILL BE DONE NOW AND FOREVER!

So, aspiring Spiritual Trillionaires have an opportunity to repent, practice the act of doing without doing, apply ourselves honestly, put on an incorruptible spirit, and seek eternal life through the **Messiah Yashu'a (Jesus, Isa, Iesous, Yasue')** by accepting him as your savior. **The act of doing without doing does not mean to not have a strong work ethics, and it does not mean to be lazy and do nothing. It means to be at peace while accomplishing the most difficult of tasks and all other tasks every day with maximum effort, active discipline, skill and efficiency while being in a zone, or only concentrating on the task at hand while acquiring, maintaining and sustaining positive spiritual health and positive spiritual wealth in pursuit of becoming a Spiritual Trillionaire.**

358

SPIRITUAL TRILLIONAIRE:
**Cherishing the Breath of Life while Simultaneously
Preparing for the Blow of Death!**

CHILDREN OF THE MOST HIGH:
PRISTINE YOUTH AND FAMILY SOLUTIONS, LLC.
SONS AND DAUGHTERS OF THE MOST HIGH PUBLISHERS &

OH, GRACIOUS MOST HIGH HEAVENLY FATHER, HOLY IS YOUR
NAME, YOUR WILL BE DONE NOW AND FOREVER!

In the KJV bible book of John chapter 3 verses 16-18; the Messiah Yashu'a (Jesus) said: "For God so loved the world, that he gave his only begotten Son, that whosoever believeth in him should not perish, but have everlasting life. For God sent not his Son into the world to condemn the world; but that the world through him might be saved. He that believeth on him is not condemned: but he that believeth not is condemned already, because he hath not believed in the name of the only begotten Son of God."

In the KJV bible book of 1st Corinthians chapter 15 verses 50-54; it states: "Now this I say, brethren, that flesh and blood cannot inherit the kingdom of God; neither doth corruption inherit incorruption. Behold, I shew you a mystery; We shall not all sleep, but we shall all be changed, in a moment, in the twinkling of an eye, at the last trumpet: for the trumpet shall sound, and the dead shall be raised incorruptible, and we shall be changed. For this corruptible must put on incorruption, and this mortal must put on immortality."

SPIRITUAL TRILLIONAIRE:
**Cherishing the Breath of Life while Simultaneously
Preparing for the Blow of Death!**

OH, GRACIOUS MOST HIGH HEAVENLY FATHER, HOLY IS YOUR
NAME, YOUR WILL BE DONE NOW AND FOREVER!

"So, when this corruptible shall have put on incorruption, and this mortal shall have put on immortality, then shall be brought to pass the saying that is written, death is swallowed up in victory." If a person lives by the standards of the Most High Heavenly Father, a person does not have to be afraid to die. A person fears death if they are not following the standards of the Most High Heavenly Father. In the KJV bible book of 1st Corinthians chapter 15 verse 56; it states: "The sting of death is sin; and the strength of sin is the law." You have no reason to fear death because the Messiah Yashu'a (Jesus) already suffered for you. In the KJV bible book of 1st Corinthians chapter 15 verse 57; it states: "But thanks be to God, which giveth us the victory through our Lord Jesus Christ." "And walk in love, as Christ also hath loved us, and hath given himself for us an offering and a sacrifice to God." (KJV bible book of Ephesians chapter 5:2).

In the KJV bible book of John chapter 17 verses 15-22; the Messiah Yashu'a (Jesus) said: "I pray not that thou shouldest take them out of the world, but that thou shouldest keep them from the evil. They are not of the world, even as I am not of the world. Sanctify them through thy truth: thy word

360

SPIRITUAL TRILLIONAIRE:
Cherishing the Breath of Life while Simultaneously
Preparing for the Blow of Death!

CHILDREN OF THE MOST HIGH:
PRISTINE YOUTH AND FAMILY SOLUTIONS, LLC.
SONS AND DAUGHTERS OF THE MOST HIGH PUBLISHERS ®

**OH, GRACIOUS MOST HIGH HEAVENLY FATHER, HOLY IS YOUR
NAME, YOUR WILL BE DONE NOW AND FOREVER!**

is truth. As thou hast sent me into the world, even so have I also sent them into the world. And for their sakes I sanctify myself, that they also might be sanctified through the truth. Neither pray I for these alone, but for them also which shall believe on me through their word; That they all may be one; as thou, Father, art in me, and I in thee, that they also may be one in us: that the world may believe that thou hast sent me. And the glory which thou gavest me I have given them; that they may be one, even as we are one: I in them, and thou in me, that they may be made perfect in one; and that the world may know that thou hast sent me, and hast loved them, as thou hast loved me."

In the KJV bible book of 1st Peter chapter 4 verse 13; it states: "But rejoice, inasmuch as ye are partakers of Christ's sufferings; that, when his glory shall be revealed, ye may be glad also with exceeding joy." In the KJV bible book of Philippians chapter 2 verse 2; it states: "Fulfil ye my joy, that ye be likeminded, having the same love, being of one accord, of one mind."

361

SPIRITUAL TRILLIONAIRE:
**Cherishing the Breath of Life while Simultaneously
Preparing for the Blow of Death!**

CHILDREN OF THE MOST HIGH:
PRISTINE YOUTH AND FAMILY SOLUTIONS, LLC.
SONS AND DAUGHTERS OF THE MOST HIGH PUBLISHERS ®

OH, GRACIOUS MOST HIGH HEAVENLY FATHER, HOLY IS YOUR
NAME, YOUR WILL BE DONE NOW AND FOREVER!

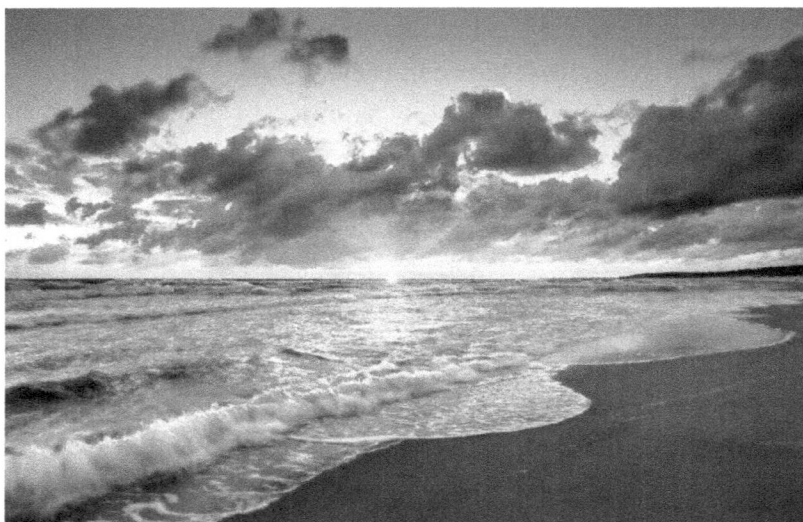

In the KJV bible book of 1st Corinthians chapter 14 verses 13-16; it states: "Wherefore let him that speaketh in an unknown tongue pray that he may interpret. For if I pray in an unknown tongue, my spirit prayeth, but my understanding is unfruitful. What is it then? I will pray with the spirit, and I will pray with the understanding also: I will sing with the spirit, and I will sing with the understanding also. Else when thou shalt bless with the spirit, how shall he that occupieth the room of the unlearned say Amen at thy giving of thanks, seeing he understandeth not what thou sayest?"

362

SPIRITUAL TRILLIONAIRE:
**Cherishing the Breath of Life while Simultaneously
Preparing for the Blow of Death!**

CHILDREN OF THE MOST HIGH:
PRISTINE YOUTH AND FAMILY SOLUTIONS, LLC.
SONS AND DAUGHTERS OF THE MOST HIGH PUBLISHERS

OH, GRACIOUS MOST HIGH HEAVENLY FATHER, HOLY IS YOUR
NAME, YOUR WILL BE DONE NOW AND FOREVER!

In the KJV bible book of Matthew chapter 6 verses 6-8; the Messiah Yashu'a (Jesus) said: "But thou, when thou prayest, enter into thy closet, and when thou hast shut thy door, pray to thy Father which is in secret; and thy Father which seeth in secret shall reward thee openly. But when ye pray, use not vain repetitions, as the heathen do: for they think that they shall be heard for their much speaking. Be not ye therefore like unto them: for your Father knoweth what things ye have need of, before ye ask him."

363

SPIRITUAL TRILLIONAIRE:
Cherishing the Breath of Life while Simultaneously
Preparing for the Blow of Death!

CHILDREN OF THE MOST HIGH:
PRISTINE YOUTH AND FAMILY SOLUTIONS, LLC.
SONS AND DAUGHTERS OF THE MOST HIGH PUBLISHERS ®

OH, GRACIOUS MOST HIGH HEAVENLY FATHER, HOLY IS YOUR
NAME, YOUR WILL BE DONE NOW AND FOREVER!

So, the Children of the Most High: Pristine Youth and Family
Solutions, LLC., ask that all Aspiring Spiritual Trillionaires,
make amends with our Heavenly Father if you have not already
done so before you experience the **Blow of Death!** In the KJV
bible book of John chapter 3 verses 3-7; Yashu'a (Jesus) said:
"Verily, verily, I say unto thee, except a man be born again,
he cannot see the kingdom of God.

364

SPIRITUAL TRILLIONAIRE:
**Cherishing the Breath of Life while Simultaneously
Preparing for the Blow of Death!**

CHILDREN OF THE MOST HIGH:
PRISTINE YOUTH AND FAMILY SOLUTIONS, LLC.
SONS AND DAUGHTERS OF THE MOST HIGH PUBLISHERS ®

OH, GRACIOUS MOST HIGH HEAVENLY FATHER, HOLY IS YOUR
NAME, YOUR WILL BE DONE NOW AND FOREVER!

Nicodemus saith unto him, how can a man be born when he is old? **can he enter the second time into his mother's womb, and be born**? Yashu'a (Jesus) answered, Verily, verily, I say unto thee, except a man be born of water **(which occurred when we were in our mother's wombs when she was pregnant with us)** and of the Spirit, he cannot enter into the kingdom of God. That which is born of the flesh is flesh; and that which is born of the Spirit is spirit. Marvel not that I said unto thee, Ye must be born again."

In the KJV bible book of Matthew chapter 3 verse 11; John the Baptist who was preaching in the wilderness of Judaea stated: "I indeed baptize you with water unto repentance: but he that cometh after me is mightier than I, whose shoes I am not worthy to bear: **he shall baptize you with the Holy Ghost**, and with **fire**." In KJV bible Greek Strong's Concordance#40, the word for "**Holy**" in this verse is: ἅγιος hagios. The word for "**Spirit**" and the word for "**Ghost**" in this verse is: the KJV Bible Greek Strong's Concordance#4151 is the **word, πνεῦμα "Pneuma"** and means "**Spirit**". So, in this verse, the **Holy Ghost** is the **Holy Spirit**.

SPIRITUAL TRILLIONAIRE:
Cherishing the Breath of Life while Simultaneously
Preparing for the Blow of Death!

CHILDREN OF THE MOST HIGH:
PRISTINE YOUTH AND FAMILY SOLUTIONS, LLC.
SONS AND DAUGHTERS OF THE MOST HIGH PUBLISHERS ®

OH, GRACIOUS MOST HIGH HEAVENLY FATHER, HOLY IS YOUR
NAME, YOUR WILL BE DONE NOW AND FOREVER!

In the verse, the same word: "**fire**" is in reference to the KJV bible book of Acts chapter 2 verses 1-4; it states: "And when the day of Pentecost was fully come, they were all with one accord in one place. And suddenly there came a sound from heaven as of a rushing mighty wind, and it filled all the house where they were sitting. And there appeared unto them **cloven tongues** like as of **fire**, and it sat upon each of them. And they were all filled with the **Holy Ghost**, and began to speak with other tongues, as the Spirit gave them utterance."

In the aforementioned verses, the **Holy Spirit** is translated as "**Holy Ghost**" which is the KJV Bible Greek Strong's Concordance**#40**, the word for "**Holy**" in this verse is: ἅγιος **hagios**. The word for "**Ghost**" in this verse is: the KJV Bible Greek Strong's Concordance**#4151**, πνεῦμα "**Pneuma**" and means "**Spirit**" as mentioned in the KJV bible book of Matthew chapter 3 verse 11 and in the KJV bible book of Acts chapter 2 verses 1-4. So, **John the Baptist who was preaching in the wilderness of Judaea baptized with water, and the** Messiah Yashu'a (Jesus, Iesous, Issa, Yasue'), baptizes with the Holy Spirit, which can occur at any given time!

SPIRITUAL TRILLIONAIRE:
Cherishing the Breath of Life while Simultaneously
Preparing for the Blow of Death!

CHILDREN OF THE MOST HIGH:
PRISTINE YOUTH AND FAMILY SOLUTIONS, LLC.
SONS AND DAUGHTERS OF THE MOST HIGH PUBLISHERS ®

OH, GRACIOUS MOST HIGH HEAVENLY FATHER, HOLY IS YOUR
NAME, YOUR WILL BE DONE NOW AND FOREVER!

Therefore, **Aspiring Spiritual Trillionaires** must decrease, so that the Messiah Yashu'a (Jesus) teachings and spirit can increase within in them. Thereby, everything we do, we do in the name of the first and the last. In the process of them learning how to overcome fear, they become aware that real fear is the lack of true-faith in the Most High Heavenly Father. Aspiring Spiritual Trillionaires learn that to love your enemies does not mean to not recognize them, it does not mean not to seek refuge in our Most High Heavenly Father from them, it means to not hold onto or have any negative feelings about them or toward them, thereby allowing the light of life to shine through you at all times, that all those that see that light shine through you, not from you; may glorify our Most High Heavenly Father! Aspiring Spiritual Trillionaires learn to control their emotions rather than allowing their emotions to control them. They also learn that anger is the desire of the heart and the sin of the soul. It makes the spirit ill and anger always seeks sin! Love replenishes everything without limitations, and sometimes when being **rebuked**, Spiritual Trillionaires look in the mirror and asked themselves: Do I give love the way I want to be loved?

367

SPIRITUAL TRILLIONAIRE:
Cherishing the Breath of Life while Simultaneously
Preparing for the Blow of Death!

In the KJV bible book of Revelation chapter 3 verses 19-20; Yashu'a (Jesus) stated: "As many as I love, I rebuke and chasten: be zealous therefore, and repent. Behold, I stand at the door, and knock: if any man (the word for "man" is the **KJV bible Greek Strong's Concordance #5100 word: τις tis**, which means **any person**) hear my voice, and open the door **(of your heart)**, I will come in to him **(that person)**, and will sup with him (the word for "him" is the **KJV bible Greek Strong's Concordance#846 word: αὐτός autos which means he or she**), and he **(KJV bible Greek Strong's Concordance #846 word: αὐτός autos meaning he or she)**, with me."

What does the word "**rebuke**" mean? "According to the **KJV bible Greek Strong's Concordance#1651 word: ἐλέγχω elegchō**, "rebuke" means to reprimand, correct, to reprehend severely, chide, admonish, reprove, to call to account, show one his fault, to chasten, and to punish." In the KJV bible book of Matthew chapter 6 verse 33; the Messiah Yashu'a (Jesus) said: "But seek ye first the kingdom of God, and his righteousness; and all these things shall be added unto you."

SPIRITUAL TRILLIONAIRE:
Cherishing the Breath of Life while Simultaneously
Preparing for the Blow of Death!

CHILDREN OF THE MOST HIGH:
PRISTINE YOUTH AND FAMILY SOLUTIONS, LLC.
SONS AND DAUGHTERS OF THE MOST HIGH PUBLISHERS ®

OH, GRACIOUS MOST HIGH HEAVENLY FATHER, HOLY IS YOUR
NAME, YOUR WILL BE DONE NOW AND FOREVER!

In conclusion, some millionaires and some billionaires are not seeking the Kingdom of God or the Messiah Yashu'a (the True Vine, Jesus), they are seeking more millions and billions of dollars, control of the world, and all of the earth's natural resources. According the KJV bible book of Job chapter 1 verse 7; it states: "And the LORD said unto Satan, Whence comest thou? Then Satan answered the LORD, and said, from **going to and fro** in the earth, and from walking up and down in it." So, Satan and his children are moving around on the planet. The phrase "**going to and fro**" is the **KJV bible Hebrew Strong's Concordance #7751 word, שׁוּט shuwt, meaning to go, go or rove about, or walk or run)**. Satan and his children or the children of the devil are the ones who do not have the love of the Heavenly Father in them, they don't want to live by the laws and commandments of **God (Elohiym)**, they reject the Messiah Yashu'a (Jesus). Their elite work themselves into the highest man made or woman made positions of power to kill, destroy, lie to, neglect, unfairly treat, and to abuse the most vulnerable populations of people on the planet earth. The children of Satan are the most wicked trouble makers on the planet earth.

SPIRITUAL TRILLIONAIRE:
**Cherishing the Breath of Life while Simultaneously
Preparing for the Blow of Death!**

CHILDREN OF THE MOST HIGH:
PRISTINE YOUTH AND FAMILY SOLUTIONS, LLC.
SONS AND DAUGHTERS OF THE MOST HIGH PUBLISHERS ®

OH, GRACIOUS MOST HIGH HEAVENLY FATHER, HOLY IS YOUR
NAME, YOUR WILL BE DONE NOW AND FOREVER!

This is why in the KJV bible book of Matthew chapter 6 verse 24; the Messiah Yashu'a (Jesus) said: "No man [person] can serve two masters: for either he will hate the one, and love the other; or else he will hold to the one, and despise the other, Ye cannot serve God and mammon." The KJV bible Greek Strong's Concordance#3126 word for "mammon" is: μαμωνᾶς mamōnas which means: "**wealth; riches where it is personified and opposed to God; avarice (deified)**."

In the KJV bible book of John chapter 14 verse 6; the Messiah Yashu'a (Jesus) said: "I am the way (**Ani, means "I am the way" in the ancient Egyptian language and "Egypt" is the word: מִצְרַיִם Mitsrayim in the KJV bible Hebrew Strong's Concordance#4717**), the truth, and the life: no man cometh unto the Father, but by me." However, according to the KJV bible book of John chapter 6 verse 44; only the Most High Heavenly Father can lead a person to the Messiah Yashu'a (Jesus).

SPIRITUAL TRILLIONAIRE:
Cherishing the Breath of Life while Simultaneously
Preparing for the Blow of Death!

CHILDREN OF THE MOST HIGH:
PRISTINE YOUTH AND FAMILY SOLUTIONS, LLC.
SONS AND DAUGHTERS OF THE MOST HIGH PUBLISHERS ®

OH, GRACIOUS MOST HIGH HEAVENLY FATHER, HOLY IS YOUR
NAME, YOUR WILL BE DONE NOW AND FOREVER!

The Messiah Yashu'a (Jesus) said: "No man [person] can come to me, except the Father which hath sent me draw him: and I will raise him up at the last day." In the KJV bible book of John chapter 14 verse 21; the Messiah Yashu'a (Jesus) said: "He [or she] that hath my commandments, and keepeth them, he [or she] it is that loveth me: and he [or she] that loveth me shall be loved of my Father, and I will love him [or her], and will manifest myself to him [or her]."

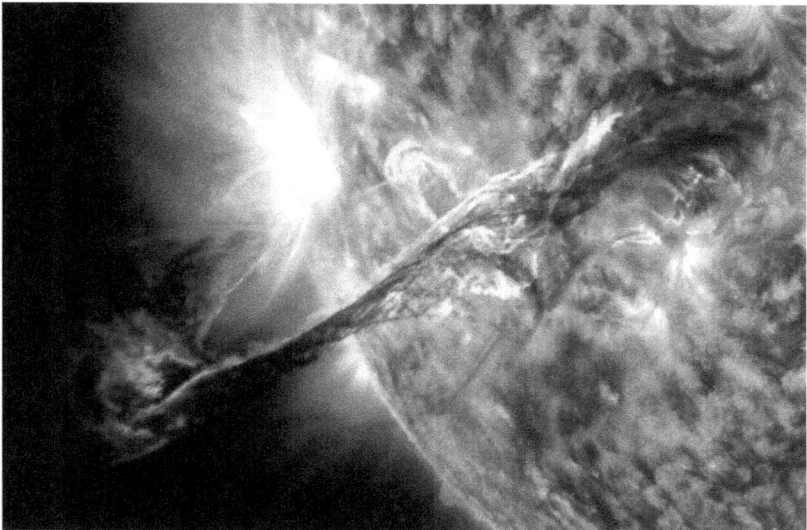

SPIRITUAL TRILLIONAIRE:
Cherishing the Breath of Life while Simultaneously
Preparing for the Blow of Death!

CHILDREN OF THE MOST HIGH:
PRISTINE YOUTH AND FAMILY SOLUTIONS, LLC.
SONS AND DAUGHTERS OF THE MOST HIGH PUBLISHERS ®

OH, GRACIOUS MOST HIGH HEAVENLY FATHER, HOLY IS YOUR
NAME, YOUR WILL BE DONE NOW AND FOREVER!

In the KJV bible book of John chapter 14 verse 6; where the Messiah Yashu'a (Jesus) said: "I am the way" which **in the ancient Egyptian language is "Ani" and means "I am the way;"** is there a correlation between Yashu'a **and "Egypt"** in the KJV bible as it relates to him being **the Key to Eternal Life**?

In the KJV bible book in the book of Isaiah chapter 22 verse 22; it states: "And the **key** of the house of David will I lay upon his shoulder; so, he shall open, and none shall shut; and he shall shut, and none shall open." In the KJV bible book of Hosea chapter 12 verse 9; it states: "And **I that am the LORD thy God from the land of Egypt** will yet make thee to dwell in tabernacles, as in the days of the solemn feast."

SPIRITUAL TRILLIONAIRE:
Cherishing the Breath of Life while Simultaneously
Preparing for the Blow of Death!

CHILDREN OF THE MOST HIGH:
PRISTINE YOUTH AND FAMILY SOLUTIONS, LLC.
SONS AND DAUGHTERS OF THE MOST HIGH PUBLISHERS ®

OH, GRACIOUS MOST HIGH HEAVENLY FATHER, HOLY IS YOUR
NAME, YOUR WILL BE DONE NOW AND FOREVER!

In the KJV bible book in the book of Hosea chapter 13 verse 4; it states: "Yet **I am the LORD thy God from the land of Egypt, and thou shalt know no god but me: for there is no savior (יָשַׁע Yashu'a) beside me**."

In the KJV bible book in the book of Revelation chapter 11 verse 8; it states: "And their dead bodies [shall lie] in the street of the great city, **which spiritually is called Sodom and Egypt, where also our Lord was crucified**."

373

SPIRITUAL TRILLIONAIRE:
Cherishing the Breath of Life while Simultaneously
Preparing for the Blow of Death!

CHILDREN OF THE MOST HIGH:
PRISTINE YOUTH AND FAMILY SOLUTIONS, LLC.
SONS AND DAUGHTERS OF THE MOST HIGH PUBLISHERS ®

OH, GRACIOUS MOST HIGH HEAVENLY FATHER, HOLY IS YOUR
NAME, YOUR WILL BE DONE NOW AND FOREVER!

In the KJV bible book in the book of Isaiah chapter 19 verse 25; it states: "Whom the LORD of hosts shall bless, saying, **Blessed be Egypt my people**, and Assyria the work of my hands, and Israel mine inheritance." The aforementioned KJV bible verses make it very clear that the Messiah Yashu'a is **the Key to Eternal Life, "the LORD thy God from the land of Egypt, the truth, and the life: no person cometh unto the Father, but by Yashu'a** (Jesus). **The True Vine "Yashu'a (Jesus) is the Perfect and Best Example of a Spiritual Trillionaire!** All Aspiring Spiritual Trillionaires are seeking the Kingdom of God and the Messiah Yashu'a (the True Vine, Jesus), who will take those who have repented, and who have accepted him as their personal savior, and received the holy spirit, to the Most High Heavenly Father.

SPIRITUAL TRILLIONAIRE:
**Cherishing the Breath of Life while Simultaneously
Preparing for the Blow of Death!**

CHILDREN OF THE MOST HIGH:
PRISTINE YOUTH AND FAMILY SOLUTIONS, LLC.
SONS AND DAUGHTERS OF THE MOST HIGH PUBLISHERS ®

OH, GRACIOUS MOST HIGH HEAVENLY FATHER, HOLY IS YOUR NAME, YOUR WILL BE DONE NOW AND FOREVER!

Once a person has accepted the Messiah Yashu'a (Jesus) as their personal savior, there is a Kingdom of God inside of them, but not there exclusively; and they are always being attacked by the children of the devil. In the KJV bible book of Luke chapter 17 verse 21; Yashu'a (Jesus) said: "Neither shall they say, Lo here! or, lo there! for, behold, the kingdom of God is within you."

**"The kingdom of heaven is within you;
whosoever shall know thyself shall find it."
Ancient Egyptian Proverb.**

In the KJV bible book of Revelation chapter 21 verse 24; it states: "And the nations of those **who are saved** shall walk in its light." So, as living souls, the children of the Most High are made aware that the Supreme Creator of the Boundless Universes, manifests through us as the breath of life! Therefore, those of us who are working to acquire, maintain and sustain positive spiritual health and positive spiritual wealth on the path of becoming a Spiritual Trillionaire; are intentionally, cherishing **the breath of life before we inevitably will experience the <u>blow of death, when we take our last breath</u>!**

SPIRITUAL TRILLIONAIRE:
Cherishing the Breath of Life while Simultaneously
Preparing for the Blow of Death!

CHILDREN OF THE MOST HIGH:
PRISTINE YOUTH AND FAMILY SOLUTIONS, LLC.
SONS AND DAUGHTERS OF THE MOST HIGH PUBLISHERS ®

OH, GRACIOUS MOST HIGH HEAVENLY FATHER, HOLY IS YOUR NAME, YOUR WILL BE DONE NOW AND FOREVER!

Nothing would exist if you Oh Gracious Most High Heavenly Father, The Creator didn't create it. You are alone in Your Greatness; you have no partners that share in your grace. To you all sovereignty is due and you are all powerful over everything. We seek refuge in you, the ever watchful Most High who hears and knows all things! Glory be to you as many times as the number of things you have created! All gratitude is due to you oh gracious Most High Heavenly Father, you are the Creator and Sustainer of all the boundless universes. You are the Yielder, and the most Merciful. The Ruler of the Day of Decision. It's you whom we worship and it is you alone whom we beseech for help, oh Guide, guide us to the narrow path (which reflects moral integrity and positive character traits in action) of the ones who stand straight, the narrow path of those who earned your grace not inclusive of those who brought an everlasting curse on themselves, those who conceal the facts of that which they know to be true in order to lead the sincere-hearted seekers of your truth astray. Amen

376

SPIRITUAL TRILLIONAIRE:
Cherishing the Breath of Life while Simultaneously
Preparing for the Blow of Death!

CHILDREN OF THE MOST HIGH:
PRISTINE YOUTH AND FAMILY SOLUTIONS, LLC.
SONS AND DAUGHTERS OF THE MOST HIGH PUBLISHERS ®

OH, GRACIOUS MOST HIGH HEAVENLY FATHER, HOLY IS YOUR
NAME, YOUR WILL BE DONE NOW AND FOREVER!

About the Author

CHILDREN OF THE MOST HIGH:
PRISTINE YOUTH AND FAMILY SOLUTIONS, LLC.
SONS AND DAUGHTERS OF THE MOST HIGH PUBLISHERS ®

WOODIE HUGHES JR.
CEO & FOUNDER
M.S. & B.S. IN CRIMINAL JUSTICE, ED.D. CANDIDATE

Mr. Hughes is a Servant of the Most High, Teacher of the
Most High's Doctrine, and a Youth and Adults Workshop
and Presentation Consultant.

📞 478-538-1918
✉ INFO@CHILDRENOFTHEMOSTHIGH.COM
🌐 CHILDRENOFTHEMOSTHIGH.COM
🐦 @WOODIEHUGHESJR9
f CHILDRENOFTHEMOSTHIGHPRISTINEYOUTHANDFAMSOLUTIONS

377

SPIRITUAL TRILLIONAIRE:
Cherishing the Breath of Life while Simultaneously
Preparing for the Blow of Death!

CHILDREN OF THE MOST HIGH:
PRISTINE YOUTH AND FAMILY SOLUTIONS, LLC.
SONS AND DAUGHTERS OF THE MOST HIGH PUBLISHERS ®

OH, GRACIOUS MOST HIGH HEAVENLY FATHER, HOLY IS YOUR NAME, YOUR WILL BE DONE NOW AND FOREVER!

Mr. Hughes and Mrs. Tonya Hughes have been happily married for 19 years and have a son and a daughter. Mr. Hughes is a veteran who has received a United States Army honorable discharge for his 8 years of service with the Illinois Army National Guard. Mr. Hughes is the son of Mrs. Annette Hughes and Mr. Woodie Hughes Sr. who have been happily married for 49 years (as of 2019)! For over 26 years, Mr. Woodie Hughes Jr. has continued to be a devout student and teacher of the Most High's doctrine who is guided by the will of the Heavenly Father, and the Messiah Yashua's (Jesus) spirit of knowledge, spirit of wisdom, and spirit of true-faith all working as the same spirits (KJV bible book of 1st Corinthians chapter 12 verses 8-9) of the Messiah Yashu'a (Jesus) which has graciously been bestowed upon him. Mr. Hughes has accepted the Messiah Yashu'a (Jesus) as his savior and is in the Body of Christ!

SPIRITUAL TRILLIONAIRE:
Cherishing the Breath of Life while Simultaneously
Preparing for the Blow of Death!

CHILDREN OF THE MOST HIGH:
PRISTINE YOUTH AND FAMILY SOLUTIONS, LLC.
SONS AND DAUGHTERS OF THE MOST HIGH PUBLISHERS ®

OH, GRACIOUS MOST HIGH HEAVENLY FATHER, HOLY IS YOUR
NAME, YOUR WILL BE DONE NOW AND FOREVER!

References

Bible, H. (2004). Holman Christian Standard Bible. Nashville: Holman Bible.

Bible, H. (1970). The new American bible. Catholic Bible Publishers. Contemporary English Bible Version.

Carroll, R., & Prickett, S. (Eds.). (2008). The Bible: Authorized King James Version. OUP Oxford.

Craft, M. 1984. Education for diversity. In Education and cultural pluralism, ed. M. Craft, 5–26. London and Philadelphia: Falmer Press.

De Gámez, T. (1973). Simon and Schuster's international dictionary: English-Spanish Spanish-English.

Dubois-Charlier, F., & King, E. L. (1986). The American Heritage Larousse Spanish dictionary. Houghton Mifflin Company.

SPIRITUAL TRILLIONAIRE:
Cherishing the Breath of Life while Simultaneously
Preparing for the Blow of Death!

CHILDREN OF THE MOST HIGH:
PRISTINE YOUTH AND FAMILY SOLUTIONS, LLC.
SONS AND DAUGHTERS OF THE MOST HIGH PUBLISHERS ®

OH, GRACIOUS MOST HIGH HEAVENLY FATHER, HOLY IS YOUR
NAME, YOUR WILL BE DONE NOW AND FOREVER!

References

Duncan, O. D. (2018). Methodological issues in the analysis of social mobility. In *Social structure and mobility in economic development* (pp. 51-97). Routledge.

Elliott, L. (1966). George Washington Carver: the man who overcame. Prentice-Hall.

Fox, J. A., Levin, J., & Quinet, K. (2018). The will to kill: Making sense of senseless murder. SAGE Publications.

Gibran, K. (1968). Secrets of the Heart. Hallmark Cards Inc.

Goren, L. (2018). Ten strategies for building emotional intelligence and preventing burnout. Family practice management, 25(1), 11-14.

Google Harvard Heart Letter (2015) entitled: "Can deep, slow breathing lower blood pressure?"

Harper, D. (2001). Online etymology dictionary.

SPIRITUAL TRILLIONAIRE:
**Cherishing the Breath of Life while Simultaneously
Preparing for the Blow of Death!**

CHILDREN OF THE MOST HIGH:
PRISTINE YOUTH AND FAMILY SOLUTIONS, LLC.
SONS AND DAUGHTERS OF THE MOST HIGH PUBLISHERS

OH, GRACIOUS MOST HIGH HEAVENLY FATHER, HOLY IS YOUR
NAME, YOUR WILL BE DONE NOW AND FOREVER!

References

Hendricks, LaVelle, Bore, Sam, Aslinia Dean, & Morriss, Guy. (2013). The Effects of Anger on the Brain and Body. National Forum Journal of Counseling and Addiction Volume 2, Number 1.

Hiesberger, J. M. (2006). Catholic Bible. Oxford University Press, USA. Good News Translation.

Houghton Mifflin Company. (2019). Online American Heritage Dictionary. Fifth Edition.

Hughes Jr., Woodie. (2001). Hughes Mind Journal.

Kinley, Henry Clifford. (1931). The Gospel of The Kingdom True Names and Title.

Leaf, C. (2009). Who Switched Off My Brain? Controlling toxic thoughts and emotions.

Leaf, C. (2013). Switch on your brain: The key to peak happiness, thinking, and health. Baker Books.

SPIRITUAL TRILLIONAIRE:
Cherishing the Breath of Life while Simultaneously
Preparing for the Blow of Death!

CHILDREN OF THE MOST HIGH:
PRISTINE YOUTH AND FAMILY SOLUTIONS, LLC.
SONS AND DAUGHTERS OF THE MOST HIGH PUBLISHERS ®

OH, GRACIOUS MOST HIGH HEAVENLY FATHER, HOLY IS YOUR
NAME, YOUR WILL BE DONE NOW AND FOREVER!

References

Lehrer, M., & Schmid, S. (2019). Strategic discipline: inconspicuous lessons from Germanic Mittelstand firms. Journal of Business Strategy. Origin of article: www.inc.com/marcel-schwantes/warren-buffett-says-this-is-1-simple-habit-that-separates-successful-people-from-everyone Schwantes, Marcel. (2018).

Levine, S. R., & Crom, M. A. (1993). The leader in you: How to win friends, influence people, and succeed in a changing world. Simon & Schuster.

Lyubomirsky, S., King, L., & Diener, E. (2005). The benefits of frequent positive affect: Does happiness lead to success? Psychological bulletin, 131(6), 803.

Mahoney, K. (2016). Latdict, Latin dictionary and grammar resources. *Retrieved July*, *5*, 2016.

Mchie, Benjamin (2019). African American Registry® (the Registry).

SPIRITUAL TRILLIONAIRE:
Cherishing the Breath of Life while Simultaneously
Preparing for the Blow of Death!

CHILDREN OF THE MOST HIGH:
PRISTINE YOUTH AND FAMILY SOLUTIONS, LLC.
SONS AND DAUGHTERS OF THE MOST HIGH PUBLISHERS ®

OH, GRACIOUS MOST HIGH HEAVENLY FATHER, HOLY IS YOUR
NAME, YOUR WILL BE DONE NOW AND FOREVER!

References

Miller, I. I., & Francis, P. (1990). Rev. Dr. Martin Luther King, Jr.: Portrait of a Prophet.

Soga, M., Gaston, K. J., & Yamaura, Y. (2017). Gardening is beneficial for health: A meta-analysis. Preventive Medicine Reports, 5, 92-99.

Sustainable Agriculture Research & Education Website. (2012). https://www.westernsare.org/About-Us/What-is-Sustainable-Agriculture.

Traina, Angelo, B. (1963). The Origin of Christianity.

Unterman, A. (1991). Dictionary of Jewish lore & legend. Thames & Hudson.

Varmah, A.J., (2004), Solar Biology or Lunar Astrology?

Viveros, J., & Schramm, D. G. (2018). Why Stress Management Strategies Work.

SPIRITUAL TRILLIONAIRE:
Cherishing the Breath of Life while Simultaneously
Preparing for the Blow of Death!

CHILDREN OF THE MOST HIGH:
PRISTINE YOUTH AND FAMILY SOLUTIONS, LLC.
SONS AND DAUGHTERS OF THE MOST HIGH PUBLISHERS ®

OH, GRACIOUS MOST HIGH HEAVENLY FATHER, HOLY IS YOUR
NAME, YOUR WILL BE DONE NOW AND FOREVER!

References

Williams, B., & Le Menestrel, S. M. (2013). Social capital and vulnerability from the family, neighborhood, school, and community perspectives. New directions for youth development, 2013(138), 97-107.

Zodhiates, S. (Ed.). (1991). The Hebrew-Greek Key Word Study Bible: King James Version, Zodhaites' Original and Complete System of Bible Study World Bible Publishers, Incorporated.